Tyndale Old Testament Commentaries

Volume 21

TOTC

Jeremiah and Lamentations

Tyndale Old Testament Commentaries

Volume 21

General Editor: Donald J. Wiseman

Jeremiah and Lamentations

An Introduction and Commentary

R. K. Harrison

Inter-Varsity Press

IVP Academic
An imprint of InterVarsity Press
Downers Grove, Illinois

Inter-Varsity Press, England
Norton Street
Nottingham NG7 3HR, England
Website: www.ivpbooks.com
Email: ivp@ivpbooks.com

InterVarsity Press, USA
P.O. Box 1400
Downers Grove, IL 60515-1426, USA
World Wide Web: www.ivpress.com
Email: email@ivpress.com

Inter-Varsity Press, England, is closely linked with the Universities and Colleges Christian Fellowship, a student movement connecting Christian Unions in universities and colleges throughout Great Britain, and a member movement of the International Fellowship of Evangelical Students. Website: www.uccf.org.uk.

InterVarsity Press®*, USA, is the book-publishing division of InterVarsity Christian Fellowship/USA*® *<www.intervarsity.org> and a member movement of the International Fellowship of Evangelical Students.*

First published 1973
Reprinted in this format 2009

British Library Cataloguing in Publication Data
A catalogue record for this book is available from the British Library.

UK ISBN 978-1-84474-335-3

Library of Congress Cataloging-in-Publication Data
Harrison, R. K. (Roland Kenneth)
Jeremiah and Lamentations: an introduction and commentary / R. K.
Harrison.
  p. cm.—(Tyndale Old Testament commentaries ; v. 21)
Originally published: Downers Grove, Ill.: Inter-Varsity
Press, 1973. Includes bibliographical references. ISBN
978-0-8308-4221-6 (pbk.: alk. paper)
1. Bible. O.T. Jeremiah—Commentaries. 2. Bible. O.T.
Lamentations—Commentaries. I. Title.
BS1525.53.H37 2009
224'.207—dc22

                                                                    2009013991

USA ISBN 978-0-8308-4221-6

Set in Garamond 11/13pt
Typeset in Great Britain by Avocet Typeset, Chilton, Aylesbury, Bucks
Printed and bound in the United States of America ∞

P 18 17 16 15 14 13 12 11 10 9 8 7 6 5 4 3 2 1
Y 24 23 22 21 20 19 18 17 16 15 14 13 12 11 10 09

CONTENTS

LAMENTATIONS

GENERAL PREFACE

The aim of this series of Tyndale Old Testament Commentaries, as it was in the companion volumes on the New Testament, is to provide the student of the Bible with a handy, up-to-date commentary on each book, with the primary emphasis on exegesis. Major critical questions are discussed in the introductions and additional notes, while undue technicalities have been avoided.

In this series individual authors are, of course, free to make their own distinct contributions and express their own point of view on all controversial issues. Within the necessary limits of space they frequently draw attention to interpretations which they themselves do not hold but which represent the stated conclusions of sincere fellow Christians. The experience of the prophet Jeremiah and his teaching, with its emphasis on a bold personal and practical faith in God in a time of stress and opposition, are as relevant to our time as they were when he spoke and wrote some 2,500 years ago.

In the Old Testament in particular no single English translation is adequate to reflect the original text. The authors of these commentaries freely quote various versions, therefore, or give their own translation, in the endeavour to make the more difficult passages or words meaningful today. Where necessary, words from the Hebrew (and Aramaic) text underlying their studies are transliterated. This will help the reader who may be unfamiliar with the Semitic languages to identify the word under discussion and thus to follow the argument. It is assumed throughout that the reader will have ready access to one, or more, reliable renderings of the Bible in English.

Interest in the meaning and message of the Old Testament continues undiminished and it is hoped that this series will thus further the systematic study of the revelation of God and his will and ways as seen in these records. It is the prayer of the editor and publisher, as of the authors, that these books will help many to understand, and to respond to, the Word of God today.

D. J. Wiseman

AUTHOR'S PREFACE

The two books which comprise this commentary deal with one of the most tragic events in the life of the Chosen People. The first gives the reader a picture of the carefree Judeans of the pre-exilic period as they indulged shamelessly in the grossest forms of idolatry, ignored the many warnings of impending destruction given by their compatriot Jeremiah, and finally brought their long-promised ruin down on their heads. The second book shows something of the devastation and agony which accompanied divine judgment on national sin when Jerusalem fell in 587 BC. Together they formulate a theology of disaster commensurate with the nature of the catastrophe, but by their insistence upon the ethos of the Sinai covenant they point the way through suffering to spiritual renewal.

Relevant archaeological discoveries have been brought to bear upon the material under consideration, and the most significant textual problems have been discussed in the appropriate places in the commentary sections. Dates have been written in the form 605/4 BC because the Hebrew year did not coincide with the January-to-December period of our Western civil year.

I wish to express my thanks to the Rev. Norman Green, Assistant Director of the McLaughlin Planetarium in Toronto, for his great kindness and skill in correcting the proofs of this book, and to Professor D. J. Wiseman for his general oversight of the work.

R. K. Harrison
Wycliffe College, University of Toronto

CHIEF ABBREVIATIONS

ANET	*Ancient Near Eastern Texts relating to the Old Testament* edited by J. B. Pritchard, 1950.
AV, KJV	English Authorized Version (King James), 1611.
CCK	*Chronicles of Chaldaean Kings (626–556 B.C.) in the British Museum* by D. J. Wiseman, 1956.
EVV	English Versions.
HIOT	*Introduction to the Old Testament* by R. K. Harrison, 1969.
JBL	*Journal of Biblical Literature.*
JNES	*Journal of Near Eastern Studies.*
JQR	*Jewish Quarterly Review.*
LXX	The Septuagint (pre-Christian Greek version of the Old Testament).
MT	Massoretic (Hebrew) Text.
NBD	*The New Bible Dictionary* edited by J. D. Douglas, 1962.
NEB	New English Bible, 1970.
RSV	American Revised Standard Version, 1952.
RV	English Revised Version, 1881.

SHORT BIBLIOGRAPHY

Jeremiah

J. Bright, *Jeremiah* (1965).

A. Condamin, *Le Livre de Jérémie* (1920).

H. Freedman, *Jeremiah* (1949).

J. P. Hyatt, *The Interpreter's Bible* (1956), V, pp. 777–1142.

H. T. Kuist, *The Book of Jeremiah* (1960).

J. Muilenberg, *The Interpreter's Dictionary of the Bible* (1962), II, pp. 823–835.

T. W. Overholt, *The Threat of Falsehood* (1970).

J. Skinner, *Prophecy and Religion* (1922).

D. W. Thomas, 'The Prophet' *in the Lachish Ostraca* (1946).

J. G. S. S. Thomson, *The New Bible Dictionary* (1962), pp. 606–611.

H. Torczyner, *Lachish I, The Lachish Letters* (1938).

A. C. Welch, *Jeremiah* (1928).

G. E. Wright, *Biblical Archaeology* (1957).

Lamentations

B. Albrektson, *Studies in the Text and Theology of the Book of Lamentations* (1963).

S. Goldman, *Lamentations* in A. Cohen (ed.), *The Five Megilloth* (1959).

N. K. Gottwald, *Studies in the Book of Lamentations* (1954).

R. K. Harrison, *Introduction to the Old Testament* (1969), pp. 1065–
1071.

D. R. Hillers, *Lamentations* (1972).

A. S. Peake, *Jeremiah and Lamentations* (1912).

A. W. Streane, *Jeremiah and Lamentations* (1913).

JEREMIAH

INTRODUCTION

1. Title and place in canon

The book of Jeremiah received its name from its attributive author, the celebrated seventh-century BC prophet of Judah. It occupied a consistent position between Isaiah and Ezekiel in the Hebrew canon, although a rabbinic tradition, preserved in *Baba Bathra* 14*b*, mentioned the three works in the order of Jeremiah, Ezekiel and Isaiah. Numerous European manuscripts, especially from French and German sources, have adopted this tradition and placed Jeremiah at the head of the Latter Prophets.

In the LXX the book occupied the place in which it occurs in the English versions, but in the Peshitta Syriac it was found immediately after the twelve minor prophets. The name Jeremiah appeared in Hebrew either as *yirmĕ̌ya* or *yirmĕ̌yahu*, which was rendered by the LXX as *Ieremias* and by Latin versions as *Jeremias*. The precise meaning of the name is unknown, with suggested interpretations including 'the Lord founds', 'the Lord exalts' and 'the Lord throws down'.

2. Historical and archaeological background

It has been correctly observed that, at times of great moment in the
history of his people, God has called men of outstanding spiritual
stature to guide the nation according to the divine will and to foster
a vision of its destiny as the Chosen People. Jeremiah was one of
those summoned to discharge this important task, made all the
more difficult by the continued state of political and religious crisis
in the southern kingdom during his ministry. The prophet spoke at
a time when the ancient Near East was in an almost unparalleled state
of ferment. Within his lifetime he witnessed the collapse of the
mighty Assyrian empire and the rise of a virile Babylonian régime
which swept across the Near East and battled the powerful Egyptian armies to a standstill. In his own country he experienced a succession of political crises, interspersed with only the briefest periods
of hope for national stability. As the moribund Assyrian empire relin-
quished its grasp upon former spheres of political influence, the
southern kingdom enjoyed a welcome period of independence and
freedom from external control. This respite, however, ended all
too quickly when Egypt endeavoured to assert its former power in
Palestine and Syria. As though subjugation of this kind was not
enough, Judah was compelled to exchange a bad master for an even
worse one when the Babylonian and Chaldean armies brought an
end to the existence of the southern kingdom by a relentless de-
population of the land. The various agonizing crises through which the
nation passed are clearly evident in the utterances of one of Judah's
most loyal sons. By their anguish and pathos the sombre words of
Jeremiah mirror the stark tragedy attached to national extinction.

In order to appreciate the significance of the position which
Jeremiah held in Judah and the personal sorrow which he experienced as he proclaimed the fate of a wilful and unheeding nation,
it is necessary to be acquainted to some extent with the events
which culminated in the collapse of the southern kingdom. In 639
BC, about the time that Jeremiah was born, Josiah came to the
throne of Judah at the tender age of eight as the outcome of a popular movement which also liquidated those who had assassinated his
father Amon (2 Kgs 21:24; 2 Chr. 33:25). The passages which
described Josiah's reign (2 Kgs 22:1 – 23:30; 2 Chr. 34:1 – 35:27) were

concerned predominantly with the great religious reformation which he instituted. The first stage of this programme occurred in the eighth year of his reign (c. 631 BC), not long before the death of Ashurbanipal (c. 626 BC),[1] the last great Assyrian ruler. Jeremiah seems to have been influenced profoundly by the way in which Josiah consistently renounced the corrupt polytheism which his father Amon and his grandfather Manasseh had espoused.

After the death of Ashurbanipal the Assyrians were so beset by internal weaknesses that they were unable to prevent Josiah from moving towards independence by his summary repudiation of Assyrian suzerainty. Others also capitalized on the overextended position of the Assyrians, including the barbarous Cimmerians and Scythians from the Caucasus region. The Medes of western Iran, against whom the Assyrians had fought earlier with indifferent success, began to pose a serious threat to the very existence of the empire, and this became acute when Babylon asserted her own independence under Nabopolassar (626–605 BC). Although Assyria had experienced some military success in Egypt under Ashurbanipal in 663 BC, this situation was reversed in an upsurge of Egyptian power following the accession of the pharaoh Psammetichus (664–610 BC).

About five years after Josiah instituted his reforms in Jerusalem, Jeremiah received a divine call to prophesy to the people of Judah. Between this time (c. 626 BC)[2] and the religious reformation of 621 BC, Jeremiah concentrated upon warning the nation about the imminent invasion from the north (1:13f.) and denouncing the

---

1. For discussions of this date see A. Poebel, *JNES*, II, 1943, pp. 85f.; W. H. Dubberstein, *JNES*, III, 1944, pp. 38ff.; F. M. Cross and D. N. Freedman, *JNES*, XII, 1953, pp. 56ff.; C. J. Gadd, *Anatolian Studies*, VIII, 1958, pp. 35ff.; W. F. Albright, *The Biblical Period from Abraham to Ezra* (1963), p. 79.

2. Cf. J. P. Hyatt, *JBL*, LIX, 1940, pp. 112, 121; *JNES*, I, 1942, pp. 156ff.; and in *The Interpreter's Bible* (1956), V, pp. 779f., postulated a date of between 614 and 612 BC for the prophet's call by rejecting the evidence of Jer. 1:2. Cf. the reply of H. H. Rowley in *Studies in Old Testament Prophecy presented to T. H. Robinson* (1946), p. 158, and *Men of God* (1963), pp. 136ff.

various corruptions of contemporary life. When a law-scroll was discovered in the temple during renovations to the fabric of the building it was brought to the attention of the king, and the resultant reformation which Josiah instituted brought Jeremiah to the forefront as a vocal exponent of the covenant relationship between God and Israel (11:1–8).

In Assyria events were approaching a climax. About 617 BC the Babylonians under Nabopolassar allied with the Medes and began to launch attacks upon all the principal Assyrian cities. The capital Assur was conquered in 614 BC and two years later mighty Nineveh capitulated to the invaders. The disorganized Assyrians fled to Harran and found an ally in Psammetichus, who doubtless wished to maintain Assyria as a buffer state against resurgent Babylonia. Harran fell to the Babylonians and Medes in 610 BC, the year in which Psammetichus died, and further Assyrian resistance to Babylon ended abruptly.

Determined to assert Egyptian power in Syro-Palestine, the pharaoh Necho (610–594 BC), the successor of Psammetichus, marched into the Palestinian coastal plain with the intention, made clear from the Babylonian Chronicle, of coming to the assistance of the Assyrians who were making a desperate stand against the Babylonians at Harran. This move caused great concern to Josiah of Judah, since he had no desire to see Egyptian armies supporting the hereditary enemies of the southern kingdom. Accordingly he marched to Megiddo in 609 BC in an attempt to block the advance of the Egyptian forces, but was killed in the ensuing battle. The loss of both its ruler and its independence at one blow was the first major tragedy to overtake the kingdom of Judah, and the calamity received its full expression of sorrow when the body of Josiah was brought back to Jerusalem in his chariot (2 Kgs 23:29f.; 2 Chr. 35:20–25).

Jehoahaz II, son of Josiah, succeeded his father in a wave of popular feeling, but Necho felt threatened by this arrangement and precipitated yet another crisis in Judah three months after the accession of Jehoahaz by deposing him and replacing him with Jehoiakim, his elder brother. Jehoahaz was taken to Egypt (2 Kgs 23:31–35), presumably as a hostage to ensure the continued subservience of Judah, which was placed under heavy tribute to Egypt, thus losing its political independence.

For the next three years Necho maintained considerable military strength in Palestine and Syria, being helped by the fact that the Babylonians were busily regrouping their forces and making their northern flank secure against attack from mountain tribes. As a result of this, apart from sporadic raids, no serious military engagements were undertaken by the Babylonians against the Egyptians. During this period the personal fortunes of the prophet Jeremiah were at as low an ebb as those of the people of Judah. His troubles were precipitated by the so-called 'temple address' (7:1 – 8:3) which was delivered in Jerusalem about 609 BC. With great boldness the prophet ridiculed the popular idea that a naive trust in the temple as the shrine of God would automatically guarantee the people deliverance in a time of crisis. This stand in itself was bad enough, but when he went on to prophesy that the much-revered temple would meet the fate which had overtaken the shrine at Shiloh centuries earlier, the people could stand his denunciations no longer, and the storm of protest which resulted almost cost him his life.

A person less conscious than Jeremiah of his mission as a divinely-appointed prophet to a disbelieving, apostate and wanton generation might well have abandoned the situation at that point as being absolutely hopeless. But Jeremiah was nothing if not an ardent and loyal patriot, and therefore he felt it his duty to inform his countrymen of the dangers lurking in the current international situation. With the collapse of the Assyrian empire a powerful Babylonian régime arose to challenge all comers in the military sphere. Under vigorous leadership the international aspirations of the Egyptians had also been renewed after more than a century of quiescence, and a conflict with Babylon was a foregone conclusion.

Judah had now been reduced to a buffer state, and the foretaste of battle experienced in 609 BC did not indicate an encouraging future. Indeed, it appeared to Jeremiah that whatever happened politically, Judah was destined to become a battleground. With this deplorable prospect in mind the prophet announced to all who would listen that the southern kingdom would fall victim to the might of Nebuchadnezzar (25:9). So firm was his insistence upon the imminence of this catastrophe that out of deep loyalty to his country he made strenuous attempts to persuade his compatriots to become vassals of Babylon immediately, and so escape the carnage which would occur should other counsel prevail (27:6–22). Unfortunately for his patriotism and his convictions the trend of popular feeling was against him, an attitude which ultimately sealed the doom of the nation.

Though obviously aware of the political crises which had overtaken Judah, Jehoiakim showed little appreciation of the alarming extent to which the morality fostered by Josiah's reformation was collapsing. While there is no evidence that the pagan excesses of Manasseh's reign arose once more in Judah, some of the current Canaanite religious practices came into vogue at this time (7:16–18; 11:9–13). That this trend appears to have had at least semi-official backing seems evident from the fact that those who opposed it did so at the risk of their lives (26:20–23). His lack of ability to see matters in proper perspective led Jehoiakim to construct a larger and more splendid palace for which forced labour was employed (22:13–19), an act which did not endear him to Jeremiah. This occurrence showed that the callous disregard which this puppet-ruler actually had for the welfare of his people and for the prophet was typical of the man himself.

Events of profound international significance were precipitated when Necho marched to the Euphrates from Megiddo in 605 BC and regrouped his forces at Carchemish, a city guarding the main ford across the river sixty-three miles north-east of Aleppo. His aim was to recapture the city and make it a base for harassing the Babylonians. To his surprise the latter entered the city suddenly in the late spring of 605 BC under the vigorous leadership of Nebuchadnezzar II. The Egyptians were completely routed in fierce combat around the city (46:2), and retreated in considerable disorder to Hamath on the Orontes. The battle of Carchemish thus demonstrated the military superiority of the Babylonians, and marked the point at which the hegemony of the Near East passed into their hands. Consequently Jeremiah was more convinced than ever that Judah should become a Babylonian vassal if it was to survive as a nation. Since all the trading-routes to Egypt were now irrevocably under Babylonian control, the prophet saw clearly that it was only a matter of time before the Babylonians made a further devastating attack upon Egypt.

Unwilling to allow his enemies time for regrouping, Nebuchadnezzar marched into the Palestinian coastal plain in 604 BC, sacked
Ashkelon and took many of its inhabitants captive to Babylon.[3] This
tragic event had been anticipated by Jeremiah (47:5–7) and also by
Zephaniah (Zeph. 2:4–7), and seems to have had a profound effect
upon the outlook of the people of Judah. Doubtless they began to
sense that further calamities could not be long delayed, and accordingly a fast was proclaimed in Judah (Jer. 36:9). It may be significant
that the date of this fast coincided with Nebuchadnezzar's campaign
against Ashkelon. At all events in 604 BC, Jehoiakim, along with some
other rulers, decided to submit to Nebuchadnezzar and become his
vassal (36:9–29). Although Jehoiakim was a weak king who pandered
to his own vanity and selfishness, he was also very much of a political opportunist. His abandonment of Egyptian suzerainty was
clearly designed to gain temporary respite for Judah, and at that out
of sheer necessity. Once the immediate political crisis had eased he
would again court the favour of Egypt, as the events of 601 BC
proved.

    Late that year the Babylonians marched against the frontier out-
posts of Egypt and met surprisingly firm resistance. Babylonian
cuneiform sources indicate that Nebuchadnezzar returned home for
a year to re-equip his forces, an eventuality made necessary by the
virility of Egyptian resistance. Encouraged by this turn of events,
Jehoiakim committed the fatal error of casting in his lot once more
with Egypt and rejecting the suzerainty of Babylon (2 Kgs 24:1),
despite the urgent warnings of Jeremiah (cf. Jer. 22:13–19). Since the
main Babylonian armies were not yet to hand, Nebuchadnezzar dis-
patched local garrison troops, along with Syrians, Moabites and
Ammonites, to raid the southern kingdom (2 Kgs 24:2).

    In December of 598 BC the re-equipped Babylonian army
marched on Palestine, and at this juncture Jehoiakim died, some three
months before Jerusalem actually fell. How he met his end is
unknown, and thus it cannot be said for certain that he was assassinated in the hope that the Babylonians would be more lenient with

_____

3. Cf. E. F. Weidner, *Mélanges syriens offerts à M. René Dussaud* (1939), II,
pp. 923ff.

the people of Judah. However, apart from plundering the temple, Nebuchadnezzar did not ravage the city when it fell on the second day of the month Adar (March 15–16) in 597 BC, restricting his activities to the deportation of king Jehoiachin,[4] who had succeeded his father (2 Kgs 24:8ff.), the queen-mother, the royal court, and the potential leaders among the people. He even permitted Judah to continue its existence as a state under the rule of Zedekiah, the youngest son of king Josiah (Jer. 1:3) and uncle of Jehoiachin (2 Kgs 24:17). Unfortunately this act sealed the doom of the southern kingdom, for Zedekiah proved to be a weak individual who was unable to exert proper control over his subjects (Jer. 38:5, 19). In particular he found it impossible to compensate for the lack of political leadership caused by the removal of court officials to Babylonia and, although he had taken an oath of loyalty to his new masters, his current officers of state preferred to look to Egypt for political and military support.

In 595/4 BC an uprising occurred in Babylonia which may possibly have involved certain of the people deported from Judah, judging from the fact that Nebuchadnezzar seems to have executed certain Judean prophets (cf. 29:21f.). This event had other ramifications, since false prophets were predicting that the exile would last for only two years, and were attempting both from Babylonia and Jerusalem to secure the death of Jeremiah, who by contrast had foretold an exile of some seventy years.

Outside Judah the revolt in Babylonia, though quelled quickly, had stirred up hopes of a collapse of Babylonian power. With this expectation representatives from Edom, Ammon and Moab came to Jerusalem in 594/3 BC to discuss, along with emissaries from Tyre and Sidon, the possibility of rebelling against Babylon (27:3). Popular feeling was unquestionably influenced by the utterances of false prophets, which seemed to point to an imminent return of the exiles (28:2ff.). Jeremiah, however, was vigorously opposed to any abandonment of Babylonian suzerainty, and it may have been as a result of his utterances that Zedekiah visited Babylon that same year (51:59), doubtless to allay the suspicions of Nebuchadnezzar.

---

4. Cf. W. F. Albright, *BA*, V, 1942, No. 4, pp. 49ff.

When the pharaoh Hophra came to the throne of Egypt in 589 BC, he ushered in a new period of political uncertainty for Judah by interfering in Palestinian affairs much as his father Psammetichus II (594–589 BC) had done earlier. Zedekiah yielded to pressure from his own inexperienced ruling class and reluctantly entered into negotiations with Hophra. Not unnaturally the Babylonians viewed this as an act of rebellion which demanded the most serious of punishments. In 587 BC the Babylonian and Chaldean armies swept down upon the small states of Syria (cf. 25:9) and reduced the fortified cities of Judah one by one. Within three months only Lachish (Tell ed-Duweir) in south-west Judah and Azekah (Tell ez-Zakariyah) stood in the path of an onslaught upon Jerusalem. Vivid illustration of the contemporary political and military situation has been provided by the discovery of some inscribed pottery at Lachish, which shows among other things the extent to which morale in Jerusalem had been weakened by the crisis.

Just as all hope seemed lost, news came to the capital that the Egyptians were marching to the relief of the city. The Babylonians immediately diverted their forces from blockaded Jerusalem to meet this threat to their grip on southern Palestine (37:3, 5), and within a short time they had sent the Egyptians fleeing to their own borders. Jerusalem continued to resist the Babylonian siege for some months and, though Jeremiah urged Zedekiah to surrender (37:3–10; 38:14–23), the king was unwilling or unable to do so.

When his advice was rejected Jeremiah endeavoured to leave the city, but was accused of deserting to the enemy and was thrown unceremoniously into prison (37:11–21), where he remained until the city fell. Just as famine took hold in 587 BC the Babylonians captured Jerusalem and brought Judah's existence as a kingdom to an end. The city was pillaged, Zedekiah himself was blinded and taken captive to Babylon along with many of his people, and the invading Chaldean forces occupied Jerusalem and its environs. By contrast, Jeremiah was removed from his prison and on the orders of Nebuchadnezzar was treated with great deference.

When Gedaliah was appointed governor of Judah under the provincial system of the Babylonian empire, Jeremiah joined him at Mizpah (40:6) and supported his attempts to restore some order to society. But intrigue among supporters of the old royal house resulted in the murder of Gedaliah, whereupon the remnant at Mizpah fled to Egypt, taking Jeremiah with them (42:1–22). In 581 BC a third deportation from Judah took place on the orders of Nebuchadnezzar, perhaps in reprisal for the murder of Gedaliah, and the once-prosperous kingdom of Judah was absorbed into the neighbouring province of Samaria.

Archaeological discoveries have thrown a good deal of light upon the last days of the southern kingdom, and have corroborated the historicity of the biblical narrative in several important areas. The history of the period between 626 and 594 BC was illumined from an extra-biblical standpoint when D. J. Wiseman discovered in 1956 four additional tablets of the Babylonian Chronicle in the archives of the British Museum.[5] This material furnished the first secular account of the fall of Jerusalem, and also supplied important information about the campaigns of the Babylonian armies from 626 BC.

The Chronicle recorded the shattering defeat of the Egyptians at Carchemish in 605 BC and the subsequent Babylonian occupation of 'the whole area of Hatti'. A previously unrecorded engagement between Egypt and Babylon occurred in 601 BC, in which, according to the Chronicle, both sides sustained severe losses. In consequence Nebuchadnezzar was compelled to withdraw to Babylon for a year to re-equip his army, and the following twelve months were spent in probing the strength of defences in Syria. From the evidence furnished by the Chronicle it is now possible to date the fall of Jerusalem on March 15–16, 597 BC with complete accuracy.[6] These and other facets of this highly important secular source helped to confirm the accuracy of the biblical narrative as well as furnishing new information about the international situation in the seventh century BC.

The last days of Judah were also vividly illustrated in 1935, when eighteen ostraca or potsherds, inscribed in the same kind of ancient Hebrew script as that found on the Moabite Stone, were uncovered

---

5. D. J. Wiseman. *Chronicles of Chaldaean Kings (626–556 B.C.) in the British Museum* (1956).

6. *CCK*, pp. 32ff.

at the site of ancient Lachish.[7] The discovery was made by J. L. Starkey, who found the pieces of broken pottery in the ruins of a small guardroom situated just outside the city gate. Three years later three more inscribed potsherds were recovered from the same general area, and together they comprise letters and lists of names from the period immediately prior to 587 BC.

Most of the texts can be dated from 589 BC, and although they have been poorly preserved it is clear that a number of them are dispatches of a military nature.[8] In one of these (Ostracon IV) the writer complained that only Lachish and Azekah stood between the enemy and Jerusalem, while another letter (Ostracon VI) criticized the nobility in Jerusalem for lowering the morale of the inhabitants. There is an ironic note about this particular complaint, since it was the very thing of which Jeremiah himself had been accused by the selfsame nobility in the days of Zedekiah (38:4).

Ostracon III, written by Hoshaiah, the author of Ostracon IV, made reference to a certain 'prophet' who was otherwise not identified. Some scholars have felt that this was an allusion to the activities of Jeremiah, while others have maintained that an unknown contemporary prophet was being cited when the letter was written. Such a procedure would be by no means unusual in the Ancient Near East, since prophetic oracles were frequently sought and given in the conduct of military affairs. H. Torczyner[9] maintained that the ostraca were part of a group dealing with the fate of a prophet whom he identified with Urijah (Uriah) of Kiriath-jearim. This man had

---

7. Cf. H. Torczyner, *Lachish I, The Lachish Letters* (1938); W. F. Albright, *Bulletin of the American Schools of Oriental Research*, 70, 1938, pp. 11ff.; ibid., 73, 1939, pp. 16ff.; ibid., 82, 1941, pp. 18ff.; J. Hempel, *Zeitschrift für die alttestamentliche Wissenschaft*, XV, 1938, pp. 126ff.; J. W. Jack, *Palestine Exploration Quarterly*, 1938, pp. 165ff.; R. de Vaux, *Revue Biblique*, XLVIII, 1939, pp. 181ff.; D. W. Thomas, *Journal of Theological Studies*, XL, 1939, pp. 1ff.; *Palestine Exploration Quarterly*, 1940, pp. 148ff.; ibid., 1946, pp. 38ff., 86ff.; ibid., 1948, pp. 131ff.; ibid., 1950, pp. 1ff.

8. The texts are translated by W. F. Albright in *ANET*, pp. 321f. Cf. D. W. Thomas (ed.), *Documents from Old Testament Times* (1958), pp. 212ff.

9. Cf. H. Torczyner, *Lachish I, The Lachish Letters*, pp. 18, 38.

foretold the fall of Jerusalem and had then fled to Egypt to avoid being killed. However, he was extradited shortly after the event by order of Jehoiakim and was brought back to Jerusalem, where he was executed (26:20–23). It seems more probable, however, that the letters deal with the military crisis which had overtaken Judah as a result of the Babylonian invasion, and since the 'prophet' was unnamed it is very doubtful if his identity will ever be established.[10] It will be clear from the foregoing, however, that this correspondence constitutes a highly valuable secular 'supplement' to the prophecy of Jeremiah.

Excavations near the Ishtar Gate of ancient Babylon have uncovered a number of tablets listing the rations of grain and oil allotted to the captives living in Babylon between 595 and 570 BC. Included in the list was 'Yaukin king of the land of Yahud', who was mentioned in 2 Kings 25:29f. as a recipient of royal bounty.[11] Independent evidence of the status of Jehoiachin in Babylon was supplied by the discovery of three stamped jar handles at Debir and Beth-shemesh. They carried the inscription, 'belonging to Eliakim, steward of Yaukin', each impression having been made from the same seal.[12] This shows that the Babylonians still regarded the crown property as his, and that a steward had supervised it between 598 and 587 BC.

Another seal impression recovered in 1935 from the ruins of Lachish bore the inscription: 'to Gedaliah who is over the household'.[13] The reverse side of the seal showed traces of the papyrus document to which it had been attached originally. The owner of the

---

10. The identification with Urijah (Uriah) was denied by D. W. Thomas, *Journal of Theological Studies*, XL, 1939, pp. 5f. On this general problem see J. W. Jack, *Palestine Exploration Quarterly*, 1938, pp. 165ff.; C. H. Gordon, *The Living Past* (1941), p. 189; D. W. Thomas, *'The Prophet' in the Lachish Ostraca* (1940), pp. 7ff.; J. Hempel and L. Rost (eds.), *Von Ugarit nach Qumran* (1958), pp. 244ff.

11. Cf. R. Koldewey, *Das Wieder Erstehende Babylon* (1925), pp. 90ff. For the texts see *ANET*, p. 308; *Documents from Old Testament Times*, pp. 84ff.

12. Cf. G. E. Wright, *Biblical Archaeology* (1957), pl. 125.

13. Cf. ibid., pl. 128.

seal was unquestionably the Gedaliah who had been appointed
under Nebuchadnezzar as governor of Judah (2 Kgs 25:22). The title
'who is over the household' was carried by the senior administrative
official who stood next in rank to the king. From this and other evidence it will be apparent that the book of Jeremiah is particularly
amenable to illustration and support by modern archaeological
discoveries.

3. Ancient Near Eastern covenant forms

The prophecy of Jeremiah had a great deal to say about the covenant
with Israel, and is actually of particular importance in marking a
point where the historical covenantal observances had broken down
and were about to be replaced by new ones. The covenant in question was that enacted between God and the Israelites at Sinai, which
resulted, in broad terms, in Israel becoming the Chosen People and
heirs of the Promised Land. The terms of the agreement stipulated
that God would provide for the total needs of his people if they in
turn would be obedient to his commands and worship no other deity
(cf. Exod. 20:3). The effect of this was to establish Israel as a vehi-
cle of divine revelation in the world and constitute her as a witness
in contemporary pagan society to the nature and purposes of the one
true and living God.

While covenants of various kinds went back to the third millennium BC in the Near East, and are represented in the Old Testament
by such agreements as those between God and Noah (cf. Gen. 9:9)
and God and Abram (cf. Gen. 15:18; 17:7), the structure and form
of Mosaic and post-Mosaic covenants has come in for particular illu-
mination recently as a result of tablet discoveries at Boghazköy.[14]
These sources indicate that in the second and first millennia BC there
were two principal varieties of international treaty, namely that

14. For the main texts see E. F. Weidner, *Politische Dokumente aus Kleinasien*
    (1923), 1–11; J. Friedrich, *Staatsverträge des Hatti-Reiches* (1926–30), 1–11;
    J. Nougayrol, *Palais Royal d'Ugarit* (1956), IV, pp. 85ff., 287ff.; A. Goetze,
    Kleinasien (1957 ed.), pp. 95f.; H. Klengel, *Orientalistische Literatur Zeitung*,
    LIX, 1964, col. 437ff.

between parties bound by identical obligations (known as a parity treaty), and that between a great king and a vassal (known as a suzerainty or vassal treaty). Such sophisticated forms of agreement were apparently basic to the stability of the ancient Hittite empire, particularly that of the suzerainty treaty. Late second-millennium BC covenants of this variety followed a specific pattern, comprising a *preamble* or title, which identified the instigator of the covenant; a *historical prologue*, which reviewed past relations between the suzerain and the vassal and indicated that past benefactions by the former constituted grounds for gratitude and future obedience on the part of the latter; *basic and detailed stipulations*, imposed by the great king upon the vassal; a provision for the *deposition and public reading* of the covenant at intervals by the vassal; a list of *deities as witnesses* to the agreement; and an enumeration of the *blessings or curses* consequent upon either observance or neglect of the covenant provisions.

Almost all fourteenth- and thirteenth-century BC treaties known to the present followed this basic pattern, the only variation being in the omission of certain components. In addition to the foregoing form, some covenants were also attested by means of a ceremonial oath of obedience, a solemn ratification ritual, and a basic mode of procedure to be followed when vassals became recalcitrant. A difference of some significance which has been discovered through a comparison of second- and first-millennium BC treaties of an international nature was that, in the latter, the *historical prologue* was usually omitted.

Certain scholars[15] have argued from the evidence presented by these formulations to the conclusion that there is little fundamental change in the structure of covenants between the second and first millennia BC. While it is true that there are certain constant elements present in treaties from both periods, there can be no question that, in the treaties published to date, the order of elements in first-millennium BC treaties is far less stable and consistent than can be

---

15. E.g., D. J. Wiseman, *Iraq*, XX, 1958, p. 28; J. A. Thompson, *The Ancient Near Eastern Treaties and the Old Testament* (1964), pp. 14f.; D. J. McCarthy, *Treaty and Covenant* (1963), pp. 80ff.

observed in dateable late second-millennium counterparts. Even the 'fundamental unity' of which McCarthy speaks[16] breaks down in connection with the historical prologue, which was a typical feature of late second-millennium BC covenants, but which has to be demonstrated conclusively in many published first-millennium BC treaties.[17] The Sinai covenant corresponds remarkably to the pattern of late second millennium BC treaties,[18] containing as it does a *preamble* (Exod. 20:1); a *historical introduction* (Exod. 20:2); *stipulations* of a basic nature (Exod. 20:3–17, 22–26; 21–23; 25–31); a provision for the *deposition of the text* (Exod. 25:16; 34:1, 28–29); the presence of *witnesses* (cf. Exod. 24:4), and the *oath* and *solemn ceremony* (Exod. 24:1–11). Such a form places the Sinai covenant well within the Mosaic age, and suggests also a late second-millennium BC period for covenant renewals such as are seen in Deuteronomy and Joshua 24. The Sinaitic covenant was thus meant to be understood by Israel in a manner similar to that in which the secular treaties were regarded in contemporary society. While the covenant with Israel was unique in antiquity in linking a nation to the interests of a living God, it was just as binding as other types of treaties in so far as matters of observance were concerned. The repudiation of parity or suzerainty agreements carried certain penalties, as observed above, and this was also true of the Sinai covenant. Because of the apostasy which commenced during the wilderness period and posed a serious threat to national spirituality by the Judges period, the Israelites had long

16. D. J. McCarthy, *Treaty and Covenant*, p. 80. See also D. J. Wiseman's criticism of McCarthy's position in D. W. Thomas (ed.), *Archaeology and Old Testament Study* (1967), p. 132 n.10.

17. This statement applies to the situation described in Neh. 9 – 10, which is actually a covenant-renewal ceremony having reference to the Sinai enactment, and not the instituting of an entirely new covenant.

18. Cf. G. E. Mendenhall, *BA*, XVII, 1954, No. 3, pp. 50ff.; ibid., *The Interpreter's Dictionary of the Bible* (1962), I, pp. 714ff.; M. G. Kline, *Treaty of the Great King* (1963), pp. 42ff., 48; W. L. Moran, *Biblica*, XLIII, 1962, p. 103; J. A. Thompson, *The Ancient Near Eastern Treaties and the Old Testament* (1964); K. A. Kitchen, *Ancient Orient and Old Testament* (1966), pp. 90ff., et al.

stood under threat of punishment. The mission of the pre-exilic prophets actually constituted a sustained effort to recall disobedient Israel to an observance of the pledges given by their ancestors at Sinai in an attempt to offset the worst implications of apostasy. Since these efforts were mostly ineffective, there could be no question as to the inevitability of divine retribution, and it was this critical situation which haunted Jeremiah throughout his ministry. Though well aware that the threats of punishment were conditional upon continued national apostasy, he also knew that the obstinate disregard of the covenantal obligations made catastrophe merely a matter of time. This sensitive and patriotic Judean had the unenviable task of proclaiming a message of doom to his unheeding fellow-citizens, and it was only his intense loyalty to the ethos of the Sinaitic covenant that enabled him to discharge his prophetic office with such signal fidelity.

4. Structure, authorship and date

It is now increasingly realized that the extant writings of the prophets actually comprise anthologies of their utterances,[19] and the book of Jeremiah is no exception to this general principle. Like some other prophecies the work exhibits a wide variety of literary types and forms, the poetry appearing under such diverse guises as that of the lyric war stanzas (4:5–8, 13–16, 19–22), the stylistic diversity of the indictment of pagan nations (46:3–12; 50:35–38), and the sad pathos of out-poured grief (13:15–17), while the prose manifests such different forms as that of the acted parable (13:1–11; 18:1–6), the visionary experience (24:1–10), vivid biographical data (26:1–24; 27:1 – 28:16), and sermonic material (7:1–15; 34:12–22). Many of the prophetic oracles are cast in poetic form as in the case of other Old Testament books, and the general nature of this type of literature will be examined in the Introduction to Lamentations, towards the end of this volume. Although the prose and poetic literary units vary considerably in length, form and content, different parts of the book

---

19. Cf. W. F. Albright, *From the Stone Age to Christianity* (1957), p. 275; J. Bright, *Jeremiah* (1965), pp. xli, lxxix.

exhibit a relative consistency of style. This phenomenon has furnished a basis for the literary criticism of Jeremiah, the results of which, however, are not notably uniform, due largely to the subjective nature of the approach. Duhm[20] made the first important contribution by recognizing in the prophecy the presence of three principal types of material, namely poetic sayings, biographical prose and prose discourses. This view was expanded and applied in the light of concepts of oral tradition by other scholars, especially Mowinckel,[21] who regarded the prophecy as a compilation of three major collections of material. Some scholars have understood the extant prophecy as an accumulation of short 'books', and have taken the reference in 25:13a as indicating the end of one such 'book'.[22] Arguing from the date furnished in 25:1, the scope of this 'book' has been alleged to include the utterances proclaimed from about 626 BC to 605 BC, since chapter one is supposedly of a kind with 25:1–13a.

Because this period is approximately that covered by the scroll mentioned in chapter 36, it has been suggested that 25:1–13a comprises either the beginning or the end of such a document. Since, however, the first twenty-four chapters of the extant prophecy contain material which is considerably later than 605 BC, it is not easy to see how such narratives could have found their way into a scroll of that date.

Yet another 'book' has been postulated in terms of chapters 46 to 51, a section comprising oracles uttered against various pagan nations, and the existence of this collection in separate form has been based on the MT heading of 46:1. Because this material appears in the LXX in a different order and location from that of the MT, it has been alleged that the oracles were most probably non-Jeremianic and enjoyed a separate history of transmission.[23] All that this may

20. B. Duhm, *Das Buch Jeremia* (1901), pp. xiff. For a brief survey of theories of compilation see *HIOT*, pp. 809ff.

21. S. Mowinckel, *Zur Komposition des Buches Jeremia* (1914), pp. 7ff.

22. Cf. J. Muilenburg, *The Interpreter's Dictionary of the Bible*, II, p. 833; J. Bright, *Jeremiah*, p. lvii.

23. Cf. P. Volz, *Jeremia* (1928), pp. 378ff.; J. Skinner, *Prophecy and Religion* (1961 ed.), pp. 239f. n. 3.

mean, however, is merely that the compilers of the LXX version decided to rearrange the order of the oracles and place them in a different position in their own translation for reasons which are no more apparent to the modern scholarly mind than are those which underlay the order of the material in the MT. What should be noticed in this connection, however, is that the prophecy contains blocks of literature of a kind which can be discerned in other prophecies (cf. Isa. 13 – 23; Amos 1:3 – 2:3; Ezek. 25 – 32), so that the problem presented here is by no means unique.

A third independent 'book' has been thought to comprise chapters 30 and 31,[24] and might even include chapters 32, and 33 as well.[25] This section consists of another block of literary material of a distinctive character, and since it contains many utterances about hope for the future it has been styled the 'Book of Consolation' in some circles.

Whether something of the foregoing constituted the actual pattern which determined the growth of the extant work or not, it is very important for the reader to understand that the term 'book' as employed above has no relationship to the modern use of that word. Indeed, the idea of a 'book' in this connection can be misleading, and for this reason alone the blocks of material should be recognized instead for what they actually are, namely collections of narratives, sayings relating to specific topics, and oracles of various sorts, none of which exhibits any consistent plan of arrangement, and least of all a chronological one.

As has been noted already, the book of Jeremiah contains a number of differing literary genres, with prose and poetry being interspersed in the extant work in approximately equivalent amounts. However, both main elements appear in variant forms, with the result that different types of poetry are in evidence while the prose oracles are sometimes proclaimed in the first person and at other times in the third person. Despite this diversity there is a remarkable coherence of language and thought-forms, so that, in reading the MT, there is seldom any doubt that one is studying the book of Jeremiah, even

24. Cf. O. Eissfeldt, *The Old Testament: An Introduction* (1965), p. 361.
25. So R. H. Pfeiffer, *Introduction to the Old Testament* (1941), p. 501.

when the thought of other prophets is being reflected. This circumstance furnishes a strong argument for the integrity and unity of authorship of the composition.

Many modern scholars[26] have followed Mowinckel to varying extents in isolating three major literary types in the prophecy in terms of biographical prose, prose discourses and poetic sayings, and on the basis of a critical reconstruction of Hebrew history have suggested that the prophecy came into existence when the utterances of Jeremiah and the biographical narratives of Baruch were edited and expanded by exilic and post-exilic ('Deuteronomistic') supporters of the reform movement instituted under Josiah. This critical reconstruction has the effect of imposing a fairly late date upon the final form of the prophecy, as, unfortunately, it also does for the book of Deuteronomy. Needless to say, such an approach does not trouble to explain what possible relevance the reforms of Josiah could have had for an exilic and post-exilic situation, when the whole issue of pagan Canaanite idolatry was an absolutely dead one. However many literary types can be identified and isolated from the extant prophecy, the simple fact is that they furnish absolutely no understanding whatever of the principles by which the material was arranged.

As opposed to the internal evidence of the prophecy, which points to a reasonably short though complex history of transmission of the text, some scholars, particularly in Scandinavia, have used the concept of oral transmission to imply that the prophecy only attained its final form long after the seventh century BC.[27] They have argued that, because of a comparative scarcity of writing materials, the utterances of the prophet were handed down from one generation to another primarily by word of mouth, and only at the end of this prolonged process were the various oracles finally committed to writing.

---

26. E.g., H. G. May, *JBL*, LXI, 1942, pp. 139ff.; W. Rudolph, *Jeremia* (1947), pp. xiiiff.

27. These scholars include Birkeland, Engnell, Mowinckel, Nielsen and Nyberg. For a brief review of their studies see C. R. North in H. H. Rowley (ed.), *The Old Testament in Modern Study* (1951), pp. 76ff.

Aside from the wholly gratuitous assumption that writing materials were actually scarce at the time, a view for which there is no factual evidence whatever,[28] such arguments have the double demerit of misunderstanding the nature of oral transmission in the Ancient Near East and of assuming that the techniques used by Norse balladeers in the perpetuation of their material were also valid for oriental peoples. A vast body of comparative literary sources is now available to make it abundantly clear that, in the Ancient Near East, anything which was deemed to be of special significance was written down at or very shortly after the time of occurrence. Oral transmission was employed primarily to proclaim the material spatially to the people of that particular generation, and it was only as these individuals passed it on to their descendants that oral transmission assumed a more lineal character.[29]

In Near Eastern antiquity written and oral forms of the same event commonly existed side by side, this being possible because of the high degree of literacy in contemporary society. In Greece and Europe by contrast, where the population was largely illiterate, the sagas, legends, histories and other materials were dependent for their preservation upon the tastes and habits of wandering bards or camp fire balladeers, who were not averse to varying the content of their traditions somewhat as occasion dictated. As a result it was only at a comparatively late stage in the history of their transmission that such materials were put into written form.

It may be remarked at this juncture that in Old Testament studies, as in other branches of knowledge, it is of fundamental importance for correct procedures of method to be applied to the problems at hand. As far as the compilation and transmission of Jeremiah are concerned, it will have become apparent to the reader that the difficulties are of a surprisingly complex nature. Hence if

---

28. On writing materials and their general availability see D. J. Wiseman, *NBD*, pp. 1342ff.; R. J. Williams, *The Interpreter's Dictionary of the Bible*, IV, pp. 915ff.

29. On the Scandinavian traditio-historical school see E. Nielsen, *Oral Tradition* (1954); K. A. Kitchen, *Ancient Orient and Old Testament*, pp. 135ff.; *HIOT*, pp. 761f.

a system of arbitrary and subjective delineation of literary units is wedded to a theory of textual transmission which is patently out of harmony with the known scribal practices current in the Ancient Near East, and is applied to a matter such as the transmission of Jeremiah, the difficulties in the way of arriving at even a reasonably coherent view of the processes will be multiplied enormously. The use of oral tradition in this general context needs to be understood correctly if a proper method is to be brought to bear upon the elucidation of the problems connected with the way in which Jeremiah assumed its final form. Consequently it is salutary for the reader to note the reminder of Bright[30] to the effect that the writing down of Jeremiah's sayings began at an early stage, regardless of the nature of oral transmission.

From internal evidence it would appear that the prophetic oracles were first committed to writing in the fourth year of Jehoiakim (604 BC), when, in the words of Baruch, Jeremiah 'dictated all these words to me, while I inscribed them with ink on the scroll' (36:18). This material covered the events of the period beginning about 626 BC and ending at the point at which the narratives appeared in written form, i.e., 605/4 BC. These were the oracles destroyed by Jehoiakim in the fourth year of his reign (605/4 BC). Precisely what the scroll contained is, of course, entirely unknown, except that 36:2 suggests that it included 'all the words which I have spoken to you against Israel and Judah and all the nations'. Thus its contents must have been very similar to many of the warnings and denunciations occurring in the first twenty chapters of the canonical book.

Jeremiah subsequently dictated yet another scroll to Baruch his secretary, adding 'many similar words' to what had been included in the first scroll (36:32). This second document formed the nucleus of the extant prophecy, although again any precise delineation of the contents is impossible. Some scholars have suggested that Baruch compiled his own 'memoirs' of Jeremiah which were subsequently incorporated into the prophecy. That this possibility is doubtful, however, seems indicated by the fact that, in the extant book, Baruch

---

30. J. Bright, *Jeremiah*, p. lxxvi.

is consistently depicted as the scribe of Jeremiah, not the editor of his compositions.

Precisely how the final form of the prophecy arose is unknown. Chapters 50 and 51 may point to the activity of Jeremiah and Baruch in Egypt after the temple had fallen (cf. 50:4, 17; 51:34, 45). Chapter 52, which is almost identical with 2 Kings 24 – 25, may have been excerpted from a larger historical source of which Jeremiah was apparently not the author. There seems little doubt that it was added to the prophecy within seventy years after the occurrence of the events which it recorded.

While it is true that the prophecy in its final form constitutes an anthology of the utterances of Jeremiah, it is clear that the latter occur in a quite irregular manner without following any particular chronological pattern, and it is difficult at times to see why some oracles should occur in their present place. Perhaps the disorderly arrangement of the material reflected the strife, uncertainty and turmoil of the period, and might imply that the final form of the book was in circulation not later than 520 BC.

Despite what has been said above, however, the arrangement of the material is not quite as haphazard as might be imagined. With the exception of the historical appendix (52:1–34), the prophecy is either biographic (21 – 29; 30 – 39; 40 – 51) or autobiographic (1 – 10; 11–20) in nature, and the overall arrangement of the material made it possible for the grim theme of national sinfulness and judgment to be emphasized time and again in throbbing, poetic rhythms. Aside from this rather obvious classification of material, the analysis of the prophecy is apt to be subjective, and it is seldom that two commentators agree on the outline of contents.[31] F. Cawley and A. R. Millard have divided the prophecy up as though it had originally been a bifid composition.[32] In antiquity this device was sometimes adopted for coping with writings of considerable length, the

---

31. Cf. E. J. Young, *An Introduction to the Old Testament* (1960 ed.), pp. 250ff.; W. O. E. Oesterley and T. H. Robinson, *An Introduction to the Books of the Old Testament* (1949), pp. 291ff.; A. Weiser, *The Old Testament: Its Formation and Development* (1961), pp. 213ff.; *HIOT*, pp. 801f., et al.

32. In *The New Bible Commentary Revised* (1970), p. 628.

purpose being to circulate the material in two approximately equal halves so that whichever section was read, the thoughts of the writer would be conveyed adequately.[33]

The present author prefers to entertain the prophecy, in so far as some of the oracles can be dated, against the following historical background:

a.	Under Josiah	1:1–19; 2:1 – 3:5; 3:6 – 6:30; 7:1 – 10:25
b.	Under Jehoiakim	11:1 – 13:14; 14:1 – 15:21; 16:1 – 17:27; 18:1 – 20:18; 22:1–30; 23:1–8, 9–40; 25:1–14, 15–38; 26:1–24; 35:1–19; 36:1–32; 45:1–5; 46:1–12, 13–28; 47:1–7; 48:1–47
c.	Under Jehoiachin	31:15–27
d.	Under Zedekiah	21:1 – 22:30; 24:1–10; 27:1–22; 28:1–17; 29:1–32; 30:1 – 31:40; 32:1–44; 33:1–26; 34:1–7, 8–11, 12–22; 37:1–21; 38:1–28; 39:1–18; 49:1–22, 23–33, 34–39; 50:1 – 51:64
e.	Under Gedaliah	40:1 – 42:22; 43:1 – 44:30
f.	Historical Appendix	52:1–34

There are obvious difficulties associated with the dating of some of the foregoing sections, although it seems probable that there were no oracles given during the reign of Jehoahaz (the Shallum of 22:11), who occupied the throne of Judah for three months only.

5. The man and his message

Jeremiah is unusual among the Hebrew prophets because of the extent to which he revealed his personal feelings. Whereas others delivered their oracles without disclosing much of their inner selves, Jeremiah effectively lays bare the turbulent emotions of a man selected somewhat against his will to be God's spokesman to his generation. Very little is known of his early life apart from the information in 1:1f. He was probably born about 640 BC at Anathoth,

---

33. For Isaiah as a bifid composition see *HIOT*, pp. 787ff.

some three miles north-east of Jerusalem, being descended from priestly stock. Though proof is lacking, his father may have sprung from the line of Abiathar, a priest of David who fell into disfavour under Solomon (1 Kgs 2:26f.). If so, Jeremiah was able to trace his ancestry back to the house of Eli, and hence there may be a personal element in the reminiscences concerning Shiloh (7:1f.; 26:6), since the Elides had been in charge of the ark there (1 Sam. 1:3, 9).

There is no evidence that Jeremiah had either been trained for the priesthood or had officiated in such a capacity. Yet there can be little doubt that he was aware of the responsibilities which the priests traditionally exercised in connection with the Law, and the flagrant manner in which they disregarded them (cf. 8:8). So far from interpreting the obligations of the covenantal relationship to the people, the priests had supported the pagan worship which flourished under Manasseh and Amon (cf. 2 Kgs 21:1–22). Thus it is small wonder that Jeremiah was later to hold them responsible to such a large extent for the spiritual decay of Judah.

He seems to have been reared in the traditions of the Torah, especially so in the matter of understanding the Sinai covenant and the maledictions associated with its neglect or disavowal (Deut. 28:15–68). Like Amos and Hosea he believed that apostasy would result in dire punishment for the nation, but even if this tragedy happened divine grace could still redeem and restore a penitent people (cf. Jer. 5:18). Whatever his own background was, he appeared most diffident about the prospect of prophetic office when he was called (1:6–8), though assured of divine support. His reluctance may have been based on feelings of personal inadequacy when confronted with the almost hopeless task of recalling apostate Judah to a state of true repentance. To make matters worse, at an early stage in his ministry he was forbidden to marry (16:1–4), and the ominous reasons given made more clear than ever the fact that Judah stood under divine judgment.

The extant prophecy makes quite evident the emotional conflicts which Jeremiah endured. While he naturally had no desire to be a prophet of calamity, ardent patriot that he was, he had no choice but to proclaim to a rebellious and idolatrous nation the imminence of disaster. Consequently his pent-up mental anguish found expression in emotional outbursts against his lot in life (cf. 15:10; 20:8, 14, 18), and there were times when he would gladly have accepted release from the compelling obligations of his prophetic office. Under the strain imposed by social rejection and derision (20:7), active opposition to his message (cf. 26:9–19; 28:5–17), accusations of sedition (38:4) and constant persecution by those whose welfare he cherished most, Jeremiah went so far as to say that he would never again speak in the divine name (20:9). Yet the very realization that he had been chosen to be the supreme mouth-piece of God to his obdurate generation drove him on relentlessly towards the fulfilment of his prophetic mission. One important part of his spiritual legacy to mankind was his ability to make his religious life a matter of an essentially personal relationship with God, a situation largely forced upon him by the nature of the persecution which he had to endure.

His patriotism can be seen in the ardent manner with which he desired a permanent spiritual union between Judah and her God, based upon the provisions of the covenantal relationship. But the resolute apostasy of the nation made such a prospect extremely remote, and consequently Jeremiah lived for a harrowing forty years in anticipation of the divine punishment which must surely overtake Judah. Much of his emotional conflict was governed by the fact that, as one who loved north and south alike, he was understandably reluctant to proclaim the doom shortly to descend upon a nation sunk in the morass of idolatry and apostasy. Yet so strong was his fidelity to his prophetic mission that he pronounced impending calamity fearlessly, despite the outraged cries, the vituperation and the incessant hostility alike of the nobility and the general populace.

In making pointed pronouncements against Jerusalem and the temple Jeremiah resembled Micah before him (7:1–15; 26:1–15 and Mic. 3:9–12). One of these utterances led to his arrest and trial for sedition, and the situation was only saved by an appeal to the prophecy of Micah from the preceding century (26:16ff.). A lover of nature, he drew upon agricultural life to bring force and clarity to his message, as did Amos (e.g. 24:1–10 and Amos 8:1–3). Like that celebrated Judean prophet Jeremiah also asserted the supreme lordship of God over nature and nations alike (32:16–25 and Amos 4:13). His wide spiritual vision combined the fearlessness of Amos, the loving concern of Hosea, and the stern grandeur of Isaiah. An heir to this great tradition of spirituality, he was as uncompromising in his message as John the Baptist was in calling his people to bear fruits worthy of repentance (Luke 3:8). The statements concerning divine wrath were for both of them as acute as a fiery ordeal (cf. 5:14; 11:16 with Matt. 3:7–12; Luke 3:15–17), while their forthright attitude towards an unworthy ruler provoked a violent reaction in both cases from the authorities (36:20–31; 38:1–13; Matt. 14:1–12; Mark 6:14–29).

The tragic picture of Jeremiah as a man of God lamenting with great sorrow of heart the tribulations soon to overtake an unrepentant nation spanned the centuries and etched itself deeply into the consciousness of New Testament writers. There are about forty direct quotations of his prophecy, half of which occur in the book of Revelation, principally in connection with the fall of Babylon (cf. 50:8 and Rev. 18:4; 50:32 and Rev. 18:8; 51:49f. and Rev. 18:24, etc.). Jeremiah's forthright denunciation of his people as uncircumcised in heart and ear (6:10; 9:26) was repeated with equal force by Stephen (Acts 7:51) in an address which cost him his life. The lessons derived from the visit to the potter's house (18:1–10) were applied by Paul to God's calling of the Gentiles (Rom. 9:20–24).

Most impressive of all, however, is the way in which Jesus Christ was associated in the popular mind with Jeremiah. When on one occasion Christ took a sampling of public opinion from his disciples (Matt. 16:13f.), some reports identified him with the outstanding prophetic figure of the seventh century BC. It is hardly surprising that some mistook the Man of sorrows for the prophet of the broken heart, for Jeremiah and Christ both lamented and wept over their contemporaries (cf. 9:1 and Luke 19:41). Jeremiah's uncompromising condemnation of iniquity brought him rejection and suffering as it did to Christ, and Jeremiah actually compared himself to a lamb or an ox led to the slaughter (11:19). Both men made the temple at Jerusalem a centre for their teachings, and on the memorable occasion when Christ cleansed the Herodian temple he quoted in part the denunciation in 7:11 as having finally become a reality (Matt. 21:13). Understandably, however, there are some differences between these two towering personalities. Whereas Christ remained steadfast to his vocation even to the point of surrendering his life on the cross, Jeremiah displayed somewhat less resolution in pleading to be spared when threatened with imprisonment and its consequences (37:20).

By comparison with Christ, who in dying prayed for his enemies to be forgiven (Luke 23:34), Jeremiah was insistent in his desire that the wicked should be punished (cf. Jer. 12:3; 18:23). Yet throughout their ministries both men exemplified the covenant ideal of a close personal relationship with God based on holiness of life, and demonstrated by their actions that their highest commission was to perform the will of God fully and responsibly.

In his teachings Jeremiah upheld the absolute character of the old Sinaitic covenant, and looked forward to a time when it would be replaced by a more individual approach to fellowship with God. It is clear from the prophecy that by his own life-experiences he anticipated that event, and from the depths of his anguish and grief pointed the way to what has since become one of the most prized of human spiritual blessings. Jeremiah had been compelled to find personal refuge in his God because of an enforced dissociation from normal social contacts, compounded by the emotional stresses with which he was oppressed for most of his ministry. Victory and defeat, sorrow and joy, exaltation and humiliation, diffidence and boldness, all beset him continually; yet despite every obstacle he remained firmly committed to his prophetic calling. In the end the reality of his vocation as a prophet of God was vindicated, almost as a matter of course, by the events of history.

The Old Covenant

The covenantal concepts which Jeremiah advocated so consistently reflected firmly the ideals of the book of Deuteronomy, which is itself a covenant-renewal document. The extent to which this is the case has been a matter of some debate among scholars,[34] but despite this there can be no doubt that Jeremiah understood the content of Deuteronomy in a manner similar to that of other prophets, and in certain respects even more precisely so (cf. 11:1–5). The fact that a special type of covenantal relationship existed between God and Israel was one of the most strongly marked aspects of Jeremiah's teachings. He held that Israel was deliberately chosen (cf. Deut. 4:37, 7:6–8, etc.) and adopted by God in general fulfilment of the

---

34. Cf. H. H. Rowley, *From Moses to Qumran* (1963), pp. 187ff.

Abrahamic covenant into a special filial relationship (Deut. 8:5; 14:1; 32:6). The covenant constituted an act of sovereign grace (cf. Deut. 4:13f.; 29:13) and was made with a redeemed people (Deut. 9:26; 13:5; 21:8). Under its provisions Israel became the adopted people of God and committed themselves to the necessity of observing the covenantal stipulations (Exod. 24:7). Such obedience involved a correlative expression of divine holiness in Israelite life as a regulatory feature of fellowship between the nation and her God (Deut. 6:4–15; Lev. 19:2). If this holiness was exemplified in terms of obedience, the covenantal blessings would continue (Deut. 4:40; 6:16ff., etc.). While the participators in the Old Covenant, like their counterparts in the New, were redeemed by divine grace, this did not mean that they were not liable to divine judgment if they sinned; and the consequences of disobedience and infidelity which overtook them have a disconcerting relevance for more modern times.

Apostasy and formal religion

Following the pattern of Hosea, Jeremiah threw deficiencies in the covenant relationship into sharp focus by using the imagery of marriage and contrasting a faithful husband with an adulterous wife (2:1f.; 3:1–13; 31:32 and Hos. 1:2 – 2:5).

Jeremiah proclaimed the divine message to his contemporaries against a background of political and moral crisis in Judah. He made abundantly clear his conviction that the apostasy of the nation was the real reason that devastation was imminent. Instead of adhering to the high moral and spiritual concepts of the Sinai covenant, the Israelites had accommodated themselves to a large extent to the debased and idolatrous religion of Canaan. So pervasive had this influence become that idols were actually located in areas of the temple (32:34), while at various sites near Jerusalem young children were being sacrificed periodically to Baal and Molech (7:31; 19:5; 32:35), in defiance of the prohibitions found in the Law (Lev. 18:21; 20:2ff.). Although these idolatrous practices had been suppressed in the time of Josiah, they had emerged once again after he died.

Because apostasy represented a fundamental rejection of the covenant relationship, Jeremiah saw that the coming of divine judgment upon Judah was inevitable (cf. Deut. 28:15, 58f.; 30:17–19). The sovereign Lord of the universe (Jer. 23:23f.) who governed all things

according to his will (18:5–10; 27:6–8) loved his people tenderly and
consistently (31:1–3), but by the terms of the covenant which their
forefathers had accepted he demanded their unswerving allegiance
and implicit obedience (7:1–15). Offerings made to him by an apostate people (6:20; 7:21f.) were as reprehensible as their sacrifices to
pagan deities (7:30f.; 19:5), and had brought the entire covenant relationship to the point where the destiny of the Chosen People now
hung precariously in the balance. What the Israelites were either
unwilling or unable to comprehend was the fact that the external religious forms which they were pursuing with such enthusiasm were
completely alien to the spirit of Sinai and the Law. The priests and
cultic prophets had become hopelessly corrupt (5:30f.; 6:13–15;
14:14) and instead of acting responsibly as custodians and propo-
nents of the moral and religious law were actually condoning the
spread of immorality and idolatrous worship, contrary to the explicit
injunctions of the covenant (cf. Deut. 12:1–5, 30–31; 18:9–12;
22:22–30; 27:20–23).

While the Babylonian invasion was pending, the sense of crisis
within Israelite religious life impressed itself upon the prophet. In
analysing the causes of the situation Jeremiah laid most of the
blame at the door of the priests for allowing the people to be persuaded that outward religious observances were an acceptable sub-
stitute for proper inward spiritual motivation. Jeremiah maintained
that the priests had condoned, and even actively aided, the accom-
modating of traditional Hebrew monotheism to the pagan excesses
of Canaanite religion. Finally, they had demonstrated that they were
concerned primarily with vested interests by affirming that the
temple would never fall to Babylon (6:13; 18:18; 29:25–32), despite
all that Jeremiah said to the contrary. The priests were supported in
their illusions by a number of false prophets who were associated
in some unspecified manner with the cultus (8:10–17; 23:9–40),
with the result that Jeremiah was set out in bold relief as the sole
herald of misfortune and divine judgment.

Judgment

In the light of covenant curses on such behaviour, Israel could
only expect to experience the promised pestilences, reverses and ultimate destruction. Preliminary punishment had taken the form of

famine conditions (cf. Deut. 28:20–22, 38–40; Jer. 3:3; 14:1–6), but the real threat to the people of Judah would become apparent when the Babylonian armies massed on the frontiers in preparation for the attack long promised by Jeremiah (25:9; 52:1–30). All too soon the judgment of God upon his disobedient and idolatrous people was implemented as predicted, and the utterances of Jeremiah concerning the destruction of the temple, the abrupt termination of the Davidic kingship with all its unrealized hopes, and the oppression of the nation by the Babylonians were fulfilled to the letter.

Regardless of opposition from priests and prophets he proclaimed his prophetic message without the slightest compromise. Judah would be taken captive to Babylon, though even this calamity would ultimately end (25:11; 29:10), and Babylon herself would be conquered by yet another world power. For all these sombre tidings there was still a persistent note of hope in his message (3:14–25; 12:14–17, etc.), and it is interesting to observe that, as events became more sinister and forbidding, his confidence in a glorious future for a repentant and faithful nation grew ever firmer, culminating in a dramatic act of faith at a time of great crisis (32:1–15).

His pronouncements are also of profound importance if only for the changes in Israelite life which they portended. Part of the reason for the prophet's anguish lay in the popular belief, cherished from the time of Isaiah, that the temple of Jerusalem, representing the divine presence in the midst of the nation, was inviolable (cf. Isa. 31:5; 33:20). Consequently an entirely false sense of security had grown up in Judah (7:10), leading the people to think that God would deliver them from the enemy under all circumstances. This belief overlooked the national repentance which had occurred in the time of Isaiah (Isa. 37:1–20), and which had not been matched in the following century, despite the desperate pleas of Jeremiah and his dire warning that the fate of Shiloh would be repeated in Jerusalem unless Judah repented (7:12–15).

If the city was destroyed along with the nation, the formal line of Davidic kingship with all its noble promise would also terminate catastrophically. The shattering loss of the anointed seed would be matched by other unprecedented changes in the familiar patterns of worship. Jeremiah predicted that a time would come when the sacrificial system would cease, along with the cultic ministry exercised by the Jerusalem priesthood. In his view the consistent violations of covenant grace by Israel had made the Sinai agreement void to all intents (cf. Num. 15:30), and consequently had largely nullified the sacrificial system. The outward forms of traditional Israelite religion were meaningless without those attitudes of spirit which were consistent with the ethos of Sinai. Thus for Jeremiah the rite of circumcision was a mere formality unless accompanied by a genuine circumcision of the heart (4:4; 9:26). Loyalty and obedience were fundamental to any true spiritual relationship with God, and if this kind of motivation did not characterize both life and worship there could be no real expectation of blessing for the nation.

The New Covenant
In looking for a time when people would be able to approach God on an individual basis rather than as members of a historically-covenanted group, Jeremiah was actually expecting the traditional covenant to be renewed in an even more glorious form (33:14–26). No longer would it be either desirable or necessary for an individual to express himself spiritually through the personality of the group. Instead he would be accorded the priceless possession of *a personal relationship* with God which would be valid over and above any religious forms. Under the renewed covenant the divine law would be written not upon stone tablets, as with the Sinaitic agreement, but upon the heart of the believer.

In practical terms this meant that the individual, when confronted with the new covenantal expression of divine love, would respond to it with a conscious act of will. The law of God would then be obeyed, not merely because it was known, but because it was revered, the motivating force thus coming from within rather than from outside. This expectation was fulfilled in the work of Christ on Calvary, which brought the covenant grace of the older agreements to its highest and fullest degree of exemplification. Christ pointed to the universal applicability of his sacrifice on the cross (cf. John 6:33–35, etc.), and spoke specifically of the cup drunk at the Last Supper as the new covenant in his blood (cf. Matt. 26:28; Mark 14:24; Luke 22:20; 1 Cor. 11:25) to specify the implementing of this deeper covenantal relationship and its multiplicity of blessings in terms of Christ's vicarious atonement for human sin.

The messianic hope

The messianic thought of Jeremiah linked the Righteous Branch, a descendant of the house of David (33:14–18), with the peace and prosperity which God would bestow upon a penitent, cleansed nation (33:8f.). He was thus able to look past the temporal situation of the exile into the period beyond, and contemplate a returned Israelite community establishing itself in Palestine once again (30:17–22; 33:9–13). In this future existence there would be an abundance of material gifts from God (31:12–14), while the city of Jerusalem, the restored centre of national and spiritual aspirations, would be holy to the Lord, being given the special name of 'the Lord is our righteousness' (33:16).

Having learned thoroughly the bitter lessons of exile, the restored populace would worship God penitently and wholeheartedly (31:18–20; 24:7). For this they would be forgiven their past transgressions and would be established under the rule of the messianic prince (23:5f.). So glorious would this régime be that even Gentile nations would aspire to, and ultimately receive, a portion of the blessing poured out on the restored nation (16:19; 30:9; cf. Zech. 8:22f.). This great hope of a renewed and invigorated nation (cf. the hope expressed in Deut. 28 – 30) is a sufficient answer to the objections of those who have maintained that Jeremiah is uniformly a prophet of gloom.

6. The Hebrew text and the Septuagint

Along with Job and Daniel, the book of Jeremiah exhibits striking divergences between the Massoretic Text and the LXX version. According to one estimate the equivalent of nearly seven chapters of Hebrew was omitted by the LXX translators. In addition, the LXX version included about one hundred words not represented in the Massoretic Text, though admittedly of a minor nature. The LXX omissions were due mainly to apparent condensation of the Hebrew, as in chapters 27 and 28, or to the intentional elision of Hebrew doublets (8:10–12; 30:10–11, etc.). But the most noticeable divergence is in the arrangement of the oracles against foreign powers (chapters 45 to 51), which appeared in the LXX after 25:13. These divergences go back at least to the time of Origen.

It is frankly impossible to ascertain the original order of the oracles in the prophecy, and, as noted earlier, equally difficult to see by what principles of organization they were compiled. While the shorter LXX text sometimes exhibits a regularity of rhythm lacking in the Hebrew, it is not necessarily superior on that account. From Qumran came a fragmentary Hebrew manuscript (4QJer[B]), which, where it had been preserved, followed the shorter text of the prophecy occurring hitherto in the LXX translation. However, the longer form of Jeremiah was also found at Qumran, which might suggest that more than one recension of the work was represented by these texts.

ANALYSIS

A. PROPHECIES RELATING TO CURRENT HISTORY AND DOMESTIC MATTERS (1:1 – 45:5)

1. Prophecies occurring between 625 BC and the fourth year of Jehoiakim (1:1 – 20:18)
2. Utterances relating to the kings of Judah and false prophets (21:1 – 25:14)
3. A summary of prophecies against foreign nations (25:15–38)
4. Predictions of the fall of Jerusalem (26:1 – 28:17)
5. Letter to the deportees in Babylonia (29:1–32)
6. Messages of consolation (30:1 – 31:40)
7. Prophecies from the time of Zedekiah (32:1 – 44:30)
8. A message to Baruch (45:1–5)

B. ORACLES AGAINST FOREIGN NATIONS (46:1 – 51:64)

1. Against Egypt (46:1–28)
2. Against Philistia (47:1–7)
3. Against Moab (48:1–47)
4. Against Ammon (49:1–6)
5. Against Edom (49:7–22)
6. Against Damascus (49:23–27)
7. Against Kedar and Hazor (49:28–33)
8. Against Elam (49:34–39)
9. Against Babylon (50:1 – 51:64)

C. HISTORICAL APPENDIX (52:1–34)

COMMENTARY

A. PROPHECIES RELATING TO CURRENT HISTORY AND DOMESTIC MATTERS (1:1 – 45:5)

1. Prophecies occurring between 625 BC and the fourth year of Jehoiakim (1:1 – 20:18)

Jeremiah is the most notable of the Hebrew prophets because of the almost impossible mission which God assigned to him. His task was to try to recall the people of Judah to an observance of divine law at a time when they were poised on the brink of national and spiritual catastrophe. For many years the influence of pagan Canaanite worship had exerted a corrupting effect upon the Judeans, as it had done earlier in the northern kingdom. Religious apostasy had been followed by social and moral decay, and it fell to Jeremiah to present the implications of the Sinai covenant fearlessly in a desperate attempt to stem the tide of destruction. But because the nation was indifferent and rebellious by turns, Jeremiah soon found that he had acquired a reputation for pessimism and gloom. For his fidelity to his vocation he was rejected, hated, persecuted, and even feared by those whom he was most anxious to recall to covenant spirituality. Such a prophetic mission demanded a keen and continuing sense of vocation, supported by courage, faith and determination. The first chapter describes the circumstances connected with his call as a prophet.

1:1–19. Jeremiah is called and commissioned

1–3. Superscription. Prophecies generally commence with some indication of authorship and date as a means of setting God's message in historical perspective.

1. The oracles which follow are described as *words*, but this term can also be translated 'matters', 'incidents' and 'affairs' as well as 'words' or 'sayings'. The opening phrase thus refers both to the prophecies of Jeremiah and the various events in his career. The name *Jeremiah* may mean 'the Lord exalts' or 'the Lord founds', and was borne by other biblical personages (cf. 2 Kgs 23:31; Neh. 10:2; 1 Chr. 5:24). Jeremiah's father, *Hilkiah*, was a member of a priestly family which may have ministered in the temple after the reformation of Josiah in 621 BC. This Hilkiah was not the High Priest who officiated under Josiah (cf. 2 Kgs 22:4). *Anathoth*, the home of Jeremiah, was located near the modern Anata, a village about three miles north-east of Jerusalem. It was in Benjaminite territory assigned to the Levites (Josh. 21:18), and was re-populated after the exile.

2. This verse describes the point at which the word of the Lord became a matter of great personal importance to Jeremiah. As a boy he may well have been familiar with priestly practices, but in any case there is no evidence that he ever served as a priest. It is possible, however, that what he observed in the cultus as a young man influenced his attitude towards the priesthood in subsequent days. His future life and thought were moulded to a large extent by an early acquaintance with the utterances of the eighth-century BC prophets such as Amos, Hosea, Isaiah and Micah, and probably also by the lives and sayings of Elijah and Elisha. Hosea especially seems to have gripped the imagination of the young Jeremiah with his striking illustrations of divine love for wayward Israel. In subsequent oracles Jeremiah was to employ the century-old imagery of Hosea which described Israel's apostasy as harlotry or adultery. The approximate date of Jeremiah's call to prophetic office was 627 BC, *the thirteenth year of Josiah*.

3. Josiah reigned for another sixteen years after Jeremiah's call, being succeeded by Jehoahaz, *Jehoiakim*, Jehoiachin and *Zedekiah*. Jehoahaz and Jehoiachin were probably omitted in this verse because their reigns were so short, comprising only three months each. *The captivity of Jerusalem* occurred in 587 BC, but Jeremiah continued his prophetic ministry for some time after that event.

4–10. The call of Jeremiah. God assured the prophet that he was predestined for his task, a factor which formed the basis for his unshakable conviction that his mission was indeed of divine origin. Yet despite this assurance Jeremiah still needed constant spiritual support to enable him to proclaim God's word to an unheeding, rebellious nation. As the prophecy unfolds, the way in which Jeremiah found strength by constant communion with God will become evident. As the crisis of exile draws near, his initial diffidence is replaced by a degree of boldness and forthrightness in proclaiming the divine word which shows that, as a person, he has grown in wisdom and understanding. Jeremiah dramatically depicts a servant who is faithful (cf. 1 Cor. 4:2), and whose fidelity is ultimately vindicated (Matt. 10:22). As such his life exemplifies the stability and constancy which the individual Christian ought to exhibit (cf. Eph. 6:13). It is through testing that faith grows.

4–5. Jeremiah was 'foreknown' in the best Pauline sense (cf. Rom. 8:29–30), while the imagery of sanctification (AV) parallels the promise made to Zacharias, the father of John the Baptist (Luke 1:15). There is nothing haphazard about the choice of Jeremiah as a divine messenger to Israel. Indeed, God had formulated each step of the process himself from conception to consecration, with an intimate awareness both of the need and the one who should meet it. Under such circumstances Jeremiah had little choice but to submit to his high calling. God's chosen vessels are often long in the making, as for example in the case of Moses, and they emerge at the strategic moment, the most notable instance of this being Christ himself (Gal. 4:4). The phrase *to the nations* indicates the universality of Hebrew prophecy (cf. 25:15–29).

6–7. The young Jeremiah protests his timidity and lack of experience, but to no avail. His emotional conflicts seem to begin with his call, and this verse illustrates the tension arising from his reluctance to undertake the task committed to him and the assurance from God that he had already been furnished with the requisite moral and spiritual powers. The Hebrew for *youth* (RSV) can also mean a 'child' or 'infant' (Exod. 2:6; 1 Sam. 4:21), and also a 'young man' (Gen. 14:24; 34:19), the sense of 'youth' being obviously intended here.

8. The command 'fear not' was given on many occasions in Scripture to the Lord's servants, including Abraham (Gen. 15:1), Moses (Num. 21:34; Deut. 3:2), Daniel (Dan. 10:12, 19), Mary (Luke 1:30), Simon (Luke 5:10) and Paul (Acts 27:24). Fear is one of the most paralysing of human emotions, and can only be dispelled fully by the love of Christ (cf. 1 John 4:18). This verse indicates that God always supports his servants in the missions assigned to them (cf. Exod. 3:12). While Jeremiah will not be free from opposition and even physical danger, he will survive all difficulties, because God will be with him to sustain him.

9–10. By touching the young prophet's mouth God symbolizes the communication of the divine message. The incident is reminiscent of the sanctification of Isaiah (Isa. 6:7). After Jeremiah had felt the touch of the Master's hand he was ready to begin his prophetic ministry. Note here that there is no disparity between God's words and those of the man Jeremiah. The 'word of faith' was near him, in his mouth and in his heart (Rom. 10:8). God can now proclaim his sovereign will to the nations with Jeremiah acting as spokesman. There is a decidedly negative emphasis here which sets the tone for most of the prophecy. What is corrupt in the nation must be uprooted and torn down, for only then can God undertake *to build and to plant* anew. Calamity was therefore an inevitable occurrence as long as the nation pursued its sinful ways. However, the fact that God spoke of renewal furnished some ground for hope of restoration at some future period. This is a paradigm of the spiritual life, for God has first to remove the sin before the sinner can begin to grow in grace and in the knowledge of Jesus Christ (cf. Eph. 4:15; 2 Pet. 3:18).

This section depicts in a sensitive and appealing manner the intimacy existing between God and his chosen servant. As elsewhere in Scripture God is revealed as a communicating deity who respects human individuality, speaks to people at their own level of understanding, and uses language whose intent cannot possibly be mistaken. He is also prepared for an intelligent response and will listen to explanation or argument, whether framed in the stammering tongue of Moses or the lengthy expostulations of Job. Response, however, is the important consideration when God has spoken to man, and Jeremiah, though perhaps slow and unwilling, was nevertheless by no means deficient in this respect. The thought that his very existence was a conscious part of divine purpose and not an incidental biological occurrence must have given him a special sense of destiny. This in turn doubtless contributed to his determination to fulfil his prophetic mission regardless of personal considerations.

11–16. Two visions. These incidents occurred early in his ministry, though at what precise point or how far apart is hard to say. They were probably quite separate from the call, but taken together with that occurrence they helped Jeremiah to authenticate his commission both to himself and others. By professing to 'see' what God had said to him, the prophet, like Amos (Amos 1:1; 8:1f.) and Isaiah (Isa. 2:1), was able to show how he experienced the divine word at this stage.

11–12. The first vision has a positive ring to it, having as its subject an almond rod, the first tree to bud in spring. There is a play on MT *almond rod* (*šāqēd*, 'waker') and *šōqēd* (*watching over*), which illustrates the promptness with which God keeps his promises. Just as the early stirring of the almond heralded springtime, so the spoken word pointed to its own rapid fulfilment. Like Amos, Jeremiah had an appreciation of nature (cf. 2:10; 8:7; 12:8f.; 14:4–6, etc.), and was aware that it could function as a divine agent.

13. The second vision had a more sinister tone to it, and may have been separated from the first by an interval of weeks or months. Again the prophet 'sees' a specific object designed to convey a definite meaning, the details of which, however, only become evident subsequently. The *pot* described as *boiling* (RSV) was a large vessel used for cooking or washing[1] and placed upon glowing embers which were fanned by the wind. It was *facing away from the north* (RSV),

---

1. See J. L. Kelso, *The Ceramic Vocabulary of the Old Testament* (1948), pp. 27, 48, and fig. 16.

literally, 'its face from the side of the north', implying that its contents would spill southwards from Syria into Palestine.[2]

14–15. Jeremiah here gives his first prophetic intimation of impending disaster. His chilling warning that it would be set loose on the land from a northerly direction would make his hearers apprehensive immediately about the political situation in Assyria. Ashurbanipal, the last great Assyrian ruler, died about the time of Jeremiah's call (see Introduction, Section 2), and within a decade the empire which had terrorized the Near East was on the brink of dissolution. For Judah, which was a buffer state between Egypt and the northern powers, the future was ominous. In the prophecy God stated that he was summoning the northerners as agents of his judgment. Apart from Egyptian incursions, the Hebrews were accustomed to the idea of disaster breaking out upon them from the north, and in his graphic prediction Jeremiah stated that each of the kings would *set his throne at the entrance of the gates of Jerusalem* and other fortified cities in Judah. While this could refer to the Scythian invasion,[3] it seems more probable that the allusion to Jerusalem under siege is to subsequent Babylonian attacks.[4]

16. These conquerors are divine agents carrying out God's sentence upon the Judeans for their crime of following pagan gods rather than the ideals of the Sinai covenant. The verb *qtr* (*burn incense*) is used elsewhere of the burning of fat in sacrificial offerings (1 Sam. 2:16; Ps. 66:15), the offering of meal (Amos 4:5), or the burning of incense. The tensions of syncretism between Baal worship and Israelite monotheism have now reached a climax. Jeremiah is here in harmony with other pre-exilic prophets in denouncing those who bow down before their own handiwork (cf. Isa. 46:6f.). Idolatry is just one consequence of being conformed to this world (Rom.

---

2. It is not necessary to change the MT *ûpānāyw* (*its face*) to *ûpānûy* (*turned away*) with G. R. Driver, *JQR*, XXVIII, 1937, p. 77, and NEB.

3. For the literature on this topic see *HIOT*, pp. 803f. n. 6.

4. If the Scythian invasion was as real as many have supposed, it would make unnecessary the theory that this verse was added to the prophecy by a 'Deuteronomistic' editor after the fall of Jerusalem, since the allusion could well be to the incursion of such foreign hordes.

12:2, AV), and Jeremiah makes it clear, as Christ also did, that it is impossible to serve God and mammon (Matt. 6:24; Luke 16:13).

17–19. Exhortation and promise. The apprehension felt by the prophet is met by a forthright command to be fearless, reminiscent of that given to Joshua (Deut. 31:6–8; Josh. 1:6–9). If Jeremiah loses his courage, God will shatter him for his disobedience and lack of faith, for with him, as with the Christian, whatever would not be of faith would be sin (Rom. 14:23). Though everyone would be against him God would be beside him and would make him impregnable. The Christian is bidden in exactly the same manner to stand fast (cf. Eph. 6:14) so that he will be a reliable and faithful servant at all times.

18. The imagery of structural reinforcement is applied to the moral and spiritual stand which Jeremiah has to take. God's promised presence (cf. 1:8) assures him that he will be as impregnable as a fortification, as strong as *an iron pillar* (cf. Judg. 16:29) and as resistant to attack as *bronze walls.* Such sterling qualities are necessary for the Christian also if he is to succeed in withstanding all the assaults of the devil. The *people of the land* (AV, RSV), MT *'am hā'āreṣ,* are probably the principal landowners here rather than the general populace as in some other cases.[5]

19. This is one of the richest assurances that the Lord's servant can have. It correctly ascribes the source of spiritual victory to God rather than man, and encourages the embattled believer to look consistently to the author and finisher of the faith once delivered to the saints (cf. Heb. 12:2). It also throws some light on the implications of spiritual conversion for individual personality. Here, as in verse 17, Jeremiah was warned that if he made alleged personal defects an excuse for failing to discharge his duties properly, he would be disgraced by God through those very weaknesses. As one called and sanctified, he now receives the assurance that his witness will not be impaired by any of the evil consequences of natural disability. When a man accepts Christ by faith he becomes a new

---

5. On this expression see M. Sulzberger, *JQR,* III, 1912, pp. 1ff.; N. Sloush, *JQR,* IV, 1913, p. 302; S. Daiches, *Journal of Theological Studies,* XXX, 1928, pp. 245ff.; S. Zeitlin, *JQR,* XXIII, 1932, pp. 45ff.; L. Finkelstein, *The Pharisees* (1935), pp. 25ff., et al.

creation (2 Cor. 5:17), and through sanctification of the Spirit grows up in Christ to maturity (cf. Eph. 4:13–15). Thus personality transformation through spiritual rebirth and renewal (Rom. 12:2) is mandatory for eternal salvation. Christ's atonement is intended to save from self as well as from sin (cf. Gal. 2:20).

2:1–13. Israel's past love recalled

This chapter is a powerful sermon dealing with apostasy, and was delivered with all the zeal of an evangelist, as is evident from the power and vitality of the language. While it is not easy to date precisely, the address seems most probably to have come from an early period in Jeremiah's ministry (cf. the mention of Egypt in 2:16, 18, 36). The imagery is much like that of Hosea, while the call for repentance is set firmly against the background of the historic covenant and its obligations. This address is an illuminating illustration of the way in which God spoke to ancient Israel through the prophets. It is not a detached, orderly presentation of historical fact such as the scholar or the archivist might have entertained, but a passionate yet controlled appeal to the nation to turn from idolatry and surrender to the claims of her ancestral God. The rhetorical nature of the chapter seems indicated by such things as the change of metre (2:4–13) and the person of address (cf. 2:2f., 14–19 and 4:13, especially in MT). This material was doubtless included in the original scroll compiled by Baruch (cf. 36:32), the general aim of which was to show how consistently Jeremiah had foretold the destruction of Jerusalem, even in the comparatively undisturbed days following Josiah's reformation.

1. Precisely how *the word* came is not stated, but Jeremiah makes it apparent that the prophetic message issued from the close spiritual fellowship existing between himself and God. The divine words thus become the prophetic oracle, and the personality of the sanctified speaker does nothing to invalidate or depreciate the fundamentally divine nature of the pronouncement. It is a vital part of God's saving purpose for the word to become flesh, whether in the incarnate Christ (John 1:14) or in the believer who preaches the word.

2. By contrast with her present apostasy, Israel once trusted God implicitly when she was his *bride*. The imagery is that of Hosea, and includes the characteristic term *ḥesed*, which is difficult to render in English by one word (cf. AV, RV *kindness*, RSV *devotion*, NEB *unfailing devotion*). It generally described divine favour and graciousness to men, or corresponding acts between people in human society. The Sinai relationship is depicted in terms of a marriage where the bride follows her husband in confidence to a strange land (cf. Hos. 2:2–20).

3. The ancient law of *firstfruits* (cf. Lev. 23:10, 17; Deut. 26:1–11) assigned to God a portion of the harvest which ripened first. This offering thankfully acknowledged that the earth's produce came from God, and was a token of the bounty to follow at harvest time. Israel comprised God's portion of the harvest of nations, but her neglect of covenantal responsibilities had virtually nullified her witness to contemporary society, thus depriving God of a fuller harvest. Because Israel was the Lord's hallowed portion, just as the firstfruits were (Exod. 23:19; Num. 18:12f., etc.), she was under divine protection and any who harmed her would be punished. The term 'firstfruits' is used of the Christian church in James 1:18, which as the new Israel of God (Phil. 3:3) has fallen heir to the honour ascribed to the old Israel.

4–5. The ingratitude and stupidity of the entire nation are evident here. Though Israel had been dignified uniquely by becoming God's bride, she had soon forgotten her first love (cf. 2:32; 3:21). The question *what wrong did your fathers find in me?* (RSV) actually expressed an emphatic negative. In the phrase *went after worthlessness* (RSV) the noun *hahebel* and its related verb probably constitute a play on the name 'Baal', the principal deity of Canaanite worship. In Deuteronomy and secular Near Eastern international treaties the phrase 'to go after' meant 'to serve as a vassal'.

6. God now challenges Israel to show how he had broken any promises from the Wilderness period onwards. So far from being untrue to his word, he had led them safely through desolate, forbidding terrain, safeguarding them and bringing them to the Promised Land. Jeremiah thus stresses the reliability and constancy of God's promises (cf. 2 Cor. 1:20), and implies that national ingratitude could only have arisen through Israelite forgetfulness.

7. The natural beauty of Palestine was soon polluted through indulgence in pagan worship. The *plentiful land* (RSV), literally, 'the land of Carmel', reminded the hearers of the luxurious growth of that area (cf. Amos 1:2; 9:3; Mic. 7:14; Nah. 1:4).

8. Four classes of leaders are held responsible for the idolatry and apostasy. If *the priests* had not neglected their duties, the spiritual crisis now facing the nation would never have arisen. Their function was to reconcile men to God through the sacrificial rituals, but because Canaanite religion had exerted such a corrupting influence over the ancestral Hebrew faith, they had grown lax, indifferent and irresponsible. *Those who handle the law*, namely the priests and Levites, who were responsible for teaching God's judgments to the people, were castigated for having no first-hand knowledge of the Lord. In 31:34 the prophet promises that under the new covenant information about God will be replaced by personal experience of him. Such conscious knowledge of a saving and keeping God is at the very heart of the Christian faith (cf. 2 Tim. 1:12; Eph. 3:19, etc.). The temporal *rulers* (MT *shepherds*) were just as disobedient and blameworthy as the priests, from whom they had doubtless taken their cue, while *the prophets* of the day had drawn their inspiration from Baal, not the Lord God of Israel. Despite periodic reformation, the national worship had become accommodated largely to the depraved rituals of Canaan.[6] Throughout his ministry Jeremiah was in conflict with false prophets whose idolatrous affiliations proved profitless in the end when their predictions were shown to be entirely contrary to the will of God as shown in the trend of events. The MT *lô' yô'ilû* (*things that do not profit*) may be a sarcastic play on the name Baal.

9. This unhappy situation prompts God to present a formal complaint against his people. The legal term *ryb* (RSV *contend*) is used of a plaintiff presenting his case in court (cf. Job 33:13). The verdict would unquestionably go against Israel, since the nation had violated its covenantal obligations repeatedly. Ancient Near Eastern vassal treaties provided for stiff penalties in such instances, so that the implications of the current situation would not be lost on the people of Judah. The way in which the future is inherent in the present should be noted in the reference to the descendants of Jeremiah's generation. If they persist in the apostasy of their forbears they too will be punished.

---

6. On Baal worship see W. F. Albright, *Archaeology and the Religion of Israel*, pp. 76ff.; idem, *From the Stone Age to Christianity* (1957), pp. 231ff.; *HIOT*, pp. 363ff., et al.

10–11. Jeremiah asks the populace to remember that no ancient nation had ever changed its ancestral gods, least of all for some object of veneration that proved to be less beneficial. This was true of the western isles, which derived their name Kittim (AV *Chittim*) from the Phoenician colony of Kition on *Cyprus*, and also of the eastern peoples, here represented by *Kedar*, an Arab tribe living in the desert east of Palestine (cf. 49:28f.). Unlike pagan peoples, who remained true to their national deities despite everything, Israel had abandoned the living God, its glory, for a completely useless object of worship. *Bĕlô yô'îl* (RSV *for that which does not profit*) is another play on the name Baal.

12–13 At such sacrilegious behaviour the heavens, invoked as witnesses, became aghast with horror, since they obeyed the Creator's laws implicitly. For the summoning of the heavens as God's witnesses cf. Deuteronomy 32:1 and Isaiah 1:2. Whereas the heathen are guilty only of idolatry, the covenant nation has offended on two grave counts, that of abandoning the living God and choosing to serve idols. God is here described as a *fountain of living waters*, i.e., a spring or rivulet which would flow into a cistern for storage. Christ gives this same 'living water' to all who will receive it, to be a well springing up into everlasting life (cf. John 4:10–14; Rev. 21:6). But instead of accepting a salvation based upon divine grace, the Israelites preferred one achieved by human works. Thus they had hewn out for themselves worthless idols (cf. 1:16) which in the end were unable to meet their deepest spiritual needs, just as a cracked cistern which allowed its contents to seep away was of little use for sustaining life.

2:14–30. *The infidelity of Israel*

14. With one eye on the fate which overtook the northern kingdom, Jeremiah indicates that the freeborn Israelites are soon to become slaves. He wonders why, if Israel really belonged to God, it has been so long at the mercy of the voracious Assyrian lion. The *houseborn slave* was one who had first seen daylight in the household of the master, and as such, was his personal possession as opposed to a slave obtained by purchase.[7]

---

7. On slavery as an institution see *NBD*, pp. 1195ff.

15–16. Jeremiah thinks of the threat posed to national security by the Assyrians (cf. Isa. 5:29) which culminated in the fall of the northern kingdom in 722 BC. The fact that Israel lay *in ruins* was sufficient warning of what would happen to apostate Judah. Coincidentally, after the fall of Samaria the Asiatic *lions* in the general area increased numerically so that they became a danger to life (2 Kgs 17:25). In this double allusion Jeremiah shows that God can punish a rebellious and stubborn people alike by nations and nature. Nor could Judah expect firm assistance from Egypt, for in a crisis the perfidious Egyptians would have no compunction about exploiting and robbing her (cf. 2 Kgs 23:35) instead of rallying to her cause. *Noph* (AV) is rendered *Memphis* in RSV. Located near Cairo, it was the ancient capital of Lower Egypt. *Tahpanhes* (AV *Tahapanes*) was the Greek Daphne (Tell Defneh) in north-eastern Egypt (cf. 43:7; 44:1; 46:14). According to MT the Egyptians will 'graze' or 'pasture upon' (*yirʿûk*) the Judeans. The same word with different vowel points can be read either as *yeroʿûk* ('they have fractured'), i.e., the skull, or *yeʿarûk* ('they expose'), i.e., by shaving. The first and third readings convey the idea of shame (2 Kgs 2:23; Jer. 48:45) or mourning (Isa. 15:2; 22:12) associated with baldness. No matter how appealing the prospect of alliance with Egypt might be, Judah will suffer for it if she becomes entangled.

17. The cause of all the trouble is stated bluntly here. The nation's sufferings cannot be blamed on God since they are the result of wilful disobedience. Even when they had the living God as their guide to life, the people preferred to forsake him and pursue worthless idols. Jeremiah makes clear a lesson of abiding spiritual importance, namely that the bulk of all we suffer in life is due to ignorance, stupidity, or both. The New Testament is as insistent as the Old in exhorting the believer to follow after righteousness (1 Tim. 6:11; 2 Tim. 2:22).

18. Jeremiah reiterates the theme expressed by Isaiah (Isa. 30:15) that it is futile for Judah to rely upon Egyptian aid. Her faith must be placed in God alone, but the prophet knew well that such advice was completely alien to the national temper. God had once led his people away from Egypt. To return to that land in any sense would be a move in entirely the wrong direction. Backsliding is a recurrent theme in Jeremiah (cf. 2:19; 3:6–8, 11f., 14–22; 5:6; 31:22, etc.), as also in Hosea (Hos. 4:16; 11:7; 14:4). It is a peril to the Christian (cf. Heb. 6:4–6), who is exhorted to grow to spiritual maturity (Matt. 5:48; 2 Cor. 13:9; Eph. 4:13; Heb. 6:1, etc.) and to avoid former sinful ways. *Sihor* (AV), 'blackness', is a sarcastic reference to the river Nile, one of the most highly venerated of Egyptian gods. *The Nile* and *Euphrates* here represent the Egyptian and Assyrian empires, while drinking of their waters was a metaphor for voluntary subservience to pagan ways by the Judeans (cf. Isa. 8:6f.). The mention of Assyria as a world power points to a date before 612 BC for this prophecy. Jeremiah evidently had in mind such incidents as those in 2 Kings 15:19; 16:7; 17:3, and the denunciations of Hosea (Hos. 5:13; 7:11; 8:9, etc.). Jeremiah exceeds all other prophets in citing his predecessors.

19. Neither Egypt nor Assyria has any real say about the coming disaster, even though they may be agents in various ways, since the calamity had been decreed by God as a punishment for national sin. The prophet shows that spiritual attitudes set in motion certain patterns which subsequent events confirm (cf. Hos. 8:7). Judah's wickedness as expressed in foreign political alliances will only bring trouble, not the expected security, since both Egypt and Assyria have traditionally ravaged other peoples. Jeremiah points out that apostasy inevitably carries a high price, and subsequent events lent emphasis to this assertion. The fear of the Lord begets wisdom (Prov. 9:10), but Judah had long ago abandoned this saving grace. In her folly she was depending upon treacherous mortals rather than the immutable God.

20. Judah's arrogance and wilfulness are stated with merciless clarity. *Long ago* the nation had abandoned the high moral and spiritual ideals of the covenant to indulge in lewd fertility rites at the local sanctuaries, which were situated on hilltops so as to be close to the cosmic deity Baal and other celestial members of the pantheon. So seduced were they by Canaanite religion that the people of Judah refused to assume the obligations of the Sinai covenant any longer, preferring the things of the flesh to the life of the spirit. One ultimately has to choose in this matter, and Jeremiah makes the alternative just as clear as the New Testament does (cf. Matt. 7:14; Jas 4:4, etc.).

21. How have the mighty fallen! Reflecting Isaiah 5:1–7, Jeremiah shows how the promising nation had deteriorated badly, despite all efforts at prevention. The choice stock had reverted to the original wild variety, and therefore the heavenly Husbandman had no option but to uproot it. The *noble* (AV) or *choice* (RSV) vine is literally 'Sorek vine', a high-quality red grape grown in the Wadi al-Sarar, situated between Jerusalem and the Mediterranean.

22. Behaviour leaves its mark on the personality, and this cannot be eradicated overnight. So ingrained is Judah's foul iniquity that no amount of washing with detergents can remove it. The supreme merit of Christ's work on Calvary is that it removes the dark stain of iniquity (1 John 1:7).

23–25. Perhaps in self-defence the people had been pointing to the splendid Solomonic temple and its rituals as evidence of their piety. However, they had carefully avoided mention of their blatant indulgence in the depraved fertility rites of Baal or the worship of Molech in the valley of Ben-hinnom (see on 7:32). Jeremiah illustrates the character of their sexual excesses at pagan sanctuaries by employing the analogy of a *she-camel* (the word is used here alone in this sense; AV reads *swift dromedary*) *in heat*, running to and fro in the desert looking feverishly for satisfaction from a mate. God's Chosen People should not be like animals, giving themselves over to physical lust and changing the truth of God into a lie (cf. Rom. 1:24–26). The image of the *wild ass* typified an untamed nature (cf. Gen. 16:12; Job 11:12). The animal sniffs at the wind so as to detect the male scent.[8] Similarly Judah is actively engaged in looking for incentives to idolatry and lewdness, not passively awaiting them. However, the people are solemnly warned not to go chasing after false gods until their sandals are ready to drop off, because such idolatry will ultimately be punished by a shoeless and thirsty journey into captivity. Despite this admonition, Jeremiah realizes how hopelessly infatuated Judah is with pagan Canaanite worship.

26–27. The four main social groups charged earlier with responsibility for the spiritual crisis in Judah are chastised once more. As a professional thief is embarrassed when caught in the act of stealing,

---

8. On the behaviour of camels in heat see K. E. Bailey and W. T. Holladay, *Vetus Testamentum*, XVIII, 1968, pp. 256–260.

so the Israelites will be overwhelmed with shame at the time of supreme crisis when they realize the utter futility of trust in sticks and stones. Jeremiah cannot understand how the Chosen People can worship idols so shamelessly, and he employs the term 'shame' to describe his view of Baal-veneration (cf. Jer. 3:24, etc.; Hos. 9:10). The nation's stance shows clearly a deep need for a true conversion-experience. Jeremiah reflects a situation common to many ages in noting that the apostate offenders demand immediate and effectual divine help when calamity strikes. They thus testify, however inadvertently, to God's existence and his ability to help them, undeserving as they are. A merciful and loving God has made provision for such people (cf. Luke 6:35).

28–29. At this juncture the prophet is bitterly ironic. 'Surely out of all the gods you have fashioned for your cities', he suggests, 'you are able to find one or more to redeem the plight of the worshippers.' The *many gods* and many lords (cf. 1 Cor. 8:5) of contemporary Judean society are made apparent here. Despite complaints of unjust treatment the people deserved their promised punishment, for their rebellion against God was of the essence of sin. Because Judah has been adjudged guilty of Israel's sin she must share Israel's punishment. The loyalty, consistency, and fidelity of God to the covenant obligations are continually contrasted with the perfidious, wilful behaviour of the Chosen People.

30. The heavenly Father had chastened the children he loved (cf. Heb. 12:6), but to no avail. His witnesses had been silenced ruthlessly, the allusion here being perhaps to Manasseh (2 Kgs 12:16; cf. Neh. 9:26). This resistance to the true word of God was also focused on Jerusalem by Christ (cf. Matt. 23:37; Luke 13:34; Acts 7:52), who himself met the fate which other prophets seem to have experienced in different ways.

2:31–37. The punishment of the nation indicated

31. The prophet pleads with his contemporaries to heed God's warnings while there is still time. The expostulation seems equivalent to the 'generation of vipers' expression uttered by John the Baptist (Matt. 3:7; Luke 3:7) and Jesus (Matt. 12:34; 23:33). God had led his people from the wilderness, showing that he did not have the inhospitable character of the desert, but was in fact a fount of triumph, hope and confidence for Israel. They had turned abundant promise into stark misery because of their rebellion and apostasy. While desiring freedom from covenant responsibilities they had actually been enslaved by licence through their idolatrous pursuits, and had still to learn that only in divine service is true freedom to be found (cf. Rom. 8:2; Gal. 5:1, etc.).

32. The impossible has happened. Jeremiah finds it incredible that *a bride* could *forget her attire*, yet Israel, God's bride, has long forgotten him who through the Sinai covenant had unique status in the world. The bridal *attire* was a sash or girdle proclaiming her status as a married woman (cf. Isa. 3:20). The New Testament contains allusions to the new Israel, the Christian church, as the spouse of Christ (cf. 2 Cor. 11:2; Eph. 5:25–27, 31f.; Rev. 19:7). Here Jesus is the divine bridegroom who has sought out his bride in atoning love and is entering into covenant relations with her.

33–34. The immoral pursuits of Baal worship have been sufficiently attractive to encourage the people to further licentiousness. They had planned carefully so as to accomplish their evil aims most effectively, but in consequence have become thoroughly proficient in iniquitous ways. So skilled are they that they can now instruct experienced professional prostitutes in the techniques of their nefarious trade. Wicked behaviour always involves innocent people to some extent, as Christ demonstrated in bearing the sins of humanity (cf. 1 Pet. 2:20–24). The LXX and Syriac versions of verse 34 read 'on your palms', i.e. hands, for MT 'on your skirts', which involves a slight consonantal change. The idea of polluted skirts, however, follows the sense of the preceding verse adequately. The blood had been shed illegally, for the victims had not been caught in the act of *breaking in*, otherwise they could have been killed with impunity (cf. Exod. 22:2f.). The people therefore have no excuse, and thus richly deserve divine anger.

35. Past atrocities in the days of Manasseh are conveniently overlooked as the people protest their innocence of such things. Josiah's reforms seem to have been short-lived, and the condemnations of this verse reflect the obduracy and wantonness of the Judean people who were still idolaters at heart. For this they would be brought to judgment, not for outward compliance with religious reform. The Christian needs to pay constant attention to personal motivation, remembering the kind of God with whom he has to deal (cf. Ps. 94:11; 1 Cor. 3:20; Heb. 4:12f., etc.).

36–37. God's people were thoroughly capricious, having broken their plighted troth to God, and were labouring under the delusion that they could change their course at will with complete impunity. They did not realize in their political dallyings that only the living God is eternally steadfast, whereas nations such as Assyria and Egypt are treacherous and unreliable. With a little reflection they would have known that both these foreign nations had brought only humiliation and despair upon Judah, never prosperity and blessing. Hence Jeremiah states bluntly that if Judah looks to Egypt for help she will have to retrace her steps with her hands upon her head, nursing bruises and hiding her shame. This will happen because God is overruling the course of world events in order to punish his rebellious people.

3:1–5. A plea to Israel

1. The words of 2:1 should be understood here so as to introduce the shortened form of Deuteronomy 24:1–4 properly. This statute forbade a man divorced from his wife to remarry her if she had married another in the interval, since this would defile the Chosen People. The imagery of harlotry, familiar from Hosea (Hos. 4:2, 10, 13, etc.), was applied to the nation's idolatry to show that the spiritual defilement of Israel had made reconciliation with God extremely difficult, if not actually impossible. For *will he return to her* (RSV) LXX has *can she return to him*, but this is an inferior reading. The verb *šûb* ('return') occurs also in verses 12, 14 and 22 in the sense of turning to God in true repentance. Even though, from the above analogy, the nation could not take her place again as God's wife because of her repeated adulteries, she could still be forgiven if she was truly penitent for past sin. Confession of iniquity from a contrite spirit brings for the Christian the rich blessings of forgiveness and cleansing (1 John 1:9) bestowed by a Saviour who hates the sin but loves the sinner.

2. So profligate had the people been that there was no place in the land untouched by their immorality. Jeremiah likened the national preoccupation with licentiousness to an Arab freebooter waiting in concealment to plunder a passing caravan, or to a wayside prostitute soliciting clients (cf. Tamar in Gen. 38:14. See also Prov. 7:12–15; Ezek. 16:25). This gross sensuality had defiled both the land and its people. In Acts 15:20 the primitive Christian church was warned to avoid the pollutions of idols and unchastity, lest the new Israel should repeat the mistakes of the old.

3–4. The forces of nature had been brought to bear on the nation in an effort to bring her to her senses. But brazen as any harlot, she remained completely unabashed. Then when the drought became severe, the people complained and pleaded for help, protesting that God had always been their guide. However, they could not conceal their profanation of the Sinai covenant (cf. Mal. 2:10–14).

5. Surely after such pleas and protestations a merciful God would relent and close his eyes to national iniquity. That he did not was the result of an observed disparity between lip and life. While uttering fair words she was perpetrating evil deeds, an attitude rebuked also in New Testament times by Christ (Matt. 15:8; Mark 7:6; cf. Isa. 29:13; Ezek. 33:31). Behavioural patterns are very important for those professing the indwelling Christ (cf. Eph. 4:22; Phil. 1:27, etc.), for by improper conduct the weaker brother for whom Christ also died can be destroyed (1 Cor. 8:11) and the witness to the gospel attenuated.

3:6–18. The guilt of two sisters, Israel and Judah

This section is closely connected with the preceding verses, pointing out that Israel had been put away for her apostasy. Judah had apparently not learned from this tragic experience, and was even more guilty than her sister-state. The passage stresses themes already enunciated in chapter 2, such as the worship of sticks and stones (cf. 3:9 and 2:27), the widespread harlotry (cf. 3:6 and 2:20) and the long neglect of God (cf. 3:21 and 2:32). But by contrast with previous denunciations, the nation is here invited to repent and be forgiven (3:12–14).

6–7. Here the apostate Israel is regarded as the very embodiment of the denial of God. Her indulgence in Baal worship was thoroughly ingrained, yet despite this God was prepared to wait until she had satisfied her lusts and spent her youthful passions. The LXX, Syriac, AV and NEB take the phrase *turn thou unto me* (7) as the equivalent of an MT imperative, but RSV *she will return* appears better.

Judah was characterized as infidelity personified because she was attracted by her sister's bad example.

8–10. God's hope that iniquitous Israel would return to him in penitence had proved vain. Though the nation was 'divorced' by the Assyrian captivity, Judah had failed to benefit in any way from the calamity. Instead, she treated morality so lightly that she had polluted the entire land, which had been consecrated to divine service. This attitude seems to reinforce the relationship between immorality and stupidity in Proverbs 5:1–13; 6:32; 9:16, etc. For the Christian there can be no situation-ethic, since he is commanded to flee from fornication (AV 1 Cor. 6:18; RSV *shun immorality*) and idolatry (1 Cor. 10:14). Judah's professed loyalty to God during Josiah's reformation had been superficial, and thus had failed to reverse the depravity and apostasy of the nation. This characterized her infidelity, which by its works had denied the living God (cf. Titus 1:16). Judah had yet to learn the lesson that those who deny the Creator will be denied by him (cf. Matt. 10:33).

11. While Israel had been *apostate* and had suffered the consequences, she could at least plead that she had no better example to follow. Judah, by contrast, had been warned by the events in the northern kingdom, but had compounded her infidelity by pretence and thus was condemned for being not merely apostate but *false*. No such duplicity must mar the Christian's service rendered to the living God (1 Thess. 1:9) in true holiness (cf. Eph. 4:24).

12–14. The ten tribes, carried to Assyria in 722 BC by Sargon II, are now addressed and informed that, though exiled, they should still repent, knowing that a merciful God whose anger can be appeased will not frown upon such behaviour. While apostate Israel was assured that a reversion to covenantal relations could preface a return to the homeland, there is no evidence that the suggestion was ever taken seriously. Even the very framework of the confession was furnished, and all Israel had to do was to be sincere in conceding her rebellion, immorality and disobedience. True confession, unfortunately, is a harrowing and humiliating experience, and thus seldom encountered, whether in individuals or nations. The catharsis of confession undoubtedly helps to make Christian forgiveness so rich an experience for the penitent spirit (1 John 1:9). In instructing Israel to return to her Lord, Jeremiah shows God as the true *ba'al* (meaning 'lord', 'master', 'husband') of the nation. The idea of a return by ones and twos suggests the remnant of Isaiah 10:22; 28:5. This small company, paving the way for the Israel of God in later days, would return to Zion, the centre from which, in New Testament times, the gospel of Christ spread, and which, in John's apocalyptic vision, would be presented in renewed form as the spouse of the Saviour (Rev. 21:2).

15–16. In the reshaping of the corrupt national leadership Judah will be governed by true servants of God such as David was (cf. 1 Sam. 13:14), and not by military usurpers of the Israelite variety (cf. Hos. 8:4). Leadership of the divine flock is crucial, as both the Old (cf. Ezek. 34:8–10; Zech. 10:3; 11:17, etc.) and New (Mark 13:22; 2 Pet. 2:1; 1 John 4:1, etc.) Testaments recognize. When the new covenant becomes operative God's people will be blessed and prospered. The divine presence in Zion will overshadow the ark and other cultic objects by its majesty, making the use of such symbols of God's reality unnecessary. In the heavenly Jerusalem of Revelation 22:5 the sun will be similarly outmoded. Until then, certain material reminders of divine working will be desirable as aids to faith.

17. Jeremiah looks beyond the exile to a time when idolatry is no more in Palestine, and Zion will be 'holy to the Lord' (cf. Zech. 14:20). There is unquestionably a messianic expectation here (cf. Jer. 5:18; 31:1; 33:16; Hos. 3:5, etc.). God will be enthroned among his people, who by now are loyal and obedient servants. Jerusalem is a light to the Gentiles, witnessing as the Israelites were expected to do under the Sinai covenant. When Christ came, the kingdom was indeed established in Zion, but not in material terms (cf. John 18:36; Acts 1:6, etc.).

18. The hope that Israel and Judah would be reunited ultimately is seen in Isaiah 11:12; Ezekiel 37:16–28; Hosea 2:2 (cf. Jer. 2:4), but such an event must be preceded by true repentance. Since there is no indication that the ten tribes ever repented, the projected union must point to the messianic age of grace, when Jew and Gentile alike will do honour before the enthroned Lord in Zion.

3:19–25 The need for repentance
Although the prophet somehow feels that Israel's exile can be used to achieve the salvation of Judah, he points out that God's hopes for

the southern kingdom were not realized, due to national apostasy and immorality.

19–21. A look at the covenantal blessings reminds the Israelites of what they failed to receive through wilful disobedience. Instead of promised blessings implemented by a loving heavenly Father, they suffered punishment for their apostasy. In the same way God's hopes for Judah have been thwarted because, like a woman playing false with her husband, she has merely paid lip-service to covenantal ideals while pursuing immorality. In his mind Jeremiah hears from the north a plaintive voice *on the bare heights*. This phrase (cf. Jer. 3:2; 4:11; 7:29; 12:12; 14:6) denotes naturally bare areas of land, and typifies the spiritual qualities of the pagan rituals conducted on hilltops. Such elevations were often used for mourning (cf. Judg. 11:37), and it is this which the prophet hears. The mourners are lamenting the folly and futility of worship at Canaanite shrines up and down the land, and in this figure the locale of idolatry was fittingly the scene of penitence. In the spiritual life lost power can only be regained when the sinner retraces his steps to the point where he sinned, and seeks forgiveness and restoration with God.

22. The call to return is accompanied by a promise that the divine Physician will heal the backsliding nation (cf. Hos. 6:1). The MT *šôbāb* and its related forms is variously rendered *backsliding* (AV, RV), *faithless* (RSV) and *wayward* or *apostate* (NEB), all of which express varying aspects of the nation's sin.

23–25. Jeremiah sees clearly what Judah has yet to learn through the harsh experience of captivity, i.e. that the friendship of the world is enmity with God (Jas 4:4), and that the carnal mind is a particular threat to the believer in all ages (Rom. 8:7). Hence the prophet belabours his generation for their abhorrent Baal worship, described as *the shameful thing* (RSV), or more explicitly, *Baal, god of shame* (NEB). The pre-exilic prophets consistently regarded Canaanite worship as Israel's great shame (cf. Hos. 9:10). Jeremiah states flatly that continuance in this way of life will bring ruin on the nation, and that what was so avidly sought for as a way of life will be seen ultimately to have been sin all along. The consequences of obedience to unrighteousness for both Jew and Gentile are stated in Romans 2:8f.

4:1–4. The prospect of unconditional return

If the people are truly penitent, God promises to implement the provisions of the ancient covenant.

1–2. God is concerned that any repentance by idolatrous Israel shall be genuine and lasting, and the opening words show that the situation envisaged in 3:21–25 was a prospect rather than a reality. There could be no return to the homeland unless previous apostasy was abandoned in true penitence. The term *abominations* was used in Hosea 9:10 and also by both Jeremiah and Ezekiel of pagan deities and their associated cultic rituals. The steadfast love of God as expressed in the Sinai covenant must be matched by equal fidelity in the repentant people. This latter quality is also demanded of the Christian (cf. 1 Cor. 15:58; 1 Pet. 5:9, etc.). The people are therefore required to take a new oath by the life of the Lord *in truth, justice* and *uprightness* as an indication of genuine repentance. It would have to be sworn truthfully – otherwise it would constitute blasphemy – and in effect would comprise a renewal of the Sinai promises. On this basis God pledges to implement the provisos of the ancient covenant, and thus will again be able to use his people in the evangelization of the nations, since it is through Israel that the latter will *bless themselves* (cf. Gen. 18:18; Isa. 2:3; 65:16).

3. The MT indicates that each *man* of Judah and Jerusalem is challenged to repent. It must thus be on an individual basis, not a corporate one as in the religious rituals of the day of atonement. This emphasis on personal religious experience is especially important for the theology of the new covenant, where repentance for sin and the acceptance of Christ as saviour is strictly individual in nature. In demanding that the fallow land be ploughed up, Jeremiah is insisting on the removal of the hard exterior of idolatry so as to expose a softer and more responsive environment (cf. Hos. 10:12, and the full meaning in Ezek. 18:31). It would be pointless to sow the seeds of repentance in unsuitable soil. Part of the reason for leaving land fallow was to help the farmer clear it of weeds. If the seed is sown among thorns it is choked and becomes unfruitful, a lesson driven home in one of Christ's parables (Matt. 13:7, 22; Mark 4:7, 18; Luke 8:7, 14).

4. Now the image changes somewhat, although the message is still the same. The people must remove the hard excrescence from the heart which has prevented the divine word for so long from taking

root (cf. Deut. 10:16). Circumcision was a sign of the covenant
between God and man, and in the light of verses 2–3 this dedication to the Lord must be essentially personal. The *foreskin* (omitted
in NEB) typified unregenerate nature with all its inbred passions and
lusts. This 'old man' or 'carnal mind' (Rom. 6:6; 8:7, AV) has no place
in the lives of those in Christ (Rom. 8:10–13). The Hebrews assigned
concomitant emotional functions to the main physical organs, the
heart being the locus of will, intelligence and purposeful action.
The plea for a changed heart thus constituted an appeal for spiritual
conversion. The gravity of spurning the divine offer of renewal consequent upon true repentance is indicated by the fiery anger and
unquenchable fury of God. Inner cleansing is the only alternative to
destruction by fire, a theme prominent also in New Testament
thought (cf. Matt. 13:42, 50; 25:41; 1 Cor. 3:13, etc.).

4:5–22. The coming judgment upon Judah

In the light of the invasion which he so clearly expects (5–18),
Jeremiah pleads for repentance and spiritual renewal in the
southern kingdom.

5–6. A note of alarm is evident as an unidentified army
approaches, and the people are warned to retreat to the safety of fortified towns. The confusion and peril of the times is reflected
admirably here. Because of the expected invasion Jeremiah attached
great importance to repentance and spiritual renewal. The blowing
of a horn signalled a state of grave danger (cf. Amos 3:6). Since
repentance was apparently not forthcoming, Jeremiah had no choice
but to announce imminent disaster. In vigorous poetic language he
describes the alarm which will spread when the enemy swoops
down and engulfs the land in a destruction which had already begun
to break out from the north (cf. Jer. 1:14).

7. The *lion* could represent both Assyria and Babylonia here as
fierce destroyers of nations. The lion was depicted elegantly in
sixth-century BC Assyrian reliefs, at a time when Assyrian art was at
its height, while beautiful representations of lions in enamel have
been recovered from the Processional Street of ancient Babylon. The
predator has broken camp (NEB *struck his tents*) and will not be satisfied until he has brought utter ruin on the land. The Christian's
spiritual enemy is described in similar terms (1 Pet. 5:8), and

successful resistance is possible only by those of steadfast faith, a quality signally lacking in sixth-century BC Judah.

8–10. An unrepentant nation cannot expect to escape its fate, since it has spurned divine grace repeatedly. There are equally ominous aspects connected with the Christian message of salvation (cf. Heb. 2:3), for in both situations there will be weeping and gnashing of teeth (Matt. 13:42; 22:13, etc.). The coming invasion will shatter the morale of the people completely, a situation reflected in the Lachish ostraca. All leadership would collapse because it had been based on wholly wrong expectations of peace and security, advocated by the false prophets who were supporting the priests and the ruling classes. Jeremiah can see how utterly deluded the people had been, and very soon they themselves would become aware of the awful truth. He protests the propriety of God allowing his people to persist in their delusions during such a crisis, but notes that God had not left himself without a witness. Since he was unable under the covenant obligations to coerce either belief or obedience, Jeremiah realizes that God has no choice but to punish apostate Judah for her disdain of covenant responsibilities. In this way they will become subject to the divine will, just as the incarnate Christ honoured his Father's plan (cf. Heb. 5:8).

11–12. The sirocco, a scorching wind from the desert, becomes a metaphor of destruction. As it sweeps in it withers vegetation and makes human existence almost unbearable. *Daughter of my people* (AV, RV, RSV) is MT *daughter-people*, the two nouns being in apposition. This unusual term expresses Jeremiah's sense of God's kinship with Israel. The blowing wind is too strong to be the gentle help required by the winnower at harvest-time. Instead it is the hot breath of divine judgment, consuming good and bad alike.

13–15. Like threatening clouds the inexorable agent of the Lord is moving towards Judah (cf. Joel 2:2), coming with countless forces and precluding any possibility of survival. Elsewhere the enemy is compared to a cloudbank in Ezekiel 38:16, a cyclone in Isaiah 5:28; 66:15, and eagles in Habakkuk 1:8 (NEB *vultures*).[9] If Jerusalem

---

9. Vultures are closely related to eagles and hawks, but have weaker claws and usually a naked head. The MT term *nešer* is the Akkadian *našru*.

wishes to be saved she must be cleansed from all iniquity, involving a thoroughgoing reformation of manners and morals. Nothing less than the purification of the temple and the nation will suffice, since the Father's house has become a lair for thieves (cf. Matt. 21:13; Mark 11:17). Since the promised punishment will only become absolute upon continued apostasy, there is still time for Judah to repent and be healed, a situation which illustrates the conditional nature of the prophecies of destruction. The coming devastation is heralded from the northern limits of the land (cf. Deut. 34:1), and echoed from a point just ten miles north of Jerusalem. Ample warning of the calamity has now been given, and the verbs of verse 15 demonstrate clearly the urgency of the matter. To *declare* the menace is merely to announce it as an item of news; to *proclaim* it is to publish it so forcefully that all must take notice.

16–17. A public statement is made concerning these *besiegers* (RSV MT 'watchers') who will shortly deploy their forces locally, howling for Judean blood. Soon their victorious cries will echo through the ruined cities of the land and enemy tents will spring up everywhere. These structures will be like the shelters or booths erected by shepherds and gardeners to protect their produce or flocks. A verb related to *keepers* (17) occurs in 2 Samuel 11:16 of besieging a city.

18. The truly patriotic nature of Jeremiah is seen in the way in which he identifies with the anguish of his people. Only because he loved his homeland so ardently could he proclaim so courageously and objectively the disasters which he foresaw. Responsibility for the calamity is placed where it properly belongs. To acknowledge that the incidence of misfortune is entirely one's own fault makes the consequent suffering all the more intense, as contrasted with the forbearance which can be exercised when one suffers innocently. Patient suffering of this latter kind, exemplified most fully in Christ's death, is acceptable with God (1 Pet. 2:20).

19–21. Jeremiah can contain his feelings no longer, and cries out in deep sorrow at the prospect of destruction. For AV *bowels* RSV reads *my anguish*. In Hebrew thought the intestines were the locale of the emotions, and in modern psychosomatic medical research they have been similarly described as 'the sounding-board of the entire emotional system'.[10] The MT reads *walls of my heart* for AV *very heart* and NEB *throbbing of my heart*. The MT *my heart moans (hmh) inside me* points to a profoundly disturbed physical condition due to shock. The prophet's experience will soon become that of the entire nation. (For other occurrences of the verb *hmh* see Ps. 59:6; Isa. 16:11; 17:12; 59:11; Jer. 5:22; 48:36.) One calamity now follows on the heels of another. There is no escape, for everything is devastated in a moment, as though by fire. The prophet wonders anxiously how much longer he can stand the emotional strain of contemplating his countrymen streaming to the fortified towns for refuge and quivering with terror at the warning trumpet blasts, for he knows that the latter will be of no uncertain import.

22. The overwhelming tempest of fear has a rational cause, based upon a combination of ignorance and stupidity. If the latter persists it can only receive an appropriate and entirely deserved recompense. So perverse have the people become that their only skills are iniquitous ones.

4:23–31. The heralding of desolation

In one of the most magnificent lyrical passages in the entire prophecy, Jeremiah experiences a dramatic moment of insight concerning the outpouring of divine anger upon Judah.

23. So devastating is the judgment upon Judah (23–28) that Jeremiah instinctively thinks of the state of primeval chaos (Gen. 1:2), except that what then became 'good' will now be turned to desolation at the divine presence. This description is one of the most dramatic of its kind in the entire Old Testament. The heedless destruction consequent upon apostasy has brought ruin upon the land, and the skies are darkened in mourning (cf. Isa. 24:10; 34:11). The imagery is that of the judgment day (cf. Isa. 13:10; Joel 2:10; 3:15; Amos 8:9, etc.) which had now arrived in all its terror, eclipsing the celestial luminaries and making the earth return to its primitive barrenness before the creative word emerged (cf. 2 Pet. 3:10).

---

10. For a comprehensive documented survey of such research see F. Dunbar, *Emotions and Bodily Changes* (1954). For an untechnical presentation by the same author see *Mind and Body: Psychosomatic Medicine* (1947).

24–25. Cosmic disturbances are matched by terrestrial upheaval. *The mountains*, symbols of stability and strength, are trembling for very weakness at the majesty of the divine visitation. People have fled from the scene, and even *the birds*, the most widely distributed of the animal species, have themselves long departed.

26. The solitude and desolation are all the more stark by contrast with the fruitfulness of the land (cf. 2:7) in earlier times. The definite article prefixing *desert*, omitted in most EVV, compares the country to some specific inhospitable waste such as the Sinai wilderness. While God's wrath is always tempered with mercy, the Chosen People had imposed upon his charity for so long that they had amassed wrath against the day of anger and the revelation of God's righteous judgment (Rom. 2:5). They had failed to see that divine forbearance was intended to lead them to repentance (Rom. 2:4), and they were, therefore, destined objects of punishment (Rom. 9:22). Under the new covenant Jesus has become the deliverer from divine wrath (cf. 1 Thess. 1:10), and the sinner, being justified by his blood, will be saved from wrath through him (Rom. 5:9).

27–28. Lest the impassioned poetic oracle should be dismissed as the irrational outpourings of an emotional bard, the prophet now speaks in solemn prose to reinforce the message of desolation. Severe though ruin was, God would still not blot out his people completely. The prognostications of doom carried with them the hope that a remnant would survive the ordeal, a hope found in other prophets also. To the present, however, God has not relented, for his word is sure, whether for destruction (cf. Rom. 2:2) or blessing (cf. Rom. 4:16; 2 Pet. 1:19).

29–31. The citizens of Judah flee when they hear the approaching enemy, taking refuge in woods and caves (cf. Isa. 2:19). Archers had long been used in Near Eastern armies, and their compound Asiatic bows made them formidable opponents.[11] Again Jerusalem's behaviour is questioned, this time under the imagery of feminine wiles. In the midst of ruin the prophet sees a woman clothed *in scarlet*, who like the Babylon of the apocalyptic vision (Rev. 17:4) was full

---

11. For various kinds of ancient bows see Y. Yadin, *The Art of Warfare in Biblical Lands* (1963), I, pp. 6ff.

of abominations and filthy fornication. But this is Zion, not sinful Shinar, the house of all evil (cf. Zech. 5:11), which is still playing the harlot by her idolatry. At the eleventh hour Jerusalem is trying hard to placate the enemy by alluring them in the manner of a prostitute. Though she has accentuated the beauty of her eyes by some cosmetic substance such as stibium, she still cannot gain favour in the eyes of her lovers. Destruction and desolation as a consequence of sin are inevitable because Zion is still looking for adulterous paramours such as Egypt and Assur (cf. 2:33f.) instead of clinging to her true spouse (cf. 3:1). Through her behaviour in courting lovers Judah has become tainted with a mortal disease, and by using the figure of a fatal miscarriage the prophet depicts the nation moribund and gasping spasmodically with arms outstretched, 'Help, the murderers have killed me.' Like the wanton she has been, Judah is now paying the price for her iniquity.

5:1–9. The depravity of Jerusalem

Jeremiah now appreciates the moral necessity for God's judgment of his people, as he sees clearly with his own eyes the iniquity, selfishness and depravity of life in Jerusalem.

1–3. The dirt and clutter found in Jerusalem's streets are but one symptom of her spiritual malaise. Jeremiah anticipates Diogenes of Greece in his quest for an honest man. But none can be found, whether in private houses or in public in the city squares. The conditions which Jeremiah sees justify the severe judgment of God on the nation, whose way of life has reflected the very opposite of *justice* and *truth*, despite the pleas of Amos (5:24) and others. Pardon, however, would be given to the just; they are the ones who live by their faith in God (Hab. 2:4; Rom. 1:17, etc.). The use by the Judeans of the divine name in oath constituted perjury, because their lives did not correspond to their lips. The consonance between these two is of great importance for the Christian (cf. Ps. 34:12ff.; 1 Pet. 3:10f.; Heb. 13:15f., etc.). God had for generations been looking for a lifestyle in Judah completely contrary to what had obtained. Despite severe chastisement the people had persisted in embitterment of spirit, and the prophet's threefold repetition of their refusal to repent stresses their obduracy and the ingrained nature of their iniquity. A threefold attempt to obtain spiritual renewal secured a better response in New Testament times (John 21:15ff.).

4–6. Jeremiah is inclined to excuse the poor because, being of lower social status, they could possibly be pardoned for their ignorance. Yet even the poor were supposed to know the law of God. When identical conditions occur among the upper classes, the prophet knows that they arise from a repudiation of God's commands, not from ignorance. All had sinned in breaking the yoke of the law, and were like animals which had snapped the ties securing the heavy yoke to their necks. As the servants of sin they deemed themselves free from the righteousness of the law (cf. Rom. 6:20). Jeremiah, by contrast, desired them to be free from sin and become servants of righteousness (cf. Rom. 6:18). However, Judah's preoccupation with sin will result in her destruction by lions, wolves and leopards, these animals symbolizing nations which had ravaged Israel periodically. In the pre-exilic period wild beasts were a real danger in parts of Canaan (cf. 2 Kgs 17:25). Here the nation is thought to be as defenceless as a city-dweller in a forest of wild animals. For other references to wolves and leopards see Habakkuk 1:8; Zephaniah 3:3; Hosea 13:7.

7–9. Jeremiah reiterates that God can hardly forgive his rebellious people freely because they had forsaken his covenant and had sworn oaths by idolatrous nonentities. They had evidently misunderstood the source of their bounty because, although God had satisfied them amply, the people had become depraved instead of grateful (cf. Deut. 32:15f.), and had dallied (reading *yiṯgōrārû*, with LXX, for MT *yiṯgōdādû*, 'gash oneself') at harlots' houses. Both literal adultery and metaphorical apostasy are implied here. Such immoral behaviour was the antithesis of the covenant ideal. Verse 8 presents some translation difficulties, with AV, RV reading *they were as fed horses in the morning* and the RV margin *roaming at large*. The American-Jewish translation has *well-fed horses, lusty stallions*, which is followed closely by NEB. Jeremiah makes it clear that God will impose stern retribution for such blatant immorality. Under the new covenant whoremongers and adulterers suffer the same fate (Eph. 5:5; Heb. 13:4) because they have violated God's moral order.

5:10–19. A summons to the destroyer

The deluded condition of the nation is outlined graphically here.

Little does Judah realize that the voracious people from the north will swallow up her crops, lands, people and fortresses as they execute God's judgment upon her.

10–11. Though Judah is God's vineyard (cf. Isa. 5:1–7), the heavenly Husbandman permits the enemy to enter and pillage it. But destruction will not be absolute (cf. Jer. 4:27), even though the Lord's choice vine will be pruned severely. The *branches* of the vine have not borne the fruits of righteousness, and so will be burned up while the stock will be saved. This figure is reflected very closely by Christ in John 15:1–6. Israel and Judah have separated themselves from their source of vitality through infidelity, and thus cannot be fruitful as branches because they do not abide in the vine. What they have in fact produced has been the very opposite of fruits meet for repentance (cf. Matt. 3:8, AV; Luke 3:8), despite the demands of God's servants working in the vineyard, and therefore they can only expect a fiery judgment.

12–14. The deluded condition of the nation is depicted graphically here. The people, forgetful that God maintains his rights (Exod. 20:5), had stressed the privileges of covenant membership at the expense of its responsibilities, thinking that punishment was incompatible with the nature of a loving God. Consequently they had scoffed at predictions of calamity (cf. Zeph. 1:12), regarding the prophets as mere windbags whose word had no higher authority than their own, and adhering instead to the soothing utterances of false prognosticators. The delusion of the nation is thus complete, since they are not able to distinguish God's true servants from the prophets of Baal. Such an attitude requires a special word from Jeremiah to Judah. Henceforth God will make the prophetic oracles like *fire* in Jeremiah's mouth and the nation as *wood*, which will be consumed in the encounter. There is a complete identity here between the prophet's words and God's word to Judah, as was also the case with Jesus (cf. John 3:34, etc.).

15–17. The unidentified invader is as stable and enduring as the hills and streams (cf. Num. 24:21; Deut. 21:4), speaking a foreign tongue and being in every respect alien in culture and religion. Though Judah might appeal for mercy, the language barrier would prevent her cries from being heeded because they would not be understood. Like the grave the deadly enemy arrows will not be satisfied (cf. Ps. 5:9) until they have decimated the people and laid the land waste.

18–19. The promise of 4:27 is repeated here, indicating that however threatening the denunciations against Judah, there is the reservation that destruction will not be complete (cf. Jer. 3:14). The outcome of the covenant relationship provides the explanation of the promised calamity. Judah had chosen an alien god, and so would find herself in bondage to foreign deities in a strange land, an obvious prediction of the Babylonian captivity. The lesson taught here is that spiritual values can never be compromised with impurity. The Christian is warned constantly to avoid every appearance of evil (cf. Rom. 12:2; 13:14; 1 Cor. 5:11, etc.).

5:20–31. Reasons for the coming catastrophe

Jeremiah rebukes the Judeans as a whole for their utter stupidity and lack of moral discernment. They have flaunted the covenant stipulations, and many ruthless individuals have prospered at the expense of the down-trodden.

20–22. Once more the Ruler of the cosmos addresses the nation, rebuking it for its stupidity and stubbornness. Reflecting Isaiah 6:9 Jeremiah rebukes them for their lack of insight into the metaphysical significance of existence. Christ made precisely the same criticism of his contemporaries (Matt. 13:14f.; John 12:40), as Paul also did (Acts 28:26). There is no necessary correlation between sight and perception, hearing and comprehension. Indeed, the people are shown to be as stupid as the nonentities which they worship (cf. Pss 115:5ff.; 135:15ff.). While God's world has been fashioned so as to obey his will unswervingly, his covenant people have exploited their liberty brazenly to repudiate his commandments and indulge in all sorts of corruption, overstepping constantly the limits prescribed by the covenant relationship.

23–25. The reason for this is the stubborn nature of the people (cf. Deut. 21:18, 20). The 'natural man' has engaged in the 'works of the flesh' (cf. Gal. 5:19ff.), and from this has harvested corruption. Christ is only the author of eternal salvation to those who obey him (cf. Heb. 5:9), and under the new covenant the wilful and rebellious cannot expect to fare any differently from their old covenant precursors. The infinite power of God arouses neither fear nor gratitude on the part of Israel, and the fact that his control of the seasons could affect their welfare materially seems of no consequence. Indeed, his richest blessings have already been prevented from reaching the people because of national sin.

26–27. Attention is now focused on a class of men, castigated from the days of Amos (Amos 2:6ff., etc.), who are parasites on society. Jeremiah uses a fowling metaphor, but MT is uncertain here and should perhaps be rendered, *each lurks like fowlers lying in wait* (cf. Mic. 7:2). Like a poacher coming home with a wicker-work cage containing the day's catch, so these iniquitous men steadily amass illegal gains. That one member of God's flock could exploit another in this way was as unthinkable to Jeremiah as it had been to Amos and Micah. Habakkuk condemned such activity (Hab. 2:6, 8), and the New Testament counsels scrupulous honesty in all social relationships (Mark 10:19; 1 Thess. 4:6; Titus 2:10, etc.).

28–29. In the orient, fatness was considered to indicate wealth (cf. Deut. 32:15; Ps. 92:14; Prov. 28:25, etc.). These wicked persons have known no restraint to their activities (cf. Mic. 7:18; Amos 7:8; 8:2), making it evident that the social corruption of the preceding century had by no means been eradicated. The rich still oppress the poor in Judah, and it is impossible for a man to obtain justice in the courts. This was serious, since the Mosaic law had strong humanitarian overtones which required the Israelites to look to the welfare of the needy and underprivileged. Because the wicked had violated these principles they would be punished.

30–31. Even worse is the travesty of prophetism as found among the cultic prophets. Because they prognosticate in the service of 'the Lie', namely Baal, they prophesy falsely. The meaning of *bear rule* (AV, RV, RSV) is either that the priests work under the direction of the prophets, or that they function on their own priestly authority (cf. NEB *hand in hand with them*). The result is a consistent pandering to a popular carnal element in contemporary religious life. When legal and religious values are perverted, there can be absolutely no stability in society. Verse 31 sums up the sin of the nation, showing that prophet and priest have been guilty of unthinkable faithlessness which in turn has been welcomed by the masses. So alien is this to the covenant ethos that the nation will have to endure punishment, a theme which, by its very familiarity, ought to have impressed itself deeply upon the Judean mind before now. False teachings remove the restraints of divine law and encourage human self-interest and the love of pleasure. This was characteristic of Judah's last days, and is promised also for the end of the Christian era (cf. 2 Tim. 3:1–7, etc.).

6:1–8. Jeremiah sounds the alarm

Jeremiah proclaims his certainty that the capital must shortly fall before the onslaught of the enemy. Flight to the Judean wilderness is the only hope left for personal survival.

1. Jeremiah utters a warning to his own tribe, *Benjamin*, to run for cover away from Jerusalem, for the city will be besieged shortly. The mention of *Tekoa* is a play on the words 'blow' and 'Tekoa', which have the same letters. The suggestion is that the people will be safer in this hilly area twelve miles south of Jerusalem, on the borders of the desert, than in the fortified capital.[12] *Sign of fire* (AV), *signal* (RSV), *beacon* (NEB), refer to the fire-signals mentioned in the Lachish ostraca. The use of such signals was an ancient Mesopotamian method of military communication. *Beth-hakkerem*, referred to here and in Nehemiah 3:14 only, is identified with the modern Ramet Rahel, two miles south of Jerusalem.[13] The calamity of invasion is already glaring down at the city from the north.

2–3. MT of verse 2 is uncertain, NEB has *delightful and lovely*, but if MT is understood interrogatively and modified slightly to read *halĕnāwāh mĕ unnagāh* it can be rendered, *Have I compared you to a pleasant pasture, daughter-Zion?* This then leads into the pastoral imagery of the following verse. The Hebrew *nāweh* (AV 'fold(s)', Isa. 65:10; Jer. 23:3) was the nomadic term for a pasture on which shepherds and their flocks settled temporarily. To this pasture of Zion the *shepherds* (for this description of invaders see 12:10) drive their flocks of soldiers, eager to feed upon the richness of the area.

4–6. NEB *declare war* is MT *sanctify*. In the Ancient Near East all warfare was sacred. Staff astrologers attached to pagan armies consulted

12. For early excavations at Tekoa see M. H. Heicksen, *Grace Journal*, X, 1969, pp. 3ff.

13. For the excavations at the site see D. W. Thomas (ed.), *Archaeology and Old Testament Study* (1967), pp. 171ff.

oracles regularly and offered ritual sacrifices before a decision to commence battle was announced. Such practitioners of the art of divination were in considerable demand in antiquity. Battles usually began in a morning when everyone had made proper preparations, and continued without interruption until nightfall, when the combatants retired until the next day. An attack under cover of darkness was therefore an unusual event. Had the weapons of Judah's warfare been other than carnal, her strongholds would not have been pulled down (cf. 2 Cor. 10:4). The usual techniques for attacking a fortification were to be employed for overthrowing Jerusalem. What the Babylonians did in the sixth century BC was repeated by the Romans in AD 70. MT *city to be punished* should be changed slightly with LXX to read *lying city*. The violation of the normal rules of warfare was the only fate which such a perfidious place deserved.

7–8. As water-springs maintain the water in a well at a constant level, so evil is springing up continually in Jerusalem. The current social evils have led to profound moral decay, represented by *sickness and wounds* (RSV). These need the healing touch of the great Physician, but Judah's indulgence in evil, which disavows any such treatment, has elements of a death-wish about it. While God still desires reconciliation with the nation, the current situation makes it virtually impossible. AV *depart from thee* is more forcefully expressed by MT *be torn from thee*. God does not willingly abandon his chosen, yet he must remain true to his own nature (2 Tim. 2:13).

6:9–15. The consequences of corruption
Jeremiah is urged to continue his search for individuals of moral worth in Judah, hopeless as the task might appear because of the utter depravity of the people.

9–10. The comprehensiveness of Judah's ruin is shown graphically by depicting the enemy as *a grape-gatherer*, picking the vine of Israel and looking for any hidden grapes which can be devoured. Israel had no surviving remnant, and a like fate seemed evident for Judah also. Yet the promise in 4:27 will still hold good, and while the majority will be harvested in bloodshed, a few will be preserved. The difficulty which God experienced in securing an audience is reflected by MT reference to an uncircumcised ear (10), an allusion found elsewhere only in Acts 7:51, since other references are to the lips and heart. All admonitions are in vain, unfortunately, because the people lack the insight to comprehend the divine word (cf. 1 Cor. 2:14), ridiculing that which is holy.

11–12. Because all of society has been corrupted by iniquity, the wrath of God is to be poured out upon everyone. Ancient Near Eastern war was essentially total in nature, so that a city which resisted a siege unsuccessfully could only expect complete destruction, without respect to property, age or sex. The content of verses 12 to 15 is recapitulated in 8:10–12 (cf. also Deut. 28:30). The stern message of destruction is aimed at the five stages of life mentioned here: the children in carefree play (cf. Zech. 8:5); the adolescents in their clubs or groups (cf. 15:17); the married adults; the more senior citizens; and finally those advanced in age. The Judeans will be deprived of all the material things which they have cherished. Property will be transferred violently to new owners, and all the old relationships of life will be changed when Jerusalem collapses before the enemy onslaught. This is the price to be paid for trust in materialism rather than in the living God. The wages of sin have indeed become death (Rom. 6:23), for the people have no hope, being without God in the world (cf. Eph. 2:12).

13–15. The utter depravity of the nation is expressed once again in a literary figure in which the extremes of *least* and *greatest* represent the totality of society. The religious leaders are just as corrupt as the general populace, with treachery, fraud and deception as hallmarks of their way of life, in stark contrast to the aspirations of Psalm 132:9, 16. At this very moment the priests should be in mourning for the sins of the nation (cf. Joel 1:9, 13; 2:17), and then the northern enemy would be removed (cf. Joel 2:20). The serious rupture in the relationship between God and Israel had been doctored superficially by prophetic and priestly nostrums, suggesting that all was well, whereas in reality the symptoms pointed clearly to a serious underlying malaise (cf. 8:11). The most blatant form of spiritual deception is to proclaim *peace* where none exists, an offence of which religious leaders have been guilty for many centuries. The prophets were condemned in precisely the same language in Ezekiel 13:10. There can be no peace for the wicked (Isa. 48:22; 57:21), for this only comes when the Prince of Peace is crowned in the individual heart. MT of verse 15 seems preferable to EVV renderings in stressing that the Judeans *should have been ashamed of their abominable behaviour.*

6:16–21. More unheeded warnings

Three 'good ways', represented by Israel's history, prophecy and the law, have not been followed by Judah. The catastrophe which will come upon her is thus the fruit of her apostasy.

16–17. The people have been urged to follow *the ancient paths* of the Mosaic tradition, which will be the best because they are tried and true. In these they would find rest for themselves (cf. Matt. 11:29) in contrast to the sorrow of being yoked to paganism. But they refused to adopt this course, preferring instead the pleasures of sin for a season. God had appointed his prophets as sentinels of the faith (cf. Isa. 52:8; 56:10; Ezek. 3:17; 33:7; Hab. 2:1) to give due warning of approaching spiritual disaster. The trumpet blast was the signal for taking refuge (cf. 6:1; Amos 3:6), but despite all warnings the people refused to flee from the wrath to come.

18–19. Now the Gentiles will see the humiliation of God's Chosen. The end of verse 18 is rather difficult, and can be rendered, *Understand, you assembly* (i.e., Gentiles), *and take good heed of what is coming upon them.* These witnesses are to hear the sentence of destruction passed because the nation has ignored God's words and rejected the covenant laws by which they were bound to him.

20–21. Since an appeal to past experience has proved fruitless, the cosmos is now to see the vindication of divine righteousness. *Sheba* in south-western Arabia (modern Yemen) was noted in antiquity for its incense (cf. 7:1). The *sweet cane* was probably imported from India. Ritual performances divorced from a proper moral attitude are worthless in God's sight, a view shared by other pre-exilic prophets (cf. 1 Sam. 15:22; Isa. 1:11; Mic. 6:8, etc.). The obstacles confronting the people are of their own making, and when retribution comes they cannot blame God (cf. Jas 1:13–15).

6:22–26. The character of the invader

The prophet here portrays in vigorous poetic language a description of the invaders from the north. They are cruel, merciless horsemen, who will usher in Judah's death-throes.

22–23. In language reminiscent of Habakkuk, Jeremiah again warns of the imminence of invasion by an anonymous northern military power (cf. 1:13–15). National apathy towards sin is challenged by a vigorous description of the cruel and relentless foe, armed with *bow and sabre* (NEB).[14] The one objective of this ruthless army is the destruction of the nation.

24. Tidings of the approaching enemy send ripples of panic through the population. The coming conflict will be as unequal as that between a fully-equipped soldier and a defenceless woman demoralized by shock. The plight of women in a conquered land was desperate, and it is no accident that Jeremiah uses the familiar phrase 'daughter-Zion' to add further poignancy to the Judean crisis.

25–26. In an urgent appeal to confront future realities, Jeremiah paints a graphic picture of the dangers about to engulf the people. Enemy armour would spell *terror all around*, another of Jeremiah's watchwords (cf. 20:3, 10), hence fugitives should avoid the countryside and the open road. Prior to a later destruction of Jerusalem its people were counselled to flee to the mountains (Mark 13:14; Luke 21:21). Because of her sin, the only posture which Judah can adopt is to *roll in ashes* (RSV) or *sprinkle* herself with ashes (NEB, following LXX). Death is always calamitous for Jews, and when the only son of a family dies the implied cessation of 'immortality' for the parents is especially catastrophic (cf. Amos 8:10; Zech. 12:10).

6:27–30. The final assay

Jeremiah is still hunting for precious metal among the dross of Judah's population, and comments sadly on the lack of moral worth of the nation as he now sees it.

27. The impending judgment is described in terms of a refining process (cf. Isa. 1:24ff.), with the prophet in the position of an *assayer* (RSV, NEB). The word *mibṣar* (EVV 'fortress') presents difficulties, but if vocalized as *měbaṣṣer* with RSV, it could be rendered 'assessor', thus constituting a gloss on *assayer*.

28–29. Jeremiah felt that his task was similar to that of a silver-refiner (cf. Mal. 3:3), but it is now clear that his prophetic 'fire' has

---

14. Cf. Y. Yadin, *The Scroll of the War of the Sons of Light against the Sons of Darkness* (1962), pp. 124ff.

been unable to remove the impurities from the natural 'silver'. Whereas ore will yield its riches to the refiner, the human will is frequently quite intractable (cf. Rom. 1:18–32). In antiquity lead was used in the smelting process as a flux, but here even that will be of no avail.

30. With the failure of the refining process, all that is left is slag or dross instead of the purified nation (cf. Ezek. 22:18). With subtle wordplay on *refuse* and *rejected* (RSV), both terms coming from the same root, Jeremiah sums up his message to the Judeans. Because they are *refuse silver* (RSV) God has 'refused' to turn their punishment away. The ore is far too adulterated to be worth further effort at refining. This sad judgment has ominous overtones for the wicked in all ages who forget God (cf. Ps. 9:17; Isa. 66:24; Mark 9:44–48).

7:1 – 8:3. The temple address

This celebrated attack upon popular confidence in the temple as an absolute guarantee of Jerusalem's inviolability was designed to draw attention away from cultic preoccupations and focus them upon the ethical demands of the covenant relationship for moral living. For Jeremiah the veneration of the temple was little short of blind superstition, since for him the presence of the building was no guarantee that God would remain in the midst of an idolatrous and rebellious people. Instead, the prophet urges his hearers to repent and live in conformity with the moral and ethical ideals of the Sinai covenant. As they experience spiritual renewal they will become aware of the gross inequalities existing in contemporary society, and out of loving concern for the helpless they will set about remedying existing abuses. But if the people of Judah refuse to return to God, their land will be made desolate and they themselves will be slaughtered.

7:1–20. A warning. This *word that came to Jeremiah from the Lord* (1) appears to have been delivered shortly after Jehoiakim's accession, i.e., about 608 BC, when pagan Canaanite rituals were appearing again in the cultic rites of Judah. It is difficult to question the genuineness of the pronouncements, or, for that matter, the furore which they created. This latter is described in 26:7–24, which comprises the historical summary of the affair. To the Judeans the temple was sacrosanct, being the house of the living God and therefore impregnable to all attack. Because of this belief it was ironic that this building was the very place where such erroneous ideas were exposed and denounced. For this purpose Jeremiah stationed himself at one of the gates of the temple courts where he would be guaranteed a large audience. According to Kimchi there were seven gates in all. His message was simple and direct: *Mend your ways and your doings* (3, NEB) if you still want to live in the land. LXX has a shorter summons than that in MT, reading: *Hear the word of the Lord, all you of Judah* (2). Jeremiah's words reflect Deuteronomy 7:12–15 and the fact that the promises given there only belong to a nation which keeps God's commandments faithfully.

4. This verse summarizes the 'temple theology' of the false prophets. Not merely had God promised an everlasting dynasty to David (2 Sam. 7:12f.) but he had also chosen Zion as his earthly abode (cf. Ps. 132:13f.). Therefore if God was to be true to himself, no possible harm could overtake his dwelling-place or any who sheltered in it. The false prophets fully believed that, in an emergency, God would intervene directly to save Zion, his sacred mount. For them, therefore, temple worship was little better than a charm for averting evil, and they had beguiled the people into trusting in material buildings, forgetful that God required living persons as his temple (cf. Isa. 57:15; 61:1f.; 1 Cor. 3:16f.).

5–7. Before the people can legitimately claim covenant benefits, a thoroughgoing reformation will be necessary. Social injustices must be remedied immediately, and the list given indicates the more important seventh-century offences. The profoundly humanitarian concerns of the Mosaic legislation had long been ignored by Israelite society (cf. Deut. 14:29; 24:19–21, etc.). The *innocent blood* might refer to such judicial murders as that perpetrated by Jehoiakim (26:23). But the basis of all the corruption was idolatry, with its attendant false values.

8–11. The 'Jerusalem theology' of the false prophets is dealt another staggering blow by being described as downright lies. The supposedly inviolable nature of the temple has no basis in reality. God demands a conversion of the mind and heart as the basis of peace and security (cf. Isa. 26:3), not the superstitious veneration of a stone building or a traditionally sacred site. The crimes listed by the prophet violate most of the provisions of the decalogue, thus amounting to a complete repudiation of covenant grace (*ḥesed*). In the midst of this gross wickedness the people are still so naïve as to imagine that they will be delivered from impending destruction by the performance of cultic rites. They have profaned God's house by making it a place of retreat between acts of crime (cf. Mark 11:17; Luke 19:46).

12–15. The people are warned that God can dispense with the Jerusalem temple just as he did with the ark when Shiloh ceased to be a religious centre (Ps. 78:60; cf. Jer. 26:6). God is thus shown to be independent of any given locality and uncommitted to a specific cultic object. However valuable as an aid to spirituality such things might be, they can never be acceptable substitutes for implicit faith in the living God. This affirmation must have seemed the worst kind of heresy to Jeremiah's superstitious hearers.

16–20. This section seems to interrupt the temple sermon somewhat, unless it is an interlude symbolizing the calamitous end of impiety and rebellion. Jeremiah is forbidden to intercede for Judah because of her persistent idolatry, which must now come under judgment. Young and old alike are participating enthusiastically in the cultic rites of *the queen of heaven*, no doubt the worship of the Assyro-Babylonian goddess Ishtar (see on 44:17). Variations of this cult apparently existed in Egypt and Canaan. The word *cakes* (*kawwanîm*) is of foreign origin, occurring again only in 44:19, where the same cult is described. Such appalling contamination of the ancestral faith will be punished severely.

7:21–28. Obedience rather than sacrifice. All sacrificial rituals would be useless if the covenantal requirements of obedience and moral purity were ignored. Here Jeremiah is not repudiating the value of sacrifice as such, but is denouncing the wicked and apostate who have made the rituals an end in themselves and have thus abused the cultic forms.[15] At the time the Sinai covenant was instituted, God required his people Israel to be obedient and to worship him alone. Only when these prime stipulations were promulgated did God prescribe a developed sacrificial system. The reference (22) does not deny that there was sacrifice in the wilderness period, but shows how

---

15. Cf. J. A. Motyer, *NBD*, p. 1043.

fundamentally important it was for Israel to keep the provisions of the covenant (cf. Amos 5:21–25; Hos. 6:6; Mic. 6:1–8; Isa. 1:10–17). To Jeremiah it seemed that there need not be the slightest connection between sacrifice and a repentant heart, a contention amply borne out by the retrogression and deterioration of contemporary society. Obedience is mandatory for the people of the new covenant, following the example of Christ (Phil. 2:8).

25–28. Jeremiah mentions God's persistence frequently (7:13; 25:3f.; 29:19; 35:14f.; 44:4) to show that the Father's aim is to lead his people away from the paths of destruction. Israel's tragedy lies in her stubborn refusal to follow this guidance. The truth which has perished from her midst was that of faith issuing in righteous works (cf. Hab. 2:4; Rom. 1:17; Gal. 3:11; Heb. 10:38), a response as necessary for the old covenant as the New (cf. Jas 2:26).

7:29 – 8:3. A call to lamentation. The address concludes with a description of the sin of Judah and its destined punishment. The people must begin mourning immediately by cutting their hair (29, cf. Mic. 1:16; Job 1:20) because God had rejected them just as they had spurned him. The placing of their hateful idols in the temple (2 Kgs 21:5) was the supreme gesture of sacrilege. The valley of Topheth (31), south of Jerusalem, had witnessed pagan sacrificial rites in the time of Manasseh (2 Kgs 23:10). *Topheth* is probably from an Aramaic word *tĕpat*, 'fireplace', while Ben-hinnom was perhaps the name of the former owner of the valley. The burning of children was one of the principal rites of Molech worship as practised by the Ammonites and others, and was strictly prohibited under the Mosaic Law (Lev. 18:21; 20:2–5). For their idolatry the Israelites themselves will be slaughtered by the invading enemy.

33–34. The horrible punishment of the nation is outlined graphically. For the body to remain unburied, thereby providing food for carrion birds and rodents, was a thing of unspeakable horror for the ancient Hebrews. Ironically, their sanctuary would become their cemetery as the treasured homeland was ravaged.

8:1–3. Still more appalling is the promise that the invaders will disinter the remains of the previously-buried inhabitants of Jerusalem. This barbarous act may have been intended as a deliberate insult to the community, or perhaps had as its aim the uncovering of valuables thought to be buried with the corpses. It could, however, be interpreted as incidental to the construction of a ramp prior to the final assault on the capital, though this suggestion is rather improbable. The sense seems to be that of deliberately exposing the fallen devotees to the astral deities worshipped, which are thereby proved powerless to prevent the gross humiliation and indignity described. A final observation reminds the Judeans that the remains will be like so much manure on the ground. Even more miserable than the fate of those who perished would be the lot of the survivors.

8:4 – 9:1 (MT 8:4–23). A disobedient and idolatrous people

The prophet detects in the arrogant, wilful apostasy of his people something quite contrary to nature. He concludes that they are deliberately stifling the instinct to obey divine ordinances in favour of indulging in the immoral rituals of Canaanite religion. Jeremiah is disgusted by the variety and multiplicity of Judah's sins, and laments her coming fate.

4–7. This poetic section dealing with the tragedy of a complacent nation hurtling headlong to destruction begins with a play on the word *šûb, turn … return*. Whereas normal people eventually learn from mistakes, the Judeans will never profit from experience because they are obstinate and wilful. However, there is still time for them to be saved if only they will repent. But the tragedy is that, while birds follow faithfully the instinctive urges of migration, the Israelites steadfastly refuse to yield to the promptings of covenant love. The *ordinance* is anything decreed by God, whether the instinct of the migratory birds or the directions given for human guidance. Jeremiah finds it incredible that a people can behave so unnaturally towards its Creator.

8–12. These verses show how the cultic officials in Jerusalem have beguiled the whole nation, maintaining that they were discharging the responsibilities of the Torah ('instruction', 'direction'). Here is the first Old Testament reference to *the scribes* as a professional class. 1 Chronicles 2:55 suggests that they were organized on the basis of families or guilds, and they were active as a group in the time of Josiah (2 Chr. 34:13). They originated in the Mosaic period, and functioned in the early monarchy under Hezekiah (cf. Prov. 25:1). In the seventh century BC Israel possessed a written Torah which it was the ostensible duty of the scribes to study and expound. But already unlearned and unsuitable teachers were wresting the Scriptures to their own destruction and that of others (cf. 2 Pet. 3:16). LXX omitted verses 10 to 12, which follow very closely the form of 6:12–15. This kind of repetition is not infrequent in Jeremiah.

13–17. Unhappily, when calamity comes, there will be no remnant left (*no grapes … nor figs*) to preserve the ancestral faith. MT of the end of verse 13 is uncertain, but perhaps reads *I shall bestow on them those who shall pass over them*, i.e., as a judgment on their sin. Although the Judeans propose flight to fortified cities for safety, yet God has decreed ruin for them, symbolized by a potion of bitter waters. The tenets enumerated in verse 11 are now seen to be hopelessly false. Already the northern reaches of the land have been ravaged.

8:18 – 9:1 (MT 8:18–23). Jeremiah sorrows over Jerusalem.
These verses show the intense agony through which Jeremiah passed as he contemplated the ruin of his people. His outpoured grief issued from the conflict between his love for the homeland and his unswerving fidelity to the commands of God. The meaningless *mablîgîtî*, the first word of verse 18, seems to belong to the end of verse 17, and some manuscripts divide it into two words, *mibbělî gěhôt*, beyond recovery. The snake bite is thus fatal. Verse 18 as amended would then begin, *Grief has overtaken me*. The captivity is here anticipated as the deportees question the reason for the degradation of Jerusalem. There will be no harvest to offset the promised famine, and no prophets or righteous men to heal the national malaise. Gilead was famous from the patriarchal period for its balsamic resin (Gen. 37:25), but the precise kind of balm mentioned here is uncertain.[16] There has been no regeneration of Judah's health because her spirit is still unregenerate.

9:2–26 (MT 9:1–25). Judah's corruption and ruin
Jeremiah catalogues his people's sins in a most poignant passage, and sorrows over the destruction that must inevitably follow continued apostasy.

2–3. From the image of continuous weeping like a perennial

---

16. For balm see J. D. Douglas, *NBD*, p. 129; R. K. Harrison, *Healing Herbs of the Bible* (1966), pp. 17f.

spring, Jeremiah passes to that of a person anxious to escape the corruption. For him the wilderness is preferable to the degradations of city life. The Hebrew of EVV verse 3 (verse 2, MT) is poorly transmitted, but should perhaps read, *Like a bow they bend their tongue; falsehood is their bow. They have prevailed in the land, but not in the interests of truth. They go from one evil to another* ... Judah's sin comes from wilful disregard of God (cf. Judg. 2:10; Hos. 4:1).

4–7. Judah's treachery and unfaithfulness towards God made Jeremiah realize that everyone was a Jacob or *supplanter*. MT *'āqôb ya'qōb* (RV *will utterly supplant*) is a pun on the name of Jacob (cf. Gen. 27:36). Lying, deceit, treachery, adultery and idolatry were everyday sins in Judah, and the people had literally worn themselves out with perversions. Still they rejected the God who had revealed himself in history, and for this betrayal of covenant love they must be punished. God has no choice but to make his people pass through the crucible of suffering.

8–11. The calamity of an apostate nation hurtling headlong to destruction stirs up powerful emotions in Jeremiah. He describes the destruction of Judah graphically, picturing the ravaged *pastures of the wilderness* on which cattle normally grazed (cf. Exod. 3:1), and the flight of birds and beasts (cf. Jer. 4:25). Soon only jackals will inhabit the ruins (cf. 10:22; 49:33; 51:37). The scene is reminiscent of Christ lamenting the fate of Jerusalem in a later age (Matt. 24:1–28; Mark 13:1–23; Luke 21:5–24), with the spiritual causes of destruction remaining constant.

12–16. The weeping and the flight of animals would surely be a sufficient word to the wise, but the people are so headstrong and anxious to live by pagan customs rather than by the covenant ethos that their very obduracy will plunge them into ruin. The list of Canaanite gods was generally thought to be headed by El and his consort Asherat. Their mythological offspring was the fertility-god Baal, a true cosmic deity who in many Ugaritic texts was regarded as the actual head of the Canaanite pantheon. This lewd, orgiastic cult had proved attractive to many generations of Israelites. Now Jeremiah points out that the wickedness of the fathers encourages their offspring to commit sin, the end-result of which is punishment (cf. Exod. 20:5), described metaphorically as *wormwood* and *bitter waters*. The wages of sin are always death (Rom. 6:23).

17–22. Jeremiah strikes a sensitive chord in depicting death as a grim reaper. In a lament over the destruction of Jerusalem he heightens the imagery of desolation by calling for the professional *mourning women* (17) to make loud wailing. These persons generally followed the bier at a funeral and loudly lamented the passing of the deceased (cf. Matt. 9:23). Now they will have to learn the real meaning of personal grief, for death has come to claim his victims in Judah without respect to age or sex. The allusion might be to a fatal epidemic resulting from siege conditions, but this is at best uncertain in a poetic passage. The first few words of verse 22 are omitted by the LXX.

23–26. Under such conditions of crisis the only rest which the wise can know is in the *mercy* (*ḥesed*) and *righteousness* of God (cf. 1 Cor. 1:13; 2 Cor. 10:17). *Ḥesed* is commonly used in the Old Testament of covenant love (AV, RV *loving-kindness*; RSV *steadfast love*; NEB *unfailing devotion*), hence God is emphasizing his own moral consistency as against the infidelity of his people. In an appended saying Jeremiah states that the Judeans, though circumcised in body, had no real inner dedication to the spiritual ideals of Sinai, having indulged in lust instead of glorifying God in body and spirit (cf. 1 Cor. 6:20). They were thus no better than their pagan neighbours, and so could only expect to be punished. The group of nations mentioned may possibly have comprised an anti-Babylonian alliance under Egyptian leadership. Trimming the hair away from the temples (cf. Jer. 49:32) was forbidden in the Law (Lev. 19:27), and the reference here may be to certain Arab tribes who did this to honour Bacchus (Herodotus iii. 18).

10:1–16. The impotence of idols

This poem comprises a scathing denunciation of idolatry from one who has seen its worst effects at first hand. The passage has been suggested as the work of Isaiah (cf. Isa. 40:18–20; 41:7; 44:9–20; 46:5–7) because of the similarity of phraseology. The sense does not flow very smoothly, as in verses 6 to 9, while verse 11, written in Aramaic, may be a gloss. In LXX verses 6 to 8 and verse 10 are omitted completely, while verse 9 occurs after the first part of verse 5, in an obvious attempt to provide better continuity of thought. Perhaps Jeremiah was quoting aphorisms coined by Isaiah relating to

idolatrous worship, but in any event the prophecy as a whole shows
that Jeremiah had first-hand acquaintance with the depraved nature
of Canaanite worship, and thus did not need to draw either on the
experience or the vocabulary of his prophetic precursors. It therefore seems unlikely that anyone other than Jeremiah was the author
of this section.

1–5. The dangers of living by pagan customs are illustrated here.
Such concepts often give an evil interpretation to events of nature
and tend to divorce the mind from reality, as with astrology. Idol-
worship makes a material circumstance out of what ought to be a
spiritual experience, and encourages the ridiculous spectacle of
people venerating their own impotent creations. Verse 5 should be
rendered preferably, *they are like a scarecrow in a patch of cucumbers*, with
RSV margin (cf. Baruch 6:70).

6–10. Whereas idols derive their position and authority solely
from human sources, the living God of Israel is unique in all the *kingdoms* (with AV, RSV) as sovereign over the world. Verse 8b is poorly
transmitted, being rendered literally *an instruction of vanities is the tree
itself*. The meaning is that the instruction received from idols is of
no more value than the idol itself. Hence nothing of moral or spiritual consequence can be expected from such material sources.
Tarshish was the westward limit of the ancient world, perhaps
Tartessus in Spain, and supplied silver, iron, tin and lead to Tyre
(Ezek. 27:12). *Uphaz* (cf. Dan. 10:5) is unknown as a location, and
may instead be a metallurgical term for 'refined gold' (cf. 1 Kgs 10:18,
mûpaz), similar to the definition of pure gold in 2 Chronicles 9:17
(*zāhāb ṭāhôr*). However attractive their appearance, idols are of
human origin, and can never possess the vitality of a true, living God.

11–16. Verse 11 is in Aramaic, and may comprise a popular anti-
polytheistic saying. Some Jewish interpreters think that it may have
been part of a letter sent to Jehoiachin in Babylon instructing him
how to combat idolatry, but this is doubtful. Verses 12 to 16 furnish
a powerful poetic description of the one true God engaged in creative activity (cf. Isa. 40:12–17). These functions demonstrate the
sovereignty of God over the world and his place in the life of his
people as their sole strength and stay. Several words have apparently
dropped out of verse 13, and LXX omits the first colon completely.
Cf. 51:16, where, however, LXX reads them. *The portion of Jacob* (NEB

Jacob's creator) is none other than God himself, and although Israel has long rejected him he still abides by the covenant promises. Verses 12 to 16 are repeated in 51:15–19.

10:17–25. The nearness of exile

The long-predicted catastrophe is now at the very gates of Jerusalem, and Judean society is in imminent danger of collapse. Jeremiah pleads that the punishment will be in proportion to what Judah can endure.

The time for weeping has ended, and the weary journey to Babylonia begins. Judah is summoned to pick up her bundle of belongings (17) and go on the long trek into captivity. This is the time when the people will be expelled from their land and receive their just deserts. Verses 19 and 20 express in the language of the semi-nomads the appalling desolation of the nation, likened to a collapsed tent. Incompetent leadership (AV *pastors*; RV *shepherds*) is regarded as the main cause of the calamity (cf. 2:8). For the expectation of restoration, cf. Isaiah 54:2. Activity in Babylonia (22) indicates that Judah's doom is at hand, and this evidently prompted Jeremiah to plead, by way of extenuation, the basic moral weakness of man and his congruent inability to overcome temptation consistently and walk uprightly before God. Therefore he prays that divine judgment will be applied without undue severity, and certainly not in anger (cf. 46:28). This latter fate should be reserved for pagan nations which have preyed on the Israelites in the past, including, presumably, those used as the retributive rod of divine anger, since in their vindictiveness they exceeded what he had prescribed. That Jacob should need to be punished in this way was the tragic consequence of continued apostasy. However, the servants of sin invariably receive their characteristic reward (cf. Rom. 1:18).

11:1 – 12:17. The prophet and the covenant

This important section of the prophecy contains the fourth message of Jeremiah along with an appendix (12:7–17). The main theme is a warning to Judah to be faithful to the covenant provisions, otherwise the promised judgments will be unleashed on her. Two dates have been suggested for this passage. The first would relate it to the time of Jehoiakim, perhaps a little before Nebuchadnezzar's victory over Egypt at Carchemish in 605 BC. The second would place it after the discovery of the law scroll by Hilkiah in the days of Josiah, about 621 BC, and thus connect it with the ensuing religious reformation (cf. 2 Kgs 22 – 23). The latter view is now generally accepted by scholars.[17] The reforms included a recall to the traditions of Mosaic religion and a determined assault upon pagan cultic forms. According to 2 Chronicles 34, centralization of worship at Jerusalem had preceded the discovery of the scroll. As a result the debased rites of Canaanite religion were discontinued at local shrines. Jeremiah may have seized on the opportunity afforded by public reading of the law scroll to recall Judah's attention to the provisions of the Sinai covenant. However, the precise nature and content of the scroll are unknown.

11:2–5. The *covenant* was the historic agreement sealed centuries earlier at Sinai, in which God promised to supply all the material and spiritual needs of the infant nation in return for undivided worship and obedience. The claim of Israel to possess the Promised Land was based upon the proposing, acceptance and ratification of these conditions (cf. Deut. 29:1 = MT 28:69). Curses (3) are called down on the person who ignores the covenantal stipulations. Ancient Near Eastern international treaties normally contained a section of benedictions and maledictions which were expected to occur according to whether or not the covenant was honoured. Pagan deities were regularly invoked as witnesses to such clauses, and were consequently respected as the executive agents. Because Jeremiah had identified himself with Josiah's reformation, he felt acutely the lack of national compliance with the obligations of the Sinai covenant. Having once left behind a *furnace* for smelting iron, a reference to the acute sufferings of bondage (cf. Deut. 4:20; Isa. 48:10), they should have taken care to avoid further enslavement. Jeremiah stresses that obedience was at the very heart of the covenant relationship, and here recapitulates the essence of that agreement, expressing his approval of it by using the familiar phrase *So be it.* The amen applies equally, of course, to the maledictions of verse 3, as in Deuteronomy 27:15–26. While God had kept his promises (Deut. 6:3; 11:9;

---

17. Cf. *HIOT*, p. 804 n. 11.

26:9), the people had neglected their own. The supreme obedience of Christ to the Father's will (Phil. 2:8) makes submission of the individual to God mandatory for growth in the spirit of Christ (cf. Rom. 6:13).

6–8. The responsibilities of the covenant relationship must be proclaimed far and wide if the terrible fate of captivity is to be averted. Verses 7 and 8 were omitted by LXX except for the phrase *yet they did not obey*. The *words* were the *terms* (NEB) of the covenant which described the penalties attached to a violation of the stipulations. For Jeremiah the imposition of an external covenant would have little point unless it secured the whole-hearted consent of its participants. The Sinai agreement had broken down in practice because the Israelites had violated its stipulations through apostasy. Only a true spiritual conversion could breathe new life into the moribund covenantal forms, and since this condition was obviously lacking, the prophet had no choice but to proclaim the approach of catastrophe.

9–13. While the nation had revolted against God's laws, the conspiracy was not of a formal character. So attractive were the depraved Canaanite fertility rites, and so widespread the resultant idolatry in Israel, that it appeared as though the people had deliberately plotted to renounce their covenantal obligations and espouse apostasy. Verse 10 shows the temporary nature of Josiah's proscriptions, while verse 13 shows the multiplicity of pagan gods and their shrines (cf. 2:28). For the meaning of *shame* (AV *shameful thing*) see on 3:24.

14–17. Jeremiah is forbidden to intercede for an idolatrous nation which insists upon the veneration of Baal. Verse 15 cannot be translated intelligibly. A suggested rendering is, *What business has my cherished one in my house, when she has perpetrated vile schemes? Can vows and sacrificed flesh remove your wickedness? Will you rejoice when disaster strikes?* Ritual sacrifices clearly offer no immunity from calamity. The appalling degree of moral corruption can be rectified only by punishment. Verse 16 also requires reconstruction in the light of LXX. The reference to blazing foliage is an allusion to a tree being damaged by lightning.

18–23. These verses describe the hostility which Jeremiah encountered among the people of his birthplace. The Anathoth priests had lived there since the time of Solomon (1 Kgs 2:26f.), and by force of circumstances were excluded from priestly functions in Jerusalem. Perhaps their jealousy of Jeremiah's support for Josiah's reforms stirred up their opposition. Although God had given the prophet some warning, his relationship to the people of Anathoth was that of an animal which is completely unaware of the intentions of its owner to slaughter it. The resentment of the townsmen was evidently aroused when Jeremiah, the son of a priest, actively supported the suppression of local shrines in conformity with Josiah's legislation. Hence the native sons wished to destroy the prophetic tree *with its fruit*, as with most EVV. An alternative rendering would be *'in flowing sap'*, reading *bĕlēḥô* ('in its sap') for *bĕlaḥmô* ('with its bread'). As another Lamb of God observed, a man's foes shall be those of his own household (Matt. 10:36). Jeremiah was not to be deterred from prophesying, however, being assured that none of the conspirators would survive. According to Ezra 2:23, 128 men of Anathoth returned to post-exilic Judea.

12:1–6. These verses introduce a formal statement of the problem of godless prosperity. The age-old question as to why the wicked should flourish receives no direct answer, however, here as elsewhere in Scripture. Instead, Jeremiah is instructed to prepare himself for a yet greater assault on his faith and courage. The statement is based upon the concept of God as being just and irrefutable in argument, though amenable to complaints. The image of planting, implying stability (cf. Isa. 40:24; Ps. 1:3), shows that prosperity is not accidental, but is part of God's general provision for human needs (cf. Matt. 5:45; Luke 6:35). Although the people use the divine name frequently in speech, they are actually hypocrites who are divorced spiritually from God. Cf. Isaiah 29:13, as quoted by Christ in Matthew 15:8 and Mark 7:6. Thus their wickedness is even more appalling by comparison with Jeremiah's own fidelity, and he demands to know how much longer such behaviour will go unpunished, coming very close in the process to the nadir of despair. God replies that his past sufferings are nothing compared to what will happen in the future. If he stumbled in home territory, how could he be expected to fare in Jerusalem? In common with Jeremiah, Christ and Paul, most Christians have to face a 'Jerusalem experience' if their witness has to have more than a purely local effect. The Jordan *jungle* (AV *swelling*; RV *pride*; NEB *dense thickets*) was the Zor or flood-plain of the river, which was covered with luxuriant vegetation (*gā'ôn*). It was the haunt of wild animals, including the Asiatic lion, in pre-exilic times (cf. Jer. 49:19), and in spring was partly flooded (cf. Josh. 3:15). A foretaste of the trials ahead is provided by the figure of his family in hue and cry behind him, as though he were a fugitive needing to be captured.

7–13. Here Jeremiah speaks of the forthcoming devastation of the land. By rendering the verbs as prophetic perfects, the reference is to a future catastrophe as though it had already occurred. This may further be construed as a reply to Jeremiah stating that, though prosperous at present, the wicked were actually poised on the brink of disaster. As Jeremiah's family had treated him, so the nation has treated its God, roaring hostility and defiance at the One whom their fathers had pledged to obey. The prophet is thus able to sense afresh the sorrow and regret of a God who is forced to reject his people. Rebellious Judah will now be as conspicuous as *a speckled bird* (NEB *hyena's lair*), whose unusual plumage provokes the enmity of other predators. So the inhabitants of the southern kingdom, being different from other nations, would be attacked by them, and God's *pleasant portion* would be no more. The *shepherds* are the leaders (cf. 2:8) who have furnished improper guidance, and they will see their homeland ravaged as God brings judgment upon the nation.

14–17. This section notes the fate which will overtake the evil neighbours of the Israelites because of their predatory behaviour. If they repent, their exile will be of short duration. The reference is to Syria, Moab and Ammon, who with Judah will be punished by a common adversary, i.e., Babylon. The prophet to the nations was fulfilling his divine commission (cf. 1:10). Like the eighth-century BC prophets, Jeremiah recognized that God was the Disposer Supreme, and Judge of the earth. Yet he also holds out to pagan peoples the blessings of the covenant relationship if only they will repudiate the Baal deities and swear by the living God. The conditional nature of prophecy is to be noted in verses 15 to 17, which at the same time restate the promises of Deuteronomy 4 and 29 – 30.

13:1–27. *Five warnings*

Verses 18–19 may be dated in 597 BC (cf. 2 Kgs 24:8, 12), and the remainder about 600 BC. A nation which should have been living in a close spiritual relationship with God is shown to have been corrupted by pagan religious influences. Judah's level of spiritual discernment has been appallingly low, and wilful pride has permeated all areas of society to produce a rebellious, apostate nation moving headlong towards destruction.

1–11. The first warning, conveyed by the acted parable of the ruined linen loincloth, made clear that idolatry, with its attendant moral corruptions, would be the ruin of the people. The nation had been attached closely to God in former days, but because of recent apostasy had become soiled and now was to be discarded. The prophetic symbolism rests upon the utility of articles in everyday life. The *waistcloth* was one of the more intimate forms of clothing, clinging closely to the body of the wearer and serving as a thigh-length underskirt. Had it been immersed in water it would have been softer and more pliable. Symbolically, the nation had to be guarded against all deleterious influences. If *Perath* was the literal Euphrates, typifying the land of captivity, it would have involved Jeremiah in a journey of at least 500 miles. Otherwise the reference could be to the town of Parah (Josh. 18:23), about three miles north-east of Anathoth, located on the modern Wadi Farah. The *cleft* (AV *hole*; NEB *Perath*) would probably be in the Carchemish area if Jeremiah actually visited the Euphrates. The damaged waistcloth indicated that proud Judah would be humbled and punished for her idolatry. God had wanted her to cling to him in loyalty and faith, but instead she had shaped her destiny of ruin through intimacy with pagan deities.

12–14. The second warning was a parable concerning wine jars. The *nēbel* was the largest earthenware container used for storing wine (cf. Isa. 22:24; 30:14; Lam. 4:2).[18] The saying about jars and wine was perhaps a popular aphorism among seventh-century BC drinkers. However, the jars would prove to be the inebriated people themselves, filled with the wine of God's fury, which would not be restricted to Judah (cf. 25:15). Drunkenness was one of the major social problems in the Ancient Near East, where the range of available beverages was

---

18. See J. L. Kelso, *The Ceramic Vocabulary of the Old Testament* (1948), p. 26 and fig. 5, p. 47.

considerably narrower than at present. It brought with it an assort-
ment of evils, as typified by Noah (Gen. 9:21–25), Nabal (1 Sam. 25)
and others. Drunken excesses were characteristic of pagan Canaanite worship. The New Testament warns against alcoholism, urging
people instead to put on Christ (Rom. 13:13f.) and be filled with
God's Spirit (Eph. 5:18). Jeremiah stresses that just as alcohol affects
judgment and impairs mobility, so in the coming crisis men will
behave as though inebriated, being unable to distinguish friend
from foe or to defend themselves (cf. Jer. 25:15–28; Ezek. 23:31–34;
Isa. 51:17; Ps. 60:3).

15–17. The third warning was against pride and arrogance
towards God. The glory must belong to Israel's Creator, not to Baal,
and the nation is urged to pay attention to the symbolic lessons previously set out. The people were already like unwary travellers stumbling in the gathering gloom as they tried desperately to reach shelter
for the night, and they are urged to return to God before the darkness of catastrophe engulfs them. In Greek thought *hybris*, the sin of
pride, tempted the gods to strike the proud person dead. The New
Testament listed pride with other vices which proceeded from the
inner man (Mark 7:22) and contrasted it with meekness (Jas 4:6,
citing Prov. 3:34; 1 Pet. 5:5). For Paul the proud sinner was a typical
product of depraved pagan society, a view reflected by Jeremiah.

18–19. The fourth warning was a lament over the king and
queen-mother, i.e. Jehoiachin (cf. 22:26) and Nehushta (2 Kgs 24:8).
The king was eighteen years old, hence the importance of the
queen-mother in the régime. In the Old Testament the mother's
name was supplied only for the kings of Judah, not of Israel, for reasons which are not clear. In bidding these royal personages to
descend from their throne, the prophet was rebuking them, as leaders of the people, for their contemptuous response to his message.
The Hebrew *Negeb* means 'dry', not 'south' (AV), although the Negeb
was located south of the Gaza-Beersheba road and merged into the
highlands of the Sinai peninsula. The cities of the area would be bar-
ricaded to prevent entry by refugees fleeing the fury of the invader.
The mention of complete exile (19) is poetic exaggeration, since
only the potential leaders and skilled artisans were actually taken
to Babylonia. These, however, were representative of the entire
nation. The principle of representation underlay the entire Hebrew

sacrificial system, and found supreme expression in the work of Christ on the cross (cf. John 11:50–52).

20–27. The fifth warning was a final reminder that punishment would be the inevitable consequence of wilful continuance in sin. The Hebrew text presents certain difficulties here. The subject of verse 20 is Jerusalem (with LXX). Verse 21 could well read, *What will you say when he* (i.e. God) *appoints as your superiors those friends whom you yourself have made your masters?* The latter, of course, were the Babylonians, who had been periodic allies of Judah. Like nominal believers in all ages, the people were incredulous that such calamities could overtake them. Jeremiah, however, places the blame firmly on their own shoulders and promises them the shameful public disgracing associated with prostitutes (cf. 13:26; Hos. 2:10). The *heels* of AV is another euphemism, more literally rendered 'body ravished' (RSV *suffer violence*; NEB *limbs uncovered*). Verse 23 shows how impossible it is for the nation to change its idolatrous ways. Therefore it must bear the full consequences of punishment. The irony of it all is that this will be inflicted by the very people whom Judah once courted. Because of her indulgence in the unfruitful works of darkness Judah would be exposed publicly as the corrupt wanton that she was by the One who had first espoused her in covenant love. Though this calamity was still several years distant, its shadow had already fallen ominously across the southern kingdom.

14:1–22. Intercession and response in an emergency

Poetry and prose alternate in a dialogue between God and Jeremiah, in which the prophet intercedes earnestly for Judah and tries to excuse her behaviour.

1–6. Occasional periods of drought occurred in Palestine, and along with famine they formed part of the covenant curses (cf. Deut. 28:23f.). The passage describes either a prolonged drought or a succession of short, severe ones, along with their devastating consequences. The calamity had affected the entire land, thus portending complete destruction. People were covering their heads in mourning (cf. 2 Sam. 15:30). All cultivation of crops had ceased, and some animals had abandoned their young for lack of fodder. In the face of clear indications of divine displeasure Judah still refused to repent and be rehabilitated, thereby providing a stark illustration of those lost in sin and alienated from the covenant of promise (cf. Eph. 2:12). Despite warnings from God to the contrary, Jeremiah is so overcome by anguish for his people that he prays for their deliverance.

7–10. The prophet knows that confession will result in forgiveness (cf. 1 John 1:9), and if the nation will not acknowledge its sin, Jeremiah will do so vicariously. Whereas the prophet thinks of God as a traveller who has no interest in the inhabitants of the land through which he is passing, God replies by insisting upon his covenantal rights.

11–12. Again Jeremiah is forbidden to intercede for Judah, since God will ignore their pleas (cf. Hos. 8:13). *Sword … famine … disease* is a combination which occurs seven times in the extant prophecy.

13–16. Jeremiah makes an unsuccessful attempt to explain the shortcomings of his deluded compatriots, but God in reply castigates the authors of the mischief, the false prophets, and dismisses their utterances as *lying visions, valueless divinations and self-deception* (14). Such deceivers will be the first to suffer, followed by the people as a whole, who had been revelling in the deception. To lie unburied was one of the most terrible fates which could overtake a person. False prophets are promised at the close of the Christian dispensation (Matt. 24:11; Mark 13:22).

17–22. The theme of supplication is renewed, where Jeremiah stands in the tradition of Abraham (Gen. 18:23–33), Moses (Exod. 32:11–13) and Samuel (1 Sam. 7:5–9). The last clause of verse 18 is obscure, but may mean *they wandered off to a land with which they were unfamiliar.* All around is devastation and death, the grim penalty for idolatry, and in an anguished outcry Jeremiah confesses the prolonged period of apostasy, knowing that if God abandons covenant love, all is lost for Judah.

15:1–9. The final answer

God is adamant in refusing to avert punishment. Though Moses and Samuel had earlier interceded successfully for sinful Israel (Exod. 32:11–14; Num. 14:13–24; Deut. 9:18–20, 25–29; 1 Sam. 7:5–9; 12:19–25), they had first secured the co-operation of the nation, which Jeremiah still had not been able to accomplish.

1–4. Judah, the spiritual outcast, is doomed by the predetermined means of *plague, sword, famine* and *captivity.* When slain, the corpses will undergo further humiliation from dogs, carrion birds and other predators (cf. 19:7; 34:20), and this because of the gross idolatry of Manasseh (cf. 2 Kgs 21:10–15; 23:26; 24:3).

5–9. Because Jerusalem has rejected God so consistently he can relent no longer, as in the past. Judah has been shaken like a sheaf so that the wind can remove the chaff, but to no avail. Bereavement has struck but without effect, even when the widows outnumbered the sand (cf. 2 Chr. 28:6). The woman with seven (i.e. numerous; cf. 1 Sam. 2:5) children collapses from shock, thus furnishing a presage of the fate awaiting Jerusalem, the mother-city of Judah. The utterance is reminiscent of Christ's words in Luke 23:28–31.

15:10–21. **Lament and reply**
This confessional section furnishes a glimpse of the prophet's innermost being. He is alienated from his people because of his witness, yet he has no choice but to proclaim God's word to a recalcitrant nation. He is a lonely, anxious man, yet one who rejoices that God dwells in his heart.

10–14. In a burst of powerful emotion the prophet broods over his lot in life and wishes that he had never been born, complaining that, though he has lived an upright life, everyone curses him. This was hardly surprising in view of his bitter attacks on his countrymen. However, in the future when calamity strikes, his erstwhile opponents will hurry to him, asking for intercession on their behalf. Cf. 21:1–6; 37:3; 42:1–6. Verses 11–14 present certain textual problems, and seem to be based on 17:1–4. The RSV of verse 11, *So let it be, O Lord* (AV *The Lord said*) reads *'āmēn* with LXX for MT, *'āmar*. The finest quality iron (*northern iron*) in the seventh century BC came from the Black Sea region. Clearly the armaments of Judah would be insufficient to repel the Babylonian armies, who would bring the shame and sorrow of captivity on the nation.

15–21. In a poetic passage of great beauty Jeremiah expresses his sense of utter loneliness in the midst of a bustling people. Many of his emotional tensions arose from an inner compulsion to side with God against his compatriots. Every true servant of God is likely to experience tensions of this kind, especially if, like Jeremiah, his foes are his relatives (cf. Matt. 10:36). The degree of individual sensitivity will govern the amount of suffering involved in the choice

between the world and God (cf. Jas 4:4). When God's word came to
Jeremiah he welcomed it avidly (cf. Ezek. 2:8 – 3:3), but this also fostered his isolation. He was set apart from his fellows by the
indwelling prophetic spirit, and cut off from popular activities
because of his indignation over national sin. In his grief Jeremiah
refuses to believe that God is an *unreliable stream* (wadi, 18), which
cannot be counted on for water in the heat of summer because of
his affirmation in 2:13. God's response restates the basic principle
that obedience and true repentance will guarantee forgiveness and
blessing. Jeremiah will again stand before him in divine service (cf.
1 Kgs 1:2; 10:8) if he sifts the valuable from the worthless, thereby
removing the dross of idolatry and apostasy. The description *mouth*,
i.e., spokesman, recalls the designation (perhaps an Egyptian official
title) of Aaron in Exodus 4:16. As such Jeremiah has to bring the
people up to his own spiritual level, in the assurance that God will
deliver him (cf. 1:8, 18f.).

16:1–13. The special conditions of Jeremiah's life

The theme of 15:17 seems emphasized by this chapter, which inter-
prets Jeremiah's celibacy symbolically in the light of Judah's destiny.

1–4. The prophet was forbidden the comfort and fellowship of
marriage as yet another warning to the populace concerning future
desolation. Since marriage was the normal state of life for a healthy
adult Hebrew male, abstinence for the reasons given would furnish
a powerful object-lesson commending abstinence (cf. Matt. 24:19;
1 Cor. 7:26). The fatal diseases were presumably from epidemic
causes. The loathsome thought of decomposing corpses being
eaten by birds and rodents reflects 15:3.

5–9. The 'shrill sound' (Heb. *marzēaḥ*) refers to wailing for the dead
(cf. Amos 6:7). Jeremiah is forbidden to indulge in such wakes,
since they will be so widespread in Judah. The reference to incisions
was to pagan mourning customs prohibited in the Torah (Lev. 19:28;
21:5; Deut. 14:1). In verse 7 RSV *break bread* reads *leḥem* (with LXX)
instead of MT *lāhem* (AV *for them*). Friends of the mourners usually
provided a meal after the funeral rites were concluded (cf. 2 Sam.
3:35; Ezek. 24:17; Hos. 9:4). A consoling cup in later Judaism was a
special cup of wine drunk by the chief mourner. This practice is not
mentioned elsewhere in Scripture. Both sorrow and joy were to be

avoided, since in any case they would soon be withdrawn (cf. Rev. 18:23).

10–13. In their self-deception the people are still unable to see that the real cause of their misfortunes is apostasy, but this is now made clear in unequivocal terms. The covenant supplied their spiritual guidelines, but these had long been discarded in favour of gross idolatry. Such a rejection of covenant love demanded the sternest punishment. Whereas RSV of verse 13 reads *a land*, the definite article in MT shows that the people knew about the land where they would go as captives. The allusion to *other gods* is a sarcastic comment on the opportunities for future participation in paganism.

16:14–21. The destiny of Judah
Verses 14 and 15, repeated substantially in 23:7–8, have been seen as a scribal interpolation. However, the verses need not be regarded as displaced, since the pre-exilic prophets regularly interspersed their denunciations with expectations of a brighter future (Joel 3:18–21; Amos 9:11–15, etc.). The mighty act of deliverance from Egypt will be surpassed by an even greater 'exodus' from Babylonia. But first the helpless citizens of Judah have to be rounded up and carried off before their redemption can be achieved. The *fishers* (cf. Amos 4:2; Hab. 1:15; Ezek. 12:13) will see that few slip through the net to safety. The *double* (MT *mišneh*) recompense may, from an Alalakh tablet, be better translated 'proportionate',[19] making the punishment equivalent to the offence. Verse 19 is typical of the messianic vision of prophetism.

17:1–18. Sin and its dire consequences
The prophet here shows that Judah's apostasy is very deeply engrained in the national character. It can only be atoned for by true repentance, but the corrupt minds of the people stand in the way of contrition and forgiveness. Judah will therefore have to bear the consequences of her continued rebellion against covenant love.

1–4. Judah is so firmly rooted in transgression that her sin is indelible. The iron stylus was used for engraving upon hard surfaces

---

19. D. J. Wiseman, *NBD*, p. 67a.

(cf. Job 19:24). RSV *diamond* (NEB *adamant*) is MT *šāmîr*, a term referring to some obscure stone of impenetrable hardness characteristic of the diamond.[20] Not merely has sin formed an impenetrable layer over national life, but it has permeated the very wellsprings of thought and will. The fruition of the new covenant expectations (31:33) appears in 1 Corinthians 3:2f. MT of verse 2 presents certain difficulties, but could be read as follows, *while their children commemorate at their altars and their Asherim, beside leafy trees on high hills. Asherim* (AV *groves*) were representations of the Canaanite goddess Asherah set up beside the altar at the shrines. Such cultic objects were strictly forbidden in the Torah (Deut. 16:21). Verses 3–4 present textual difficulties, but seem to be variants of 15:13–14. For MT *your high places for sins* read LXX of 15:13, *as the price of all your sins*, and for *and in you* (AV *even thyself*) read *your hand*, involving a slight change of the consonants. Because of sin the land will be plundered and the people will lose their heritage.

5–10. Complete reliance upon God was basic to the covenant agreement, and here Jeremiah is enunciating a general principle in the light of Judah's periodic political dabblings with Babylon and Egypt (cf. Ps. 146:3). The EVV *shrub* (MT *'ar'ār*) refers to the tamarisk, a dwarf juniper of a particularly stark and naked appearance which *has no prospect of improvement* (RSV *shall not see any good come*, NEB *when good comes he shall not see it*), since its stunted roots do not penetrate to the water-levels beneath the surface. The implications of the allusion would not be lost on the people, who had they lived in a faith-relationship with God could have been flourishing like the green bay tree. For AV *see* (MT *yir'e*) in verse 8 read *fear* (*yirā'*), apparently a transcriptional mistake of one letter in the Hebrew. Unregenerate human nature is in a desperate condition without divine grace, described by the term *gravely ill* in verse 9 (RSV *desperately corrupt*, NEB *desperately sick*). Cf. 15:18 and 30:12, where the meaning 'incurable' occurs. Every generation needs regeneration of soul by the Spirit and grace of God (cf. John 3:5f.; Titus 3:5).

11–13. Retribution is grounded in divine justice (cf. 32:19; Ps. 62:12; Job 34:11). The reference to *the partridge* is to the popular belief

---

20. In *NBD*, p. 632, it is related to the Akkadian *ašmur*, 'emery'.

that it would hatch the eggs of other birds.[21] Just as the fledglings soon realize the false nature of the mother and depart from the nest, so riches unjustly acquired all disappear just when the owner is counting on them for security. The *fool* is one delinquent in moral appreciation, a characteristic emphasis of the ancient Hebrew sages. Verse 12 could be rendered, *a glorious throne, a primeval height, is the location of our sanctuary.* This symbol of God's presence is only valid as long as his people respond to him in covenant love. For the expression *fountain of living waters* see on 2:13.

14–18. This elegant poetic section is a plea by Jeremiah for vindication. Since God is Israel's only hope, it is natural for the prophet to appeal to him for healing and restoration. RSV *let it come* (15) is better rendered *if only it would happen*, a taunting remark, since his prophecies of doom had so far failed to materialize. The MT of verse 16 contains textual corruptions. The sense seems to be that Jeremiah was not going to abandon his prophetic functions simply because he had been persecuted. Instead he prayed for grace to withstand opposition until the truth should be manifested, when all would see that it was God's word, not his own, that he had been proclaiming faithfully.

17:19–27. An appendix on the sabbath
This short prose section again demonstrates the conditional nature of the prophecies of doom, which could be revoked if the sinner evidenced true repentance. Jeremiah makes it clear that the people held their destiny in their own hands. *The Benjamin Gate* or Gate of the Laity (MT *sons of my people*) is of uncertain location, but was apparently used by persons other than priests and Levites. At all events the prophet would be assured of an audience. The *kings* of Judah were the ruler and the royal princes. A little later on, one of the Lachish Ostraca (Ostracon VI)[22] was to record a complaint about the demoralizing effect which certain communications sent out by these royal

---

21. *Qôrē'*, however, may not mean 'partridge' (genera *Alectoris* and *Ammoperdix*), but could refer to some variety of sand grouse (*Pteroclididae*). Cf. G. R. Driver, *Palestine Exploration Quarterly*, 1955, p. 133.
22. See *ANET*, p. 322.

officials and notables (*śārîm*) were having upon the populace as a whole. Profanation of the sabbath (21) had become commonplace, in defiance of God's commands to keep it holy. If the ethical ideals of the covenant are observed, the legitimate Davidic dynasty will be maintained, and from the north will come only peaceful migrations of people. If not, the complete destruction of Jerusalem is portended (cf. 21:14; 49:27; 50:32; Amos 1:3 – 2:5).

18:1–17. The prophet visits the potter's house

This passage shows how Jeremiah, as a result of watching the potter throwing his clay, perceived how the divine Potter shaped his human clay. Pottery-making was a familiar activity throughout the Near East, and the lessons taught here would be appreciated readily enough in Judah. The material probably dates from the earlier days of Jehoiakim.

3–6. The Hebrew form of the *wheel* is dual, 'the pair of stones'. On a vertical axis two circular stones were fitted, the lower one being spun by the potter's feet. This caused the upper disc to rotate also, and the clay which was placed in the middle was shaped by hand as the wheel revolved (cf. Ecclus. 38:29f.). In verse 4 some MSS read *kaḥōmer* ('like the clay') instead of MT *baḥōmer* ('in (with) the clay'). The former would then read, *Whenever a vessel which he was fashioning became misshapen, as clay occasionally does in the potter's hands* ... However, the MT reading seems preferable: *Whenever the vessel which he was fashioning from the worked clay was disfigured by the potter's hands* ... Quite frequently in the process of throwing the clay, some defect in design, size or structure would arise. The potter then squeezed the developing pot into an amorphous mass and recommenced his task of shaping the raw material into some other suitable container. Jeremiah was impressed by the control which the potter exercised over the clay. Whatever the reasons for dissatisfaction, he took the material and worked on it until it met his specifications. In the same way God has absolute control over his people, and will dispose their destiny according to his purposes (cf. Rom. 9:19ff.).

7–11. Jeremiah asserts the sovereignty of God over all humanity (cf. Amos 9:7; Mic. 1:2–4, etc.), though without the capriciousness associated with many earthly rulers, since God is governed by certain principles consistent with his self-revelation at Sinai. Verse 8 is

awkward textually, and is shorter in form in LXX and versions. A suggested rendering is: *But if that nation should repent of its iniquity because
I have threatened it, I would modify the punishment which I had planned to inflict
upon it.* The anthropomorphic term *repent* indicates not so much a
change of mind as of the treatment to be accorded Israel because
of her modified behaviour (cf. Num. 23:19). Again the responsibility is laid upon the people themselves, since they determine their destiny. In verse 11 the Hebrew verb *yôṣēr* (RSV *shaping*) has the same root
as 'potter'. The choice is deliberate so as to reinforce the connection.
The nation is to be moulded by means of the Exile.

12–17. Time has run out for Judah (cf. 2:25). National sin is so
ingrained that repentance is out of the question. Virgin-Israel (cf.
14:17) should have kept herself untainted by pagan orgiastic rites, just
as an unmarried woman keeps herself chaste for her future husband.
In the circumstances, however, her conduct has been revolting in the
extreme. In verse 14 some translators associate *śādāy, field,* with the
Akkadian *šadu, mountain,* while others read *śiryôn* here, the ancient
name of Mount Hermon (cf. Deut. 3:9). The latter then reads, with
RSV, *Does the snow of Lebanon leave the crags of Sirion?* If *ṣûr (pebble)* is read
for *miṣṣûr (from the rock)*, the verse would commence: *Do pebbles ever
leave the fields?* Both renderings are uncertain, however. The verb
yinnātĕšú is also problematical. It is frequently treated as a form of
nātaš, 'to root up', and hence rendered *are plucked up*, but by a trans-
position of two root letters could be read *yinnašĕtû, are dried up*,
from the root *nāšat.* This latter is preferred increasingly by scholars.
Mayim zārîm, literally 'foreign waters', is sometimes modified to
mayim zābîm, 'flowing waters', while RSV has substituted *hārîm*, 'mountains', for MT *zārîm* to read: *Do the mountain waters run dry, the cold flowing streams?* All translations of this verse are conjectural, however. The
sense seems to be that the nation's sin is completely irrational in character, as contrasted with the course of nature, which is steadfast and
consistent. Such unnatural and apostate behaviour from a covenant
people can only result in punishment. The RSV *they have stumbled* (15)
reads *wayyikšĕlû* and removes the enclitic *m*. Travellers will shake their
heads in astonishment at Israelite stupidity in forsaking the old
covenantal paths for the worship of fraudulent, non-existent deities.
The *east wind* (17) is the sirocco, a hot dry wind coming from the
eastern deserts (cf. 4:11; 13:24).

18:18–23. A second plot against Jeremiah

Cf. 11:18–23; 12:1–6; 15:10f., 15–21. The prophetic utterances had
evidently aroused such indignation in influential circles that a conspiracy was the result. In this section Jeremiah prays passionately for
his enemies to be punished. The allusion (18) to priestly instruction
(RSV *the law shall not perish from the priests*; NEB *there will still be priests to
guide us*) seems to imply that people were quite satisfied with the
depraved leadership given by their own priests and false prophets,
thus scorning Jeremiah's proclamations of doom, and using his
message as a basis for charges of treason. The RSV *hearken to my plea*
(19) reads *ribi*, with LXX, for MT *yĕribay* ('of my contenders'). This
vehement cry for vindication has been assumed to be so out of character with Jeremiah's other utterances as to be the work of an
entirely different author. However, it is not just a matter of wounded
pride demanding revenge. Jeremiah is so committed to the ideals of
Sinai that he is pleading for the divine cause, and not its mere
embodiment in his utterances, to be vindicated. This latter is particularly evident in verses 21–23. *Nepeš* (20) here means *self*, not *soul*
or *life*, as in most EVV. The *pit* was intended to trap large animals. In
a passionate response Jeremiah prays for dire penalties upon his enemies, rather than the populace as a whole. While such utterances
may constitute a rather shocking revelation of Jeremiah's humanity,
they are consistent with other maledictions uttered in the Lord's
name (cf. Ps. 137:9). The Christian attitude towards one's enemies is
markedly different (cf. Matt. 5:44; Rom. 12:20).

19:1–15. A parabolic oracle of an earthenware bottle

This utterance was to be acted out in two places – the temple court
and the valley of Ben-hinnom.

1–3. Whereas a spoiled vessel on the potter's wheel could be
reshaped, once it had hardened it was beyond reconstruction, and
only fit for breaking. The earthenware container symbolized the final
form of Judah's spiritual obduracy (cf. Rev. 22:11), and the act of
shattering it in the presence of senior citizens and priests indicated
the coming doom. The valley of Ben-hinnom (cf. Jer. 7:31), south
of Jerusalem, was a contemporary locale for Molech worship. Under
Josiah the shrine was destroyed and later on the valley was used for
burning garbage and cremating the bodies of criminals. The site is

probably to be identified with the Wadi al-Rababi. The *Potsherd Gate* (AV *East*), leading into the valley, was probably the place where broken pottery was deposited.

4–9. Jerusalem, where God's house was located, had been profaned by an indulgence in pagan cultic rites which were alien to the ethos and intent of the covenant relationship. The *blood of innocents* (RSV) might allude to the murders of 2 Kings 21:16. In that valley the people had killed and burned their sons when, following the rites of Molech worship, they required a sacrifice of particular efficacy in an emergency (cf. 7:31f.). The MT *baqqōtî, I will make void* (7), contains a play on 'bottle' (*baqbuq*). The prophet may have emptied the flask symbolically as he spoke these words. The horrors of 7:33 are repeated for emphasis, indicating that the devastated city will appear so appalling that those who see it will be completely bewildered, sucking their breath in (8). The plight of the besieged citizens will be so desperate that they will resort to cannibalism (cf. Deut. 28:53). In Lamentations 4:10 the prediction was fulfilled.

10–13. The smashing of the bottle forms the climax to the prophetic enunciation. The flask has proved useless, and is therefore shattered into fragments, thus graphically illustrating the fate of a nation which had flagrantly violated God's purpose for his people to be 'vessels for noble use' (2 Tim. 2:20f., RSV). The sentence beginning *men shall bury* (11) is omitted in LXX. Though Topheth is unclean, it will be needed to accommodate all the corpses resulting from the siege. Jerusalem will be made like the high place in the valley of Ben-hinnom, which had been desecrated during Josiah's reforms (cf. 2 Kgs 23:10). The rooftops of houses would also be destroyed because of their place in the idolatry of the nation. The flat roofs of oriental houses had a varied usage, as the biblical narratives show (cf. Judg. 16:27; 1 Sam. 9:26; 2 Sam. 11:2; Neh. 8:16; Matt. 10:27; Acts 10:9), and before the Exile they were apparently the normal places for the worship of astral deities such as Astarte (Ashtaroth) (cf. 32:29). Cuneiform texts recovered from Ras Shamra included a ritual to be used when offerings were made on rooftops to astral deities and celestial luminaries (cf. Zeph. 1:5).

14–15. As a punishment for this blatant idolatry the sentence of doom is pronounced on the nation. From 19:14 to 20:6 the narrative is written in the third person, suggesting that this section may have been the work of Baruch. Having delivered his prophecy, Jeremiah returned to the temple area to recapitulate the sentence upon Jerusalem and other Judean cities. Again the citizens are made responsible for their own destruction. Having refused to obey the revealed will of God, they have thereby committed the most serious violation of covenant love.

20:1–6. Jeremiah in the stocks

Jeremiah's utterances against Jerusalem promising divine punishment were met with a prompt and humiliating response from the temple overseer. However, the persecutor is given a name which reinforces the message of doom already proclaimed.

1–3. The boldness of the prophet in standing in the precincts of the temple to deliver a message of desolation brought immediate retaliation from the authorities. *Pashhur ben Immer* was the chief officer of the temple at the close of the monarchy. Pashhur and Immer are personal names here, but later on they became family designations (cf. Ezra 2:37f.; 10:20). From the references to Pashhur in 21:1 and 38:1 the name would seem to have been fairly common. As *pāqîd nāgîd* (AV *chief governor*) the *chief officer* (cf. 29:26) was apparently the immediate subordinate of the High Priest and maintained order in the area of the temple. The beating was perhaps with forty stripes, which in St Paul's day had been reduced slightly (cf. 2 Cor. 11:24) for fear of exceeding the legal limit (Deut. 25:3). The *stocks* (MT *mahpeket*, from a root 'to distort') were a form of scaffold in which prisoners were detained in a crooked or confined position which produced cramped muscles (cf. 29:26; 2 Chr. 16:10). The location was at a gate on the north side of the temple, not the city gate of Benjamin in 37:13; 38:7. Despite opposition from various sources, Pashhur apparently thought better of his deed, releasing Jeremiah after an overnight stay in confinement. If he thought that this act of clemency would modify the stern prophetic message he was mistaken, however, for the prophet was determined to remain true to his vocation, no matter what the cost to himself. Pashhur is himself made the symbol of the universal terror which will grip Judah once the Babylonians enter the southern kingdom. The phrase *māgôr missābîb* (RSV *Terror on every side*) recurs in 6:25; 20:10; 46:5 and 49:29.

4–6. *I will make you a terror* (RSV) might imply that Pashhur was the leader of a pro-Egyptian faction in Judah. This situation would recoil on his own head in days to come. However, the phrase can also be rendered, 'I will deliver you up to terror'. The calamity will occur in his lifetime and he will see the plundering Babylonians taking the goods of king and private citizen alike. To be interred outside the beloved homeland (6) was indeed a sad fate for any patriotic citizen. This apparently happened to both Pashhur and Jeremiah. Pashhur seems to have been one who prophesied falsely (cf. 14:14f.) that famine and the sword would never overtake Judah. For such lies he was now to be punished.

20:7–18. The dissatisfaction of the prophet with his lot

This is a powerful poetic section which contains unusual psychological insights, not merely in relation to Jeremiah himself but for canonical prophecy as a whole because of the self-disclosure of profound emotional conflict. Jeremiah's sensitive nature appears in his reaction to the sarcasm and ridicule with which his message was received. His situation was all the more acute because his burning prophetic vocation compelled him to testify concerning covenant spirituality despite all opposition from his beloved countrymen. Thus it is hardly surprising that the emotional tension and conflict which resulted found occasional expression in an outburst of intense feeling such as that indicated here.

7–10. God had induced Jeremiah to exercise a prophetic function when under other circumstances his personality would have been expressed quite differently. He prophesied at a time when the popular view demanded that the predictions be fulfilled within a fairly short interval, otherwise they would be dismissed as false. Because Jeremiah's words remained unfulfilled for so long, people just ridiculed him whenever he spoke about the future. For a person of sensitive disposition this was particularly embarrassing and offensive. The consistent theme of his message is expressed in the phrase *violence and destruction* (8), which provoked the derision of his audience. Yet so overpowering was the prophetic urge that, even if he tried to suppress it, the words flared up like fire inside him and burned until he made the pronouncements. The whisperings were either plots against his life or the sarcastic use of *māgôr missābîb* as a nickname for Jeremiah. Those who sought Christ's downfall schemed in a similar manner (cf. Mark 3:2; 14:58; Luke 6:7; 14:1; 20:20).

11–13. Despite all opposition he is evidently emboldened by realizing that God fights on his side as a mighty champion (11), and this gives him the assurance of ultimate vindication. Verse 12 is very similar in content to 11:20, reflecting the prophet's indignation at Judah's rejection of her God. In verse 13 a brief note of hope and joy pervades the gloom of the section as a whole.

14–18. The remaining verses lapse again into a state of profound depression, seeming to suggest that in the future Jeremiah will be separated even further from his people. Judah will continue her wanton ways while the prophet will stand helplessly in her midst as destruction engulfs her. *The cities* (16) are Sodom, Gomorrah and the other cities of the plain (cf. Gen. 19:24–28). Had her foetus never come to birth, Jeremiah's mother would have had her womb at full term indefinitely. Yet nature is inexorable, and in due time the infant Jeremiah had to leave the security of pre-natal existence and enter the world of humanity. As an adult he is again deprived of the resources of home, and has to face life alone, embarrassed and made the object of ridicule because of his burning prophetic vocation. This section depicts a man loudly complaining about his lot in life, yet showing that he is still submissive, loyal and obedient to God's will.

2. Utterances relating to the kings of Judah and false prophets (21:1 – 25:14)

Whereas the earlier chapters dealt with affairs under Jehoiakim, the scene now shifts to the time of Zedekiah (597–587 BC) and to the fulfilment of the prophecies of destruction.

21:1–7. The appeal of Zedekiah to Jeremiah

This passage comes from a time when Jerusalem was under siege, probably between 589 and 588 BC. A similar incident recording a message from Zedekiah to Jeremiah is contained in 37:3–10. This is not a doublet, however, but alludes to the temporary lifting of the siege by the Egyptians just before the full weight of the Babylonians was imposed on Jerusalem. The events of 597 marked the occasion when, according to the Babylonian Chronicle, Nebuchadnezzar II marched to Palestine, besieged Jerusalem, and captured it on the second day of Adar (16 March), thereby demonstrating to the Judeans that the words of Jeremiah had been the word of God to them. So changed is the situation that the state officials are now consulting the prophet about their future.

1–2. This Pashhur is not the individual mentioned in 20:1. For Zephaniah cf. 29:25; 37:3. Perhaps a different person was named in 52:24. Now they are anxious for Jeremiah to intercede, hoping that God would relent and cause the Babylonians to withdraw. The MT *Něbûkadre'ṣṣar*, usually employed by Jeremiah, transliterates the Babylonian *Nabûkudurri-uṣur* ('Nabu has protected my inheritance'?). The alternative Hebrew form *Něbukadre'ṣṣar* may perhaps be an Aramaic variant of the name.

3–7. The Chaldeans were originally a semi-nomadic tribe occupying the district between northern Arabia and the Persian Gulf. The tenth-century BC Assyrians gave the name *Kaldu* to the territory earlier known as the 'Sea-Land', and in the following century several Chaldean chiefs were included among the vassals of Adadnirari III (c. 805–782 BC). Subsequently the designation of 'Chaldaea' was used to include Babylonia as a whole (cf. Ezek. 23:23; Dan. 3:8). The siege of the capital is still in its initial phases. Those resisting the Babylonians in Judah will be forced to retreat to Jerusalem to await the final enemy onslaught. God has destined the Babylonians as his agents for the punishment of recalcitrant Israel (5). No quarter will be given to the besieged, and their resistance will be weakened further by a devastating plague (6), the survivors of which will fall captive to the Babylonians. Because the city has elected to resist the aggressor, death will overtake its inhabitants (7), in accordance with normal rules of warfare in the Near East, and the whole area will be pillaged as the ultimate punishment of apostasy.

21:8–10. Capitulation to the invaders

Total war, as practised in the Near East, meant that a threatened city could only be saved by surrendering to the aggressors. While the Judeans understood this well enough, Jeremiah's advice still sounded suspiciously like treason. The figure of a choice between two ways comes from Deuteronomy 30:15, 19. In Matthew 7:13f. Christ also spoke of 'two ways', and the difficulty which many people experienced in finding the one leading to eternal life. The *life* which Jeremiah proclaimed merely meant 'escape from death'. The expression *have his life as a prize of war* is unusual, and recurs in 38:2; 39:18. It may mean that, just as a hunter grabs his prey quickly, so he who surrenders will be able to snatch his life from the enemy who would otherwise take it. However, the phrase is uncertain in meaning. Cf. the promise to Baruch in 45:5, implying that he would emerge unscathed.

21:11–14. A message to the royal house
Bearing in mind the conditional nature of prophetic fulfilment, these verses actually comprise a last-ditch appeal to the king and his advisors. The message is in two parts, an exhortation (11–12) and a declaration (13–14), which echo the words of the eighth-century prophets. Social justice and righteousness were integral both to the ethos of the Sinai covenant and the legislative concepts of the Torah. Jeremiah still held out hope – fruitlessly, as events later proved – that swift reformation of public and private life in accordance with the covenant ideals would avert imminent disaster. The reference to *justice* being executed *in the morning* is to pre-exilic kings dispensing justice before the day's heat became too great (cf. 2 Sam. 4:5). Along with the false prophets and the immoral cultic priests, the monarchy must take its share of responsibility for the moral and social degradation of the people because the king's highest duty was the administration of justice (cf. 2 Sam. 15:4). The *inhabitant* of the valley was Jerusalem, which had valleys on three sides. *Yôšebet,* inhabitant, a feminine form, is rendered 'situated' on the basis of such passages as 1 Samuel 4:4; 2 Samuel 6:2, referring to God enthroned above the cherubim.

22:1 – 23:8. Judgment upon the royal house
This section comprises a series of utterances relating to the rulers of the southern kingdom, commencing with the reigning monarch. The original sequence of this material is uncertain.
    1–9. Exhortation to Zedekiah. From the temple precincts the prophet had to go south to the lower ground, where the royal palace was situated (cf. 36:10ff.) and demand justice and social equity for all levels of national life, for this alone could avert imminent

disaster. When God speaks of swearing by himself (cf. Gen. 22:16; Isa. 45:23; Heb. 6:13–18) he is maintaining his rights as the initiator of the covenant relationship. The solemn words of desolation recall Christ's utterance concerning Jerusalem centuries later (cf. Matt. 23:28; Luke 13:35) because it had once again rejected God's salvation.

10–12. The destiny of Shallum. This king, otherwise known as Jehoahaz, a name probably adopted on his accession, was one of Josiah's sons, succeeding after 609 BC when Josiah was killed at Megiddo. He reigned for three months before being deposed by Necho, was taken to Riblah and then to Egypt, where he eventually died (cf. 2 Kgs 23:33f.; 2 Chr. 36:4). He was the first leader of Judah to die in exile, and was told not to mourn for his father but rather for his own fate and that of his kingdom.

13–23. Denunciation of Jehoiakim. This man was the elder brother of Shallum, whom he succeeded, and was compelled to pay heavy tribute to Necho while the latter was preparing to attack the Babylonians in northern Palestine. Jehoiakim was an oppressive, covetous king who imposed heavy taxes in Judah (2 Kgs 23:35) and constructed elaborate royal buildings using forced labour. Unlike Josiah his father, Jehoiakim permitted pagan rites to flourish once again, including at this time those of Egypt (Ezek. 8:5–17), and in general behaved much as Manasseh had done (cf. 2 Kgs 24:3).

13–17. Jeremiah condemns the king's callous exploitation of his workers in defiance of the Torah (Lev. 19:13; Deut. 24:14; cf. Mal. 3:5). RSV reads verse 14b with LXX. The word *šāšar* ('cinnabar', *vermilion*) occurs again only in Ezekiel 23:14. Jehoiakim thinks he is a king because he can surpass others in the amount of Lebanese cedar in his buildings. Decorated dwellings were common in the Near East from the Ubaid period, with red being a popular colour. With this ostentation is contrasted the austere and moral way of life followed by Josiah, who was blessed by God primarily because of his spiritual qualities. Knowing God (16) demands practical expression in daily life of the highest covenantal ideals. To love God truly a man must love his brother also (cf. 1 John 4:21), not with a vague sentimentality but with Calvary love (cf. 1 John 4:10f.). LXX text of verses 15–16 diverges significantly from MT.

18–23. The normal form of lament (cf. 1 Kgs 13:30) will not be used on Jehoiakim's death, nor will he be given a royal funeral (cf.

the careful statement of 2 Kgs 24:6). Instead he will be dumped unceremoniously on the garbage heap, just as dead donkeys were dragged outside the city gate and left to rot. All through the land (20) the coming doom must be proclaimed. The shepherds of Judah (i.e., the rulers of 2:8) will be driven as by a powerful wind into exile, and Jerusalem, described under the figure of splendid Lebanon (cf. 22:6), will be destroyed, even though she thinks herself immune to attack.

24–30. The fate of Jehoiachin. This man, named Jeconiah (24:1) and Coniah (here and in 37:1), became king of Judah after his father Jehoiakim died in December, 598 BC. He ruled for three months, after which he was deported to Babylon and held as a royal hostage. He was mentioned under the name of *Ya'u-kin* in ration tablets dating between 595 and 570 BC which were unearthed near the Ishtar Gate in Babylon. A steward named Eliakim was appointed by the Babylonians to manage his estate in Judah while he was an exile. When Nebuchadnezzar II died, his successor released Jehoiachin from prison in 561 BC and allowed him to live in the royal palace (cf. 2 Kgs 25:27–30; Jer. 52:31–34). Nothing can now prevent Jehoiachin's exile, for in plucking off the *signet* God has rejected his leadership. The marking of property and documents by means of seals was an Ancient Near Eastern practice, the signet ring in this case being perhaps part of the royal insignia (cf. Gen. 41:42; Esth. 3:10).[23] God cannot remain in fellowship with the obdurate sinner, since implicit obedience is mandatory if blessing is to follow (cf. Heb. 10:36). The chilling promise of death in exile struck a sombre note.

28–30. The technical term for *pot* (28) describes a vessel of inferior grade, this being a sarcastic reference to the abilities and leadership of the young Jehoiachin. The threefold repetition of *land* shows the passionate, sorrowing love of Jeremiah for his country, soon to be devastated (cf. 7:4). Under the figure of a national census Jehoiachin is to be described as *childless*. Although he had seven sons (1 Chr. 3:17f.) his dynasty would not continue, making him in effect without succession. The promises concerning his deportation were fulfilled within three months of his accession.

---

23. For illustrations of seals and rings see *NBD*, pp. 1154f.

23:1–8. The shepherds and the sheep. Ordinarily Zedekiah, the last king of Judah, would have been next in order for consideration. He reigned from about 597 to 587 BC, succeeding his nephew Jehoiachin at the time of his deportation. Although this oracle does not mention Zedekiah by name, there is little doubt that he and his advisers were being castigated. The full weight of divine anger is shortly to fall on the corrupt Judeans.

1–4. The shepherds were the false pastors of the flock who were allowing it to be dissipated and ultimately destroyed (cf. 2:8; 10:21, etc.). Bad leadership is the ultimate attributive cause of exile. The grazing sheep reflect a pastoral image found frequently in Scripture. God the Chief Shepherd is solicitous for the welfare of his flock, while Christ the Good Shepherd (John 10:11) showed in his death how far divine love was prepared to go in redeeming sinful humanity. In verse 2 the MT *pāqad* (*attend*) is used intentionally in wordplay, as in most EVV, the second reference having the force of 'punish'. As promised by the pre-exilic prophets, a *remnant* will return and repopulate the devastated land. None of them will go astray because responsible shepherds will attend (*pāqad*) to their welfare.

5–8. Hope for the future is contained in the messianic prophecy of verses 5–8. His introductory formula, *Look, the time is coming,* appears on 16 occasions in the book as a preface to a message of hope for the future. The *shoot* (5), MT *ṣemaḥ,* the *Branch* of many EVV, is the term used to designate the messianic king (cf. 33:15; Zech. 3:8; 6:12). This personage is also referred to in Isaiah 11:1. The shoot is that which sprouts from the roots of a fallen tree. New life will thus spring forth from the fallen dynasty. Jeremiah is therefore able to proclaim that God will raise up a Davidic king whose name will indicate his true character, an expectation fulfilled in Christ, the Son of David. Unlike the successors of Josiah he will pursue a wise policy (AV *prosper*), enshrining the covenantal ideals and governing the people in justice and equity (cf. 2 Sam. 8:15). The designation *the Lord is our righteousness* means 'the one who secures our vindication'. It has been thought that the MT title *ṣidqēnû* was suggested by the name of Zedekiah (*ṣidqiyāhû*), meaning 'the Lord is my vindication', but since Zedekiah also sinned against God (2 Kgs 24:19) it seems more probable that the title was employed as a forcible contrast to his type of kingship. The shoot which will emerge in the form of a messianic personage will be quite different in character, and by his special work he will impart to men a righteousness not of works but of grace (Eph. 2:8) which will include personal holiness as the work of the Spirit after justification. The Sinaitic ideal for the nation (cf. Lev. 20:7, etc.) will be made personal through the new covenant in Christ's blood. Verse 8 contemplates a future reuniting of north and south, as entertained by some of the prophets (cf. Ezek. 37:19). The addition of *led* (EVV) or *brought back* (MT) may point to a combination of two originally distinct readings. Similarly *the seed of the house of Israel* may comprise a conflated form denoting 'Israel's descendants'. Read, *who brought the offspring of Israel back.*

23:9–40. Denunciation of the prophets of Judah
The preceding collection of oracles concerned the heads of state. Now Jeremiah deals with the leaders of religious life in the nation.

9–15. The sins of the false prophets. *Heart*, as used here, denotes a profoundly disturbed mental rather than emotional state. His mind cannot grasp the way in which these prophets have chosen to abuse their professional vocation, and he is shocked at their corrupt behaviour which is matched by the depravity of the Chosen People. MT and LXX differ in the order of the earlier clauses in verse 10, and the general arrangement is rather uncertain. In a critical assessment of those who claimed the prophetic office, Jeremiah considers the Judeans worse than their northern counterparts. They were one with the priests in condoning the pagan orgiastic rites of Baal worship. Cf. 2 Kings 21:5 and Ezekiel 8:6–18, where immoral practices and idolatrous sacrifices had infiltrated temple worship at Jerusalem. Their iniquitous path (cf. 13:16) will now disclose its treacherous nature, and they will be like men sliding on a slippery trail in the darkness, stumbling and falling on top of one another. The impropriety of the *Samaritan prophets* (13) was the sin of Baal worship; the scandal of the *Jerusalem prophets* (14) was their open espousal of adultery and falsehood, reminiscent of the wickedness of Sodom and Gomorrah. Jeremiah here sets the responsibility for the moral depravity of Judah squarely on the shoulders of these evil men.

16–20. The characteristics of false prophetism. Jeremiah stigmatizes the traits of such activity as a fundamental divorce from spiritual, moral and political reality. The false prophets are wishful thinkers, who utter false expectations of peace. Their visions are self-induced, not divinely inspired. Christ warned that in the latter days false prophets would arise, deceiving many (Matt. 24:5, 11). Had Jeremiah's false counterparts been present to hear the Lord's words and proclaim them (18), they would have been talking about judgment, as he had been, not peace (22). Verses 19–20 are repeated in 30:23f. with some variations. They contain the decisions of the heavenly court which the false prophets did not know because of their absence, and hence are not misplaced, as has been occasionally suggested. The *latter days* (20) point to the time of punishment when divine righteousness will be vindicated in Judah. The significance of the events, at present unappreciated because of self-delusion, will then become painfully apparent. The term *day* is amenable to a messianic interpretation (cf. Isa. 2:2; Hos. 3:5).

21–32. The fraudulent mission of the false prophets. Any prophetic utterances which speak of a peaceful future instead of proclaiming divine wrath are false. God, who is close by, can see all that transpires, and the false prophets cannot hide from his scrutiny. Certain classes of pagan prophets at Mari (Tell Hariri, in the Middle Euphrates) and elsewhere regarded dreams as the normal method by which revelations were given to them.[24] Verse 26 presents some textual difficulties, and the original meaning is far from clear. A suggested reading is, *How long will this continue in the minds of the prophets who are proclaiming lies, these prophets of self-deception?* Their fanciful visions distract attention from covenantal morality and focus it instead on the immoral Baal rites. Like *straw* their idle dreams lack sustenance, whereas the prophetic word, like *wheat*, nourishes its recipients. While the false prophets preface their remarks with a formula which purports to indicate divine inspiration, they use words spoken by other inspired individuals which do not apply to the present situation (30, 31).

33–40. The divine oracle and its implications. This section contains a play on the word *maśśā'* or oracle (AV, RV *burden*), used in the twofold sense of 'utterance' and 'burden'. The term also carries

---

24. For prophetism at Mari see H. B. Huffmon, *The Biblical Archaeologist*, XXXI, 1968, No. 4, pp. 101–124.

the ominous implications of calamity or divine judgment (cf. Isa. 13:1; 15:1; 17:1; Ezek. 12:10, etc.). The MT of verse 33 may have modified the original force of Jeremiah's response, and so it seems best to read, with LXX, *'attem hammaśśā', you are the burden*, instead of MT *'et mah-maśśā', what burden?* Perhaps people had been questioning Jeremiah sarcastically about future divine burdens, and so he replied that, because they had spurned the burden of covenant responsibilities, God would in turn toss them off as a burden too tiresome to be carried further. Begin verse 36, *You must never again mention this term 'divine oracle'*, pointing MT *zākar* ('remember') as though it were a causative form ('mention') with LXX. Since the *maśśā'* is so amenable to profanation, it must no longer be used as part of prophetic proclamation. For *wĕnāśîtî* (AV, RV *I will forget*) in verse 39 read, with some Hebrew MSS, the Syriac and Vulgate, *wĕnāśîtî* (RSV *I will lift you up*). In the eighth century BC there was only one symbol for the consonants *ś* and *š*. The force of the wordplay is clear when it is understood that *maśśā'* comes from the root *nāśā'*, 'to lift up'. The Judeans will be tossed forcibly out of their land in a period of unforgettable calamity.

Additional note on true and false prophets

Given two men dressed in similar clothing, each claiming to be God's messenger and prefacing his remarks with 'This is what God says', it must have been far from easy to decide from external appearances which person was proclaiming revealed truth. Closer observation, however, would have made the differences between true and false prophets apparent. Genuine prophets stood consistently in the spirit of the Mosaic law, exemplifying by their lives the ethos of the covenant relationship. Their inspired utterances formed an extension of the spiritual communion which they enjoyed with God, and his word in their minds became their word to society. Because of the corruptions of the day many of their pronouncements were highly critical, challenging people to return to the covenantal ideals of Sinai. The divine word within them was like a fire which consumed whatever was unworthy and made them persons of absolute integrity.

False prophets, by contrast, were indistinguishable from the rest of society in the matter of personal character, being essentially frauds who profaned sacred things and perverted the divine word by making it appear ludicrous. Their dreams were false, they told lies, deceived their hearers, and were spiritually irresponsible because they were not subject to a positive ethos. They proclaimed what people liked to hear, not what God had to say to them, and they invariably brought a message which would quieten the conscience and give it a delusive peace. About this latter they seemed greatly concerned, since their own worldly interests flourished best in an undisturbed environment. However, they were thinking of peace merely as the absence of turmoil or social conflict, and not as the triumph of divine righteousness among men. So far from being models of spiritual integrity, the false prophets were hypocrites who compromised the moral ethos of the Torah at every turn while professing to be God's spokesmen to the nation. Absolute loyalty and obedience to the revealed will and word of the Lord was the ultimate criterion for distinguishing between true and false prophets. The deficient spirituality of the latter led to an equally inadequate understanding of God's dealings with his people. Consequently their pronouncements were false because they did not appreciate the conditional character of Israelite covenantal traditions, and therefore they misread completely the contemporary political situation.

24:1–10. The good and bad figs

This vision occurred after the events of 597 BC, when Jeconiah (Jehoiachin) was taken captive to Babylon with the royal household and other persons from Judah. The basic message was that the exiles would be restored, while those remaining in the land would be destroyed. The skilled artisans and construction workers (1) were needed by Nebuchadnezzar to construct buildings in his imperial centres, thereby making them more splendid than their precursors. Ruins excavated from the Neo-Babylonian period (612–539 BC) show the remarkable architectural achievements of Nebuchadnezzar and his successors.[25] The meaning of *masgēr* (RSV *smiths*) in verse 1 is uncertain. The Judean leaders had been deported so as to remove potential trouble-makers. The early-ripening figs, maturing

---

25. See J. Finegan, *Light from the Ancient Past* (1951), pl. 83.

in June, were valued as a delicacy (cf. Isa. 28:4; Hos. 9:10), and contrasted sharply with the rotten figs. They symbolized two classes of people: the good, who would turn penitently to the Lord (7), and the bad, who would continue in their old rebellious ways. The former were now in Babylon, shocked into repentance, and committed to the single-minded worship of God. They would thus receive divine blessing and experience the reversal of the threats of 1:10. The latter, who were at present in Jerusalem, would feel the full weight of divine anger because of their hopeless degradation. Like bad figs they would be thrown out for all to see. In this graphic vision Jeremiah shows that fellowship with God and the blessings of divine grace need have no connection with cultic forms, national institutions or geographical locations. Whether in or out of exile, those who seek God whole-heartedly will find him (cf. Deut. 4:29ff.; Ps. 119:10; Matt. 7:7). The final accomplishment of the promise in verse 10 occurred when the Romans devastated Judea, as Christ also predicted (cf. Matt. 23:38).

25:1–14. Desolation is confirmed

This passage is dated in 605 BC, the fourth year of Jehoiakim, in which the crucial battle of Carchemish was fought. The result of this was that the Egyptians were routed and Babylon incorporated Judah into her empire as a tributary (2 Kgs 24:1). Earlier scholarly allegations of an anachronism in which the fourth year of Jehoiakim in verse 1 was equated with the third year of that same king in Dan. 1:1 are now known to have been based on a misunderstanding of Ancient Near Eastern methods of chronological compilation.[26] In seventh-century BC Palestine, the accession year was counted as the first year of the reign, whereas in Babylonia the accession year was reckoned separately, being then followed by the first year of the

---

26. For the chronology see *HIOT*, pp. 191f., 1112, and for earlier liberal views see S. R. Driver, *An Introduction to the Literature of the Old Testament* (1906 ed.), p. 498; J. A. Montgomery, *A Critical and Exegetical Commentary on the Book of Daniel* (1927), pp. 72f.; W. O. E. Oesterly and T. H. Robinson, *An Introduction to the Books of the Old Testament* (1934), p. 335; N. W. Porteous, *Daniel, A Commentary* (1965), p. 25, et al.

actual reign. Jeremiah thus reckoned according to the current Palestinian method while Daniel followed that used in Babylonia. LXX
omitted the gloss relating to Nebuchadnezzar.

1–7. Jeremiah's appeal was to the whole populace, not merely to
the ruling coterie. He was called about 626 BC and thus prophesied
for almost twenty years under Josiah, followed by three months
under Jehoahaz and three years under Jehoiakim. He was therefore
in the middle of his career at this point, having spent over two
decades urging the nation to spurn idolatrous worship and return to
the covenantal ideals. Only a truly repentant nation could expect to
receive divine blessing. God had done his part in issuing persistent
warnings to rebellious and idolatrous Israel, and now the onus must
be on them for their wilful neglect of his words. The use of manu-
factured pagan images had provoked God's anger, which had
recoiled on their users, for no idol must be permitted to be the object
of human worship, as Christ sternly pointed out during his
temptation (Matt. 4:10).

8–14. The reference to the northern tribes (9) is to the compos-
ite nature of the Assyrian empire and its Babylonian successor. LXX
reads 'a family from the north', and omits 'my servant' as a designation of Nebuchadnezzar. The disobedient nation would not listen to
God's prophetic servants, so now they must pay heed to a different
kind of servant (cf. 27:6; 43:10). The destruction of verse 9 will be
reminiscent of the obliteration of cities in the time of Joshua (cf. Josh.
6:21; 10:28, etc.). The *seventy years* of exile is a round figure, being reckoned from the fourth year of Jehoiakim (605 BC) to the start of the
return under Cyrus' régime, about 536 BC (cf. Zech. 1:12; 2 Chr.
36:20–23). Verses 12 to 14 are shorter in LXX than in MT, and do not
allude directly to Nebuchadnezzar, following the pattern of LXX
25:1, 9, 11. After the first half of verse 13 LXX inserts the contents of
chapters 46 to 51 in a modified order, prompting the suggestion that
the references to the prophecies against pagan nations in 13b served
as a heading for the section comprising verses 15 to 38. However, all
that is certain is that LXX drew upon a different textual tradition from
that of MT which need not necessarily be superior in nature. The *book*
of verse 13 is the original prophecy, which was destroyed by Jehoiakim
(36:22). The *many nations* of verse 14 are the Medes and Persians who
subjugated Babylonia under Cyrus in 539 BC.

3. A summary of prophecies against foreign nations (25:15–38)

15–29. The intoxicating cup as a symbol of divine wrath occurs in Isaiah 51:17, 22; Jeremiah 13:12f.; 49:12; Zechariah 12:2, etc. The cup is given first to Jerusalem, then to the southern nations and finally to those in the north. All the peoples mentioned in chapters 46 – 51 are included here except Damascus. Some others involved were the king of *Uz* (20), homeland of Job (Job 1:1; cf. Lam. 4:21), located in Transjordan either at Hauran, south of Damascus, or in the area between Edom and northern Arabia; *Dedan*, a tribe of merchants descended from Abraham and Keturah (Gen. 25:3); *Tema*, an Arab tribe living in the desert areas of Syria (cf. Gen. 25:15), and *Buz*, a tribe descended from Nahor, Abraham's brother (Gen. 22:21). According to ancient tradition the MT term *Sheshak* (26), RSV *Babylon*, was an *atbash* cypher for Babel. Divine wrath will fall inescapably on all these nations, beginning with God's people Judah. None can refuse to drink the cup. Even Christ was obedient to the Father's will in drinking the cup of penal suffering for man (cf. Luke 22:42).

30–38. In a poetic section Jeremiah's imagery changes to that of a ravaging lion. God is roaring vengeance against his rebellions people and the noise is like the battle-cry (*hêdād*) of warriors (cf. 51:14). As the Judge of all the earth, God reads his *indictment* of mankind: the victims of the coming disaster will lie like so much manure on the surface of the ground (33). The hour of judgment has now arrived, destroying both rulers and their peoples. The ending of verse 34 presents some difficulties. LXX omits *I will break you in pieces* (RV) and has *like choice rams* (RSV *kĕ'êlê*), whereas MT reads *like a choice vessel* (*kikĕlî*). The imagery of animals fits the context better here.

4. Predictions of the fall of Jerusalem (26:1 – 28:17)

Jeremiah is so concerned that divine judgment will overtake Judah that he attempts to warn the populace by every possible means. His attack on temple worship was meant to rescue his fellow-countrymen from self-delusion and turn them in penitence and faith to their ancestral God. But even the symbolic demonstration of captivity failed to convince either the false prophets or the people in general.

26:1–19. The temple address and its consequences

This chapter begins a record of various incidents in Jeremiah's career. With characteristic passion he promises the destruction of the temple as the price of national disobedience. This inauspicious beginning to Jehoiakim's reign (609–597 BC) occurred in the presence of people from all over Judah.

1–9. The nation is warned representatively that God will not hesitate to destroy city and temple, however sacrosanct both are believed to be. Cf. 7:1–15, which is considerably sterner. In verses 7, 8, 11, LXX adds *false* to prophets, as the context clearly implies. After *prophets* (8) MT adds *and all the people.* As an immediate savage reaction to his predictions, Jeremiah's death was demanded.

10–15. The rulers assembled to hear the case at the *New Gate* constructed by Jotham (2 Kgs 15:35), possibly the *upper gate* of 20:2. When in his own defence the prophet states that if he is killed the people will have shed innocent blood (15), the audience begins to side with him.

16–19. The ruling coterie found no fault in Jeremiah, recognizing, as Pilate did with Christ (John 19:4), that he had spoken to them in God's name. Some of the elders (17) might well have heard Micah as young men. The direct quotation from that prophecy uttered under Hezekiah (cf. Mic. 1:1) is unparalleled elsewhere in prophetic literature. In citing Micah 3:12 Jeremiah points to the harm which would result from his own death at the hands of the populace. His sincerity won over the rulers and set them in opposition to the priests and false prophets.

26:20–24. The fate of another prophet

This parenthetical passage shows the misfortune which overtook one of Jeremiah's spiritual allies. *Uriah* ben Shemaiah, an otherwise unknown individual, lived in Kirjath-jearim, identified with Kuriet el-Enab, located nine miles west of Jerusalem on the road to Jaffa. It was originally a Gibeonite city (Josh. 9:17), where the ark was deposited for twenty years (1 Sam. 7:2). Having prophesied much as Jeremiah had done, Uriah (Urijah) fled to Egypt, thus conveying the impression of sedition, which was a capital offence. Had he stood his ground like Jeremiah, his fate might well have been different. *Elnathan* (22) is mentioned again in 36:12, 25. The patronymic Achbor was fairly common in the seventh century BC. If he was identical with the man named in 2 Kings 24:8, he would be Jehoiakim's father-in-law, and thus the proper court official to proceed with Uriah's extradition. International treaties often contained extradition clauses, and this was doubtless part of the vassalage terms imposed by Egypt. Torczyner identified Uriah with the anonymous prophet mentioned in Ostracon III from Lachish,[27] but the reference is too vague to permit proper identification. Uriah's corpse was finally flung into the Kidron valley (cf. 2 Kgs 23:6). Though Jeremiah was utterly sincere, he still needed support from Ahikam ben Shaphan (24) to escape death. This insertion was evidently the work of Baruch, and contrasted the fate of the two contemporary prophetic figures. Ahikam had been a member of the deputation sent by Josiah to the prophetess Huldah (2 Kgs 22:12ff.; 2 Chr. 34:20), and was the father of Gedaliah, the governor of Judah appointed by Nebuchadnezzar (2 Kgs 25:22; Jer. 39:14). Whether Ahikam was the son of the court official known as Shaphan (2 Kgs 22:12) is not clear from MT.

27:1–22. A prophecy uttered in 594 BC

The first verse is omitted by LXX. Some Hebrew MSS and the Peshitta substituted Zedekiah for Jehoiakim, which is obviously correct chronologically (cf. 28:1). The mistake probably arose from a mis-copying of 26:1. The oracle was uttered at a time when the first captivity (597 BC) was a fact of history. Although the Babylonians had installed Zedekiah as ruler of Judah, some still thought that Babylon should be overthrown by means of political intrigue. Jeremiah shows how false these ideas were.

1–7. A powerful object-lesson is used to proclaim God's will for neighbouring nations, from which envoys had come to Zedekiah in hopes of forming an alliance against Babylon. The yoke of wooden bars laced together by thongs (cf. 28:1, 10, 12) was symbolic

---

27. Cf. D. W. Thomas (ed.), *Documents from Old Testament Times* (1961), pp. 214f.

testimony to the hopelessness of trying to throw off the Babylonian yoke. For the AV *send them* (3) RSV has *send word* (NEB *send*). One LXX MS omits the enclitic *mem* ('them'), implying that only one yoke, worn by Jeremiah, was actually made, and that news of this was to be sent to those nations plotting revolt. Most probably this is what actually happened. For *all these lands* (6) LXX reads 'the earth', implying the universal dominion of Nebuchadnezzar, to whom resistance would be completely futile. But even this great man would be judged ultimately, and humbled by an even more powerful group of nations.[28]

8–11. The false prophets who are holding out vain hopes are classed with pagan sorcerers and soothsayers. Contrary to God's will they were counselling revolt against Babylon, and were supported by false prognostications from the diviners. To be able to discern the signs of the times (Matt. 16:3) and know what the will of the Lord is (Eph. 5:17) demands close fellowship with God and an obedient, perceptive spirit.

12–15. This section comprises a message to Zedekiah urging his continued submission to Babylon, regardless of the false prophets. The nobles (*śārîm*) are included with the king in the exhortation to submission. The words of the prophets are false because they merely proclaim their own reactions to the situation, not a divinely-revealed message.

16–22. These verses repeat the previous message, this time to the priests and people. The LXX is considerably shorter here, and MT may perhaps represent an expansion. The vessels (cf. 1 Kgs 7:15–39) were from the temple, and had been carried to Babylon in 597 BC (cf. 2 Kgs 24:13). The promised restoration of cultic objects would encourage the priests to support the reactionaries who were members of the governing class under Zedekiah. Because these promises are false, the hearers are warned that, if acted upon, they will result in further destruction by Babylon. According to 52:17 the bronze pillars were damaged and taken to Babylon in 587 BC (verse 22).

---

28. On Nebuchadnezzar see D. J. Wiseman, *NBD*, pp. 873f.

28:1–17. Prophet against prophet

In 594 BC Jeremiah had a personal encounter with a false prophet who was reassuring and consoling the people.

1–4. LXX and MT diverge widely here, as elsewhere in the chapter. The former is terse and condensed, while the latter is more expanded in nature. *Hananiah* was a false prophet who is otherwise unknown. His mention of the yoke is a sarcastic reference to the one which Jeremiah was still wearing. Hananiah's promises of restoration contradicted the statements of Jeremiah in 22:24–27, thus bringing into acute focus the crucial question of truth and falsity in prophecy. The majority of the hearers would believe only what they wanted to hear.

5–9. Jeremiah's reply to this is an ironic '*Yes indeed! Would that God might do so*' (6), probably conveying his sense of doubt by his tone of voice. Future events would prove who was right, and Jeremiah knew that peace and security for Judah could only come from sincere repentance and obedience to the covenant. Truth or falsity would not be demonstrated either by enthusiasm or sincerity, but only by obedience to God. Hananiah broke Jeremiah's yoke at the same time as he predicted the humbling of Babylon within two years. When Jeremiah finally received an answer from God it was even stricter in tone than previously. LXX reads *I will make you* for MT *you will make* in verse 13. God's iron resolve to punish Judah and her neighbours makes an even stronger yoke emerge from revolt. The comparatively quick death of Hananiah (17) demonstrated the penalties of apostasy and rebellion. Cf. Deuteronomy 13:5, and the sudden deaths of Pelatiah (Ezek. 11:13) and Ananias and Sapphira (Acts 5:1–11).

5. Letter to the deportees in Babylon (29:1–32)

According to 52:28, 3,023 persons had been carried captive to Babylon in 597 BC, including Jehoiachin, his household, and certain priests and prophets. Word had reached Jeremiah in Jerusalem that some of the exiled false prophets were predicting, as Hananiah had done, a speedy collapse of Babylonian power and a consequent return of the exiles to their homeland. Jeremiah, realistic as always, felt it his duty to warn his exiled compatriots against any further self-delusion, and wrote a letter to them in 594 BC.

1–3. MT reads *the rest of the elders* (1), whereas LXX has only *to the* *elders.* The meaning of *yeter* is uncertain here, perhaps meaning 'pre-eminent', 'chief'. In such an event it would be unnecessary to suppose that several Judean elders had already been killed in Babylon for insurrection. The *elders, priests and prophets* were the whole community of exiles, of which these sections were representative. *Elasah* and *Gemariah* were the persons responsible for delivering the letter. The Babylonians evidently made no attempt to intercept communications of this kind, and there is no factual evidence for allegations of brutality towards the captives. Elasah may have been the brother of Ahikam, who came to Jeremiah's aid in a time of crisis (26:24), while Gemariah, who must not be confused with another Gemariah, son of Shaphan the secretary (36:10–12, 25), was the son of a man named Hilkiah, who is apparently otherwise unknown. One of the Lachish letters (Ostracon I) mentioned a 'Gemariah ben Hissilyahu' (c. 589 BC)[29] who must also be distinguished from the others. Obviously the name was not uncommon at the time.

The letter began with an exhortation (4–9) urging the exiles to pursue as normal a way of life as possible, and wait in submission for God to deliver them, however long that might be. Then followed a statement about the destiny of four groups: those already taken captive (10–14), those shortly to follow them (15–19), the false prophets in Babylon (20–23), and a message to Shemaiah (24–32).

4–9. The effect of this letter on the recipients can be imagined readily. The largest settlement of exiles was near Nippur, close to the Kabar canal. Two cuneiform tablets dating from about 443 BC and 424 BC referred to a large irrigation canal named *naru kabari* which flowed through Nippur, but the actual site of the exilic occupation still remains unidentified. Perhaps some exiles in desperation had already approached professional seers to have dreams supplied (cf. the causative force of MT in verse 8), but they were warned against heeding such material.

10–20. Most of verse 14, and verses 16–20 are absent from LXX. The latter section may be dittography from 24:1–10, though the reason for such dislocation is far from clear. False prophets in Babylon, who still did not understand God's will for Judah, were

---

29. See D. W. Thomas (ed.), *Documents from Old Testament Times*, p. 213.

beguiling the exiles just as they had done prior to 597 BC. Verses 15–19 plead earnestly for an end to self-deception, since those who were in Jerusalem had failed to learn the lessons of the first captivity, and therefore are to be destroyed.

21–23. *Ahab* and *Zedekiah* were two false prophets exiled in 597 BC, and about whom nothing further is known. The *curse* (22), MT *qĕlālāh*, is a wordplay on the name of *Qôlāyāh*, father of Ahab, and *roasted*, Hebrew *qālāh*. For such punishment in the fire cf. Daniel 3:20. This type of atrocity indicates a Neo-Babylonia date (612–539 BC), since under the Persians, to whom fire was sacred, a different form of punishment was adopted (cf. Dan. 6:16).

24–25. The text of verses 24–32 is in some disorder, with LXX and some other versions omitting parts of MT. Apparently these verses described the reaction of Shemaiah, a prophet exiled in 597 BC, who had protested to the Jerusalem authorities about Jeremiah's letter, asking for him to be reprimanded. On hearing the complaint read by Zephaniah the priest, Jeremiah promptly invoked judgment upon Shemaiah and his house. *Nehelam* (24) is possibly a family name, but otherwise unknown. A derivation from *ḥālam*, 'to dream' (i.e. 'dreamer', 'diviner'), seems unlikely since the form does not occur elsewhere. For *letters* (25) LXX reads, 'send a letter to Zephaniah', but the plural form can also refer to a single communication (cf. 2 Kgs 19:14).

26–28. The text of the letter by Shemaiah is given, which began by stating that Zephaniah was to replace Jehoiada as priest by divine command. Zephaniah merely relayed the contents to Jeremiah and did not comply with the request for a reprimand. *An officer* (26): for MT plural *pĕqîdîm* read the singular *pāqîd*, with the versions. Perhaps the plural was meant to signify the importance of the office. A suggested rendering is: *an officer in the Lord's house to place in the stocks and collar any crazy person who is acting like a prophet.* The *collar* held the head in a fixed position while the prisoner was in the stocks (cf. 20:2). Despite all that had already happened, Jeremiah was still regarded as mad.

29–32. Zephaniah apparently regarded Jeremiah's advice to the exiles as sound, and was doubtless impressed by the denunciation in Babylon of those very evils which had brought about captivity in the first place. Shemaiah would be deprived of the ultimate *good*, i.e. the restoration of the faithful remnant to Judea, which would otherwise have included him and his house.

6. Messages of consolation (30:1 – 31:40)

Chapters 30 – 33 interrupt the biographical material supplied by Baruch, and comprise a group of sayings about the restoration of Israel and Judah, a theme which had received some attention earlier in the book. However, to this point the tone of the prophecies has been extremely sombre, since Jeremiah was proclaiming impending disaster as a punishment for national apostasy. Jeremiah is thus contrasted forcibly with the irresponsible light-hearted attitude of the rulers and the general populace. Yet these same chapters are also frequently called the 'Book of Consolation' because of the comfort and hope for the future which they embody once the penalty of exile has been imposed. Since most of Jeremiah's optimistic statements occur in this section, it has been thought to comprise a collection of utterances from various periods of his ministry, and consequently there has been considerable disagreement on the provenance and date of the material. Some writers have held that it emerged just before the collapse of 587 BC, while others have suggested that certain aphorisms were late exilic in date and by someone other than Jeremiah. Theories of the latter kind, however, lean heavily upon critical reconstructions of Isaiah, with their entirely unwarranted assumptions and unproven conclusions.[30] Chapters 30 and 31 are unquestionably genuine sayings of Jeremiah relating to the northern kingdom and reflecting the concerns of 3:6–13. Chapters 32 and 33, written entirely in prose, seem to comprise three groups of utterances which were probably independent originally.

30:1–11. Assurances of restoration

Verses 1–3 form the superscription to the entire collection, establishing the basic theme of hope for a restoration of Israel and Judah. In exile the covenant people will learn obedience through the things they suffer (cf. Heb. 5:8). The agony of captivity is conveyed

---

30. For a survey see *HIOT*, pp. 764ff.

in the imagery of parturition (6), with men holding their thighs in intense anguish. *Like a woman in labour* (MT) is omitted by LXX. Yet even that period of hardship and disaster will be the prelude to divine salvation (cf. Amos 5:18–20; Zeph. 1:14–18). Similarly Christ's sufferings, though rigorous and cruel, brought untold spiritual benefits to mankind. The reference to *Jacob* is to Israel as a whole. Once the yoke of foreign servitude has been broken, the Israelites will serve God's messianic regent in the world (cf. Ezek. 34:23; Hos. 3:5; Luke 1:69; Acts 2:30). Verses 10–11, which are here omitted by LXX, recur in 46:27f.

30:12–17. The healing of wounds

The damage sustained to date by Israel has been dealt by a ruthless foe. Verse 13 presents difficulties, but could be rendered: *nobody pleads the case for your healing: you have no restoring medicines.* The *lovers* (cf. 22:20) were the surrounding nations on whom Judah had relied for help against Babylon. The savage punishment (14) is the just reward of Judah's wickedness. Future restoration will commence with the punishment of those who have oppressed Israel, and the nation's apparently incurable wounds will be healed (cf. 8:22; Joel 2:25). Physical and spiritual healing are essential components of God's saving work in Christ.

30:18–34. The restoration of Jerusalem

From the ruins would emerge a city which in splendour would rival that of David and Solomon. God will then lend his protection to the economy, and bless the native ruler. This passage evokes the imagery of Isaiah 35, but in the language of Jeremiah. Verse 22 is omitted by LXX. Verses 23–24 remind the hearers that divine righteousness actuates divine judgment. Apart from one word verse 23 is identical with 23:19. In the latter the text was *miṯḥôlēl*, 'whirling', whereas *miṯgôrēr* is read in the former. The meaning of this word is uncertain, but it is probably a form of *gārar*, 'to sweep away'. It is clearly synonymous with its counterpart in 23:19, and should be retained here.

31:1–40. Restoration and the New Covenant

The glorious hope of a restored nation of Israel and Judah is the main theme of this chapter.

1–6. Renewed life in the northern kingdom is promised to those who were left after the fall of Samaria in 722 BC and the subsequent deportation by Sargon II. Jeremiah sees the captivity of Israel as yet another wilderness experience, as did Hosea (2:14–16, EVV). The final colon of verse 2 occurs differently in the versions. MT can be read, *when he went to find him rest*, so that the colon can be rendered, *when Israel was seeking respite*. The term *ḥesed*, rendered *faithfulness* (RSV) or *unfailing care* (NEB), is impossible to render by one word, but expresses the divine nature as exemplified in the Sinai covenant. With this kind of mercy, compassion or love, God will again draw his exiled people to himself (cf. Hos. 11:4). In the restoration those who plant will reap the fruits for themselves (5). LXX has 'plant and give praise', but MT, 'will put to profane use', shows personal enjoyment of what has been sown, the curse of Deuteronomy 28:30, 39 being now lifted. The *watchmen* (6) are perhaps those observing the approach of festal processions going to the Jerusalem temple. Northern and southern kingdoms are united once again in this expectation of restoration.

7–14. In this joyous return Israel has pride of place among her neighbours (cf. Amos 6:1). The command to repent which was proclaimed towards the north (3:12) has resulted in the return of a penitent Israel. Even the blind will be brought by a way that they knew not (Isa. 42:16), and this second great exodus from a land of captivity will also be marked by streams gushing from the rocks (cf. Isa. 40:3–5; 43:1–7; 48:20f.; 49:9–13). On their return God will care for them like a good shepherd genuinely concerned for the welfare of his flock (cf. Isa. 40:11). Abundant offerings to the priests will reflect the productivity of the land. The importance of proper priorities is evident here (cf. Matt. 6:33). The refusal to distinguish between material prosperity and spiritual blessings is typically Semitic.

15–22. Lamentation and divine compassion. *Ramah* was a settlement in the area of Gibeon and Beeroth (Josh. 18:25). Here the captain of the guard gathered the exiles after Jerusalem fell (Jer. 40:1) and released Jeremiah from his bonds. The town was reoccupied after the return from Babylon (Ezra 2:26; Neh. 11:33). The reference to Rachel was to her tomb, located near Ramah some five miles north of Jerusalem (cf. 1 Sam. 10:2f.). Her ghost is depicted as mourning her descendants deported in 722 BC. Cf. Matthew 2:18, where the words are cited, not as a prophecy but as a type, in connection with the killing of the infants by king Herod. In the restoration God will wipe away all tears from their eyes (cf. Rev. 7:17; 21:4). Now that Israel has been disciplined she will submit to the injunctions of God, whose yoke, when worn properly, is pleasant (cf. Matt. 11:30). As a returning prodigal, Ephraim could expect to see an outpouring of God's loving concern (cf. Luke 15:22–32). *Virgin Israel* is addressed in verse 21 in the second person singular. Though she has had other masters, God still considers her to be his bride (cf. 31:3). Begin verse 22, *How long will you delay, apostate daughter?* (cf. 3:22). The innovation of a woman protecting a man describes the loving care with which a physically weaker partner surrounds and sustains the stronger one. In the new covenant the Lord descends to the level of his people, limiting himself to the point where they can lay hold upon him. This situation is described in Christ's incarnation by the phrase 'the Word became flesh' (John 1:14), whereby God became what we are in order to make us what he himself is.

23–30. The happiness of future days. In the future the people will again use phraseology which will depict Judah and Jerusalem as the locale of righteousness and true spirituality (cf. Zech. 8:3). Using the prophetic perfect, Jeremiah states how God has replenished the penitent, a prospect which afforded the prophet great satisfaction in the midst of gloom. Once the lessons of apostasy have been learned, the heavenly Sower will increase the productivity of the people and their flocks in a bustling, thriving land (cf. Ezek. 36:9–12). The popular aphorism of verse 29 reflected the scepticism of the exiles (cf. Lam. 5:7; Ezek. 18:1f.), who felt that God was judging them unjustly for circumstances which were no fault of theirs. Jeremiah repudiates this idea, showing that in the future people will be punished for their own sins. Ezekiel 18:2–4 amplifies this same theme of individual moral responsibility, already present in the Torah (Deut. 24:16).

31–34. The new covenant. The Mosaic covenant will not be sufficiently flexible for the new age of divine grace, and so will be replaced. The new covenant will be written deeply into the wills of the Israelites, who will obey it by choice rather than by compulsion. Past apostasy will be replaced by an attitude of fidelity to God, so that never again will the nation be in bondage to others. Jeremiah insists that apostasy is at the root of all Israel's troubles.

35-37. God's immutability is reflected by the fixed order of the heavenly bodies. Only the creator of the cosmos could give such a firm undertaking as that which follows. Divine love for wayward Israel is a striking and consistent theme in the prophecy. LXX begins this section of promises with verse 37 of MT.

38-40. The *tower of Hananel* was located at the north-east corner of Jerusalem and the *Corner Gate* was at the north-west corner of the city (cf. Zech. 14:10; Neh. 3:1; 12:39). Together they marked the limits of the north wall from east to west. The sites of *Gareb* and *Goah* are unknown, but the verse seems to indicate an extension of the boundary of Jerusalem on the west side. The *valley* (40) is that of the son of Hinnom (see on 7:31), while the *ashes* were the fat-soaked remains of human sacrifice. The *fields*, Hebrew marginal reading *šĕdēmôt* is uncertain in meaning, and has been related rather unconvincingly to the Ugaritic phrase *sd mt*, 'field of Mot', i.e. field of the Canaanite god of death. However unclean the locale, God will purify it just as he will purge the nation from sin. The Kidron flowed east of Jerusalem, and the Horse Gate was located at the south-east corner of the temple (cf. Neh. 3:28).[31]

Additional note on the New Covenant

The prophecy of Jeremiah marks a watershed in Hebrew religious and cultic life. From this point onwards there is a significant divergence between what has obtained in the past and what will characterize the future religious observances of Israel. Undergirding the whole of national life, and giving specification to Israel as the Chosen People, was the covenant relationship which had been established at Sinai. Basic to this agreement was the obligation of the Israelites to obey the divine stipulations, a situation familiar to them from their acquaintance with second-millennium BC secular international treaties. During the Settlement period, however, the allurements of pagan Canaanite religion succeeded in wooing away the allegiance of the Israelites from their covenantal responsibilities. This departure constituted in effect the apostasy which, in an even more

---

31. See D. F. Payne, *NBD*, pp. 616ff.

developed form, the pre-exilic prophets were to condemn so resolutely.

Part of the difficulty lay in the fact that a degree of compromise had been reached between the practice of covenantal religion and indulgence in the corrupt, depraved rites of Canaanite worship by a process of religious syncretism. Consequently pagan forms were assimilated into traditional Hebrew worship, so that at most periods in pre-exilic Israelite history the resultant blend could be said to bear some superficial resemblance to orthodox worship.

However, when the situation was examined more closely it became obvious that the pervasive immoral rituals of Canaan were completely dominant in the minds of the majority of worshippers. Not unnaturally this led to an advanced degree of popular enthusiasm for religion, but what apparently escaped the notice of generations of Israelites was that the Canaanite prostitute (*qdšû*) had nothing in common at any level with the demands of an ethical deity for a life to be pursued in terms of holiness (*qdš*). The typical Near Eastern pattern of living according to personal inclination or the traditions of one's ancestors and in independence of codified law persuaded many generations of Hebrews that the ways of their fathers were suitable for them to follow also.

In his proclamation of judgment and doom upon the nation as a punishment for apostasy and wilful sin, Jeremiah was reminding his reluctant and hostile hearers that they had consistently disregarded the obligations of the Sinai covenant. The moral and ethical nature of God demanded that his rights in the covenant agreement be observed, and when the situation took a far different turn it merely followed that punishment for Israel was in fact a manifestation of divine justice. Jeremiah saw that the Mosaic covenant had been deficient even at its best because it had been imposed externally, much as the international treaties of the day were. Although it involved a comprehensive sacrificial system for the removal of sin, it still did not provide for the forgiveness of iniquity committed deliberately and with premeditation (Num. 15:30). Sins which issued from this kind of obduracy found their highest form of development in the deliberate rejection of covenant love (*ḥesed*). Since this had been the pattern of Israelite life for many centuries it was clearly of great importance for fresh provision to be made for future generations, so that the lessons of spirituality to be learned from the experiences of captivity could be implemented in the process of subsequent national renewal.

The new covenant contemplated by Jeremiah would be one of the spirit rather than the letter (cf. 2 Cor. 3:6), and as a response to divine mercy (*ḥesed*) would spring freely from the depths of man's being. The offer by God of forgiveness and reconciliation would result in a deep surge of gratitude from the penitent Israelites, and a fuller awareness of the obligations of spiritual fellowship with God. Moses had been the means by which a glorious external covenant had been established with Israel. That this agreement had proved ineffective over the centuries was much more of a reflection upon the faults of the Israelites themselves than upon the nature of the covenant. Nevertheless, the progressively deteriorating nature of the situation involving the relationship at all levels had rendered the Sinai agreement ineffectual, and it was left to Jeremiah to proclaim the advent of a new covenant with the Israelites. Because allegiance to this covenant would be motivated internally, it would be of permanent validity and duration for the people. While the new agreement would be made with the Israelites, it would not be restricted to them, for because of the essential freedom of choice which it posited it would ultimately be operative between any willing person and God.

In acclaiming this new form of covenantal relationship both Jeremiah and Ezekiel saw that it changed the older concept of a corporate relationship completely by substituting the individual for the nation as a whole. One immediate corollary of this situation was that a man could no longer blame his misconduct upon inherited traditions or current social tendencies. Instead, under the new covenant he would have to accept personal responsibility for his own misdeeds. Probably the most significant contribution which Jeremiah made to religious thought was inherent in his insistence that the new covenant involved a one-to-one relationship of the spirit. When the new covenant was inaugurated by the atoning work of Jesus Christ on Calvary, this important development of personal, as opposed to corporate, faith and spirituality was made real for the whole of mankind. Henceforward anyone who submitted himself consciously in faith to the person of Christ as Saviour and Lord could claim and receive membership in the church of God. The new covenant in the blood of Christ, therefore, is the fruition of God's sovereign grace, conveying through a specifically spiritual relationship an adequate provision for the forgiveness of all sin, a more profound experience of divine mercy as a result of such forgiveness, and a wider sense of brotherhood among men by virtue of membership in the fellowship of Christ.

7. Prophecies from the time of Zedekiah (32:1 – 44:30)

32:1–44. A practical demonstration of faith in the future of the nation

This chapter is important because it provides a tangible demonstration of Jeremiah's faith and hope for the future restoration of his people. The incident occurred in 588/7 BC, while the Babylonians were hammering at the gates of Jerusalem preparatory to ravaging it a few months later. Jeremiah purchased the title to a piece of family property, knowing that while he himself would never settle there under the future conditions of peace and prosperity, other exiles would return and resume life on familiar soil.

1–15. The purchase. According to 39:1 the siege of Jerusalem began in the ninth year of Zedekiah's reign. It was raised for a short period when Egyptian forces approached Jerusalem (37:5) but was imposed once more when the Egyptians decided against battle. When Jeremiah was going to Anathoth from Jerusalem to attend to the purchase of the family property he was thought to be defecting to the enemy, and so was arrested (37:11–14). He was kept in close confinement, but was later given greater freedom (37:21). The guard's courtyard (cf. Neh. 3:25) was apparently a stockade within the palace grounds. Verses 3–5 are a parenthetical insertion explaining why Jeremiah was under detention. Preventing his escape was subsidiary to attempts to stifle his prophetic message. The conversation mentioning the relative's right to pre-empt (7) shows that the ancient customs governing land-tenure were still being observed. In Leviticus 25:25 a near relative could redeem property under certain conditions so as to keep it in the family. Because of the unpromising political situation Jeremiah's near relations may have shown no interest in land already occupied by the enemy. Before coinage was introduced in the sixth century BC money normally consisted of weighed amounts of gold or silver (cf. Gen. 23:16). The actual value of a shekel at this period is uncertain.[32] The proper legal procedures were observed as though the land were at peace. The deed consisted of a sealed copy comprising the contract and the conditions of sale as well as an open copy. Whether the documents were identical, or one was an abstract or 'docket' of the other, is uncertain. Probably the deed was drawn up after the fashion of similar material from Elephantine,[33] where duplicate deeds were written on papyrus, one copy being sealed and the other left open for easy reference. Verse 12 contains the first mention of *Baruch*, the amanuensis of Jeremiah who was responsible for preparing the documents. Pottery jars were widely used for storing tablets and other valuables. Some papyri from Elephantine were recovered from earthenware containers, as were certain of the Dead Sea scrolls. The jars were generally sealed with pitch to ensure indefinite preservation of the contents. Once the land was repopulated, the title-deeds would be very important for their owners. The entire transaction demonstrates the tremendous faith which Jeremiah had in the divine promises of national renewal.

16–25. Reaction and reassurance. Jeremiah's humanity is apparent here. Like many another person since, he began to have second thoughts about the wisdom of his action once he had purchased the property. In some distress he prayed to God and was reassured concerning the future. He tries to quell his rising anxieties by thinking that there is nothing too difficult for the God who created the cosmos to achieve in human life. There is, however, a serious problem with Judah, because the nation has rejected divine sovereignty (cf. Luke 19:14). Because God is open to all human actions no wickedness can escape his notice. The siege-ramps raised against Jerusalem testified that God's warnings had now become a reality. Because of this, Jeremiah could scarcely believe that a reliable and consistent deity would instruct him to acquire property when the end of organized life in Judah was at hand. Yet the prophet had been bidden to act as though the land had a glorious and prosperous future, and his faith and obedience under these circumstances are a

---

32. See D. J. Wiseman, *NBD*, pp. 836ff.
33. See D. W. Thomas (ed.), *Documents from Old Testament Times*, pp. 256ff.

model of conduct for all true believers (cf. Heb. 11:6). **26–35. God's reply to Jeremiah.** God uses Jeremiah's own words (17) to assure him that nothing is beyond the ability of the Creator. Verse 28 is considerably shorter in LXX. Roof-top idolatry (see on 19:13) had been one of the more blatant spiritual offences of the Chosen People, whose consistent wickedness throughout their history is stressed here. Jerusalem is representative of the entire nation, which in pre-Davidic days was the scene of Jebusite idolatry. The corruptions introduced under Solomon marked the start of almost continuous religious syncretism and apostasy. By the time of Jeremiah this was so much the accepted way of life that reforms such as those of Josiah had little lasting effect. The citizens had added insult to injury by their callous rejection of covenant grace and the determined espousal of pagan Canaanite religion. The *high places* (see on 7:31) witnessed the most important rite of Molech cultic worship, namely the offering of human sacrifice (cf. 19:5; Lev. 18:21).

36–44. Promise of restoration. The theme of verse 27 is resumed, indicating a glorious future for Judah consistent with the covenant mercies of God. *I have driven them* (37) is a prophetic perfect, since the exile has still not taken place. *They shall be my people* (cf. 30:22) is the essence of the covenantal formulation. The unity between God and the nation will never again be disrupted, since the returned exiles will be renewed in will and spirit. Such a revival will be a perpetual covenant (40) (cf. Isa. 55:3; Ezek. 16:60; 37:26). God will pour out blessings upon a chastened and repentant people (cf. Jer. 31:28; Deut. 30:9; Isa. 62:5). Following Jeremiah's example land will again be bought and sold (43), the *fields* of verse 44 being 'country estates', and again the procedures adopted presuppose a stable economy, flourishing under God's provision.

33:1–26. The implications of national restoration

The theme of the blessings given to the returned community continues. Parts of the text present difficulties, with verses 14–26 being omitted by LXX. Verse 1 links the sayings with the previous chapter. **1–8. Restoration of the people.** Read verse 2, with LXX, *he who made the earth and fashioned it firmly*. The second occurrence of 'the Lord' in MT and EVV is a scribal dittography, and should be omitted.

The imprisoned prophet is assured that he has only to ask in order to receive (cf. Job 13:22; Ps. 145:18; Isa. 58:9; Matt. 7:7). While God is always ready to answer the cry of the human heart, man must first request assistance. The MT *běṣurôt* (RSV *hidden things*) usually means 'that which is inaccessible', and here that which is beyond the normal reach of human knowledge. Some Hebrew MSS read *nĕṣurôt*, 'hidden things', which RSV has adopted (cf. Isa. 48:6), but the more difficult reading is preferable here. MT of verse 4 is difficult, partly because the point at which the verse ends is not clear. RSV reads *to make a defence against the siege mounds*, but this is a dubious rendering of MT, which has 'which were torn down for the siege walls and for the sword'. In verse 5 RSV has *the Chaldeans are coming in to fight*, as against MT 'they are coming to fight against the Chaldeans'. LXX has 'ramparts' for MT 'sword', and also omits 'coming', but otherwise it follows MT. Some words may have dropped out of the original, and an acceptable translation is hard to achieve. In verse 6 restoration is promised either to the city (so MT) or its inhabitants (so one LXX MS and the Vulgate), but in any case old wounds will be healed (cf. 8:22) in a time of peace and security. Some LXX MSS read 'Jerusalem' for 'Israel' in verse 7, but the emphasis on *former days* points to a time when Israel and Judah were united. The promised new covenant was to be established on the basis of the forgiveness of sin (cf. Ezek. 36:25f.).

9–13. Restoration of the land. The name of Jerusalem will be synonymous with God's loving mercies to his penitent people. The new covenant will continue to witness to God's character and saving grace, and its adherents, now purified from all idolatrous traits, will stand firm in a pagan world as witnesses to the existence and mighty acts of God. The prosperity of the restored land will evoke a spontaneous chant from those bringing thank offerings to the temple (cf. Ezra 3:11; Pss 106:1; 118:1; 136:1), and be reminiscent of the golden age of the early monarchy. Once again sheep will pass under the hands of the shepherd, this being the normal way of counting them as they entered the fold for the night. God's people will then feel the loving touch of the Master's hand.

14–26. The Davidic line restored. With the reversal of national fortunes true worship will be carried out at the temple, and all that is now lacking to complete the picture of the Golden Age is an ideal king. Jeremiah does not reveal as much about the coming Messiah as Isaiah does, but nevertheless provides glimpses of Christ as the Fountain of living waters (2:13), the good Shepherd (23:4; 31:10), the righteous Branch (23:5), the Redeemer (50:34), the Lord our righteousness (23:6) and David the king (30:9). Verses 15–16 repeat the theme of 23:5f. with some variations, promising that a king would emerge from Davidic lineage to restore the old dynasty. Here there is no contrast between the Messiah and the actual Davidic kings, as in 23:5. The new name of Jerusalem, representing all Judea, will be *The Lord our righteousness*, showing that she is finally exemplifying covenant holiness. The promised dynasty will be permanent, and will have a succession of levitical priests who will constitute a valid ministry. The persistence of God's cosmic ordinances guarantees the dependable nature of the Davidic covenant (cf. 2 Sam. 7:12–16), thereby guaranteeing the Israelites a place in the stream of history. These prophecies have been fulfilled in the work of Jesus Christ, 'the root and offspring of David' (Rev. 22:16), who alone merits the title 'the Lord is our righteousness'. If Jerusalem, the home of primitive Christianity, be taken to symbolize the church (cf. Rev. 21:2, 10), the participants in the new covenant are under obligation to manifest divine holiness (cf. Eph. 1:4; 5:27; 1 Thess. 4:3; 1 Pet. 1:15, etc.) and to witness to the world concerning Christ's justifying righteousness. As the Christian church brings men to a saving experience of Christ, it is working mediately that righteousness which Christ achieves absolutely.

34:1–22. The beginning of the end of Judah

The biographical material is now resumed, but says little of what Jeremiah did between 594 and 590 BC, though he would doubtless continue to express his sense of imminent doom and the need for submission to Babylon if the land is to be saved. The final assault has obviously commenced (34:1), provoked by Zedekiah's rebellion against Babylon in 589 BC. According to 52:4 the Babylonians commenced the siege early in 588 BC, while at the same time reducing the fortified towns in Judah as quickly as possible. This chapter describes the early stages of the final assault on Jerusalem, and shows the hopelessness of Zedekiah's position. The mention of Lachish and Azekah (7) would indicate the same period as that reflected in

Ostracon IV from Lachish, in which the commander of an out-post near Jerusalem was writing to his counterpart at Lachish stat-ing that he was waiting for fire-signals, since he could not see Azekah. If the latter meant that Azekah had already fallen, it would date from a period immediately after Jeremiah's declaration in this chapter.

1–7. A message about the fate of Zedekiah. The Chaldean armies were composed of several units from previously-subjugated kingdoms incorporated into the Babylonian empire. These forces were now crushing all opposition in Judah, and the promises of destruction show that Zedekiah's resistance will be unavailing when Nebuchadnezzar enters Jerusalem in victory. The rebellious vassal will go in captivity to Babylon, but will die peacefully there without being executed. His decease will be marked by ceremonial incense-burning, as was done for his ancestors in the homeland (cf. 2 Chr. 16:14; 21:19). God spoke again to Jeremiah during the enemy attacks on Lachish and Azekah, the former being about 35 miles south-west of Jerusalem and the latter about 15 miles south-west of the capi-tal. At its fullest development Lachish (Tell ed-Duweir) was about 18 acres in extent, and was thus larger than Jerusalem. The Babylo-nians did not advance any further south during their campaign.

8–11. An oath and its violation. During this crisis Zedekiah induced the owners of some slaves to swear solemnly that they would liberate those among them who were Hebrews, thinking that God would be suitably impressed by this charitable action and lift the blockade of the capital. At this point news arrived that an Egyptian army was marching to relieve Jerusalem, and these tidings caused the Babylonians to lift the siege temporarily so as to regroup and attack the advancing Egyptians. This distressingly short respite must have seemed little short of miraculous to the beleaguered citizens of Jerusalem, and some slave-owners were so convinced that danger was now past that they promptly revoked their earlier promises to the slaves and took them back forcibly into servitude. This act of perfidy violated the ancient Hebrew 'law of release' (Deut. 15:12ff.). The conditions of slavery were the product of the preceding cen-tury whose social injustices had been condemned so vigorously by Amos, Hosea, Isaiah and Micah. By breaking their promises the owners not merely disregarded the covenantal undertaking, but also profaned the divine name by which the oaths had been sworn. This, however, was typical of the casual and irresponsible attitude which had characterized the Chosen People for many generations, and for which stern retribution was now at hand.

12–19. Jeremiah contrasts the high moral and ethical character of God with the baseness and perfidy of the covenant people. The imposition of slavery by Hebrews upon Hebrews was castigated as a denial of the right to individual freedom established by God at the time of the exodus. Slaves were limited to six years' servitude under the law of Moses (cf. Exod. 21:2; Deut. 15:1, 12) but the *seven years* of verse 14 included the year of liberation, and should not be amended to 'six', as in LXX and RSV. MT can also be translated literally *who shall have sold himself*, reflecting the long Near Eastern tradition of the voluntary adoption of servitude by individuals for economic reasons. The mention of the *house* shows that the undertakings for release had actually been given in the temple under accredited religious auspices. In breaking their promises the slave-owners had also violated the divine law (Exod. 20:7), thus adding perjury to perfidy. In verse 18 MT reads *the calf which they cut in two*, which is rather awkward grammatically. The text could be emended to *ka'ēgel*, 'like the calf', as in RSV. However, it is better to make 'calf' the direct object of 'divided', the reference being to the ancient Babylonian method of ratifying a covenant (cf. Gen. 15:9f., 17), implying that those who violated the agreement could expect to meet the same end as the sacrificial animal. The title *eunuch* (Heb. *sārîs*; cf. 1 Sam. 8:15; Jer. 52:25, etc.) designated some royal official or state functionary, and did not necessarily denote a castrate.

20–22. To be given as food for the birds was a horrible and reprehensible fate in the eyes of the Hebrews, since corpses would not thereby receive normal interment. Such punishment clearly implied a grave offence. Jeremiah saw that the redeployment of the Babylonian armies against the advancing Egyptians was only a temporary interruption of the grim task of overthrowing Jerusalem. Final destruction, with all its attendant horrors, was about to burst furiously upon the city.

35:1–19. The prophet and the Rechabites

Events at the close of Jehoiakim's reign are reflected here, and verse 11 shows that marauding Aramaean and Chaldean forces were ravaging Judah. See 2 Kings 24:2 for the reasons for the attacks. While the Babylonians were regrouping after the battle with Egypt in 601 BC, they made sporadic raids on selected sites in Judah between 599 and 597 BC, to which verse 11 refers. Why this chapter and its successor occur here is difficult to determine.

1–11. Jeremiah tests Rechabite fidelity. The *house* (2) was the Rechabite religious community, having the sense of 'clan' or 'group'. Its founder, Jehonadab (Jonadab) ben Rechab (cf. 2 Kgs 10:15–31), was a militant participator with Jehu in the savage purge of Ahab's house (c. 840 BC) and the massacre of the Baal votaries. This violent reaction against Tyrian Baal worship was a protest of conservative religious thought in which Rechab was involved along with others (cf. 2 Kgs 10:1–10). The Rechabites were of Kenite descent (cf. Judg. 1:16; 1 Chr. 2:55), and probably lived as semi-nomads in the southern desert areas (cf. 1 Sam. 15:6) and in Israelite territory after the Settlement (cf. Judg. 4:17; 5:24). In the time of Jehu they probably pastured their flocks near Hamath in the northern kingdom, but after Israel fell in 722 BC they probably moved southwards, and by the time of Jeremiah they seem to have been located in the uplands of Judah. Their rule of life as imposed by Jehonadab enshrined the essence of the nomadic ideal, and the prohibitions against agriculture illustrated the disdain of the nomad for the burdensome, degrading manual work of the settled dweller. Under the conditions of nomadic life the production of wine was virtually unknown, and hence it was prohibited to the clan members. There seems a connection here with a similar vow which formed part of the Nazirite way of life. Excessive wine-drinking was common in the Ancient Near East, and was an inevitable part of Canaanite religious celebrations.

1–4. Jeremiah was told to bring the Rechabites from their encampment into one of the inner rooms of the temple, where cultic equipment and furnishings would normally be stored (cf. 1 Chr. 28:12). *Jaazaniah* was probably the leader of the community in Judea. His father was no relation to the prophet, and the name comes both before and after the exile (cf. 2 Kgs 23:31; 24:18; 1 Chr. 12:10, 13; Neh. 10:2; 12:1, 34). The name Jaazaniah occurred on a seal recovered from Tell en-Nasbeh and dated c. 600 BC, showing that it was not uncommon at this period.[34] Being an acted parable, the little drama was to be given publicity by being presented in the temple. *Hanan ben Yigdaliah*, otherwise unknown, may have been a prophet associated with the cultus who was partly in sympathy with Jeremiah. The title *man of God* was applied from early times to prophets such as Samuel (1 Sam. 9:6), Elijah (2 Kgs 1:9), Elisha (2 Kgs 4:9, etc.), and others. The expression is better rendered 'a godly man'. If 'sons' in this verse has the same general force as the expression 'sons of the prophets' had in the tenth and ninth centuries BC, it would appear that Hanan was the head of a group of disciples. Since, however, the term is found only in this one instance in Jeremiah, it is difficult to be certain about this matter. *Maaseiah ben Shallum*, the *keeper of the threshold*, held an ancient priestly office occupied by three individuals (cf. Jer. 52:24; 2 Kgs 25:18) who were in charge of moneys allocated for temple repair (2 Kgs 12:10), and were highly-placed in the cultus (Jer. 52:24).

5–11. The MT *gĕbi'îm* is an Egyptian loan-word (*qbḥw*) used of a large container from which the wine was poured into cups or bowls. The Rechabite explanation says much for the force of Jehonadab's personality after 200 years of community existence in obedience to his original rules, aimed at reflecting the period of wilderness wanderings when Israel walked faithfully with her God (cf. 2:1–3). LXX of verse 7 omitted 'plant' and read quite explicitly, *you shall not own a vineyard*. Being native Israelites the Rechabites were not *gērîm* (resident aliens) in the normal sense, but were to live as strangers and pilgrims in the land, being prepared to move at God's command (cf. Heb. 11:13; 12:14; 1 Pet. 2:11). Obedience to Jehonadab's regulations won divine approval for the Rechabites (18–19), whose fidelity stood in stark contrast to the perfidy of Israel.

12–19. The lessons of this incident. Having tempted the Rechabites without success, Jeremiah now uses their refusal to compromise their ideals as an object-lesson to Judah. Whereas Jehonadab's injunctions had been obeyed over the succeeding generations, the commands of God at Sinai had long been disregarded and indeed

---

34. See D. W. Thomas (ed.), *Documents from Old Testament Times*, p. 222 and pl. 13.

rejected as an acceptable way of life. The Rechabites will be blessed
for their fidelity, but their contemporaries in Jerusalem will face the
horrors of the coming slaughter. Verses 18–19 have been shortened
in LXX. The whole chapter demonstrates the meaning of fidelity and
moral obligation, and as usual reflects uncreditably upon the Chosen
People.

36:1–32. The writing of the scroll

This valuable chapter informs us as to the way in which Jeremiah's
prophecies assumed written form. Early in the reign of Jehoiakim
the prophet was ordered by God to write out his oracles. Once this
was done, the scroll was read successively, and finally destroyed by
the angry monarch. Jeremiah was later instructed to compile a new
record of his sayings and to include additions.

1–7. The first scroll was dictated in 605/4 BC, a year in which the
Babylonians won a decisive victory over Egypt. Perhaps the onset
of calamity precipitated the compilation of the oracles in the hope
that Judah would repent. The scroll was probably a parchment of
book-length (cf. Ps. 40:7; Ezek. 2:9). Ancient Hebrew books had
their text written in parallel columns, necessitating the unrolling of
the scroll as the reading proceeded. The actual contents of the
document in question are unknown, though it probably comprised
an anthology of material proclaimed between 626 and 605 BC. As
compared with the extant prophecy it was evidently fairly short, since
it could be read three times in one day (verses 10, 15, 21). *Baruch* ben
Neriah (4) was the brother of Seraiah, quartermaster to king
Zedekiah (51:59). First mentioned in 32:12f. as the attendant of
Jeremiah, he served his master faithfully (36:10), wrote down his
prophecies (36:4, 32) and read them aloud in public (36:10–15).
When Jerusalem fell he resided with Jeremiah at Masphatha, and
when Gedaliah was murdered he was arrested for influencing the
departure of Jeremiah (43:3). According to 43:6 he went with
Jeremiah to Egypt, where both apparently died. Throughout the
entire prophecy Baruch is represented as Jeremiah's scribe, not the
editor of his work. The Hebrew verb *'āṣûr* describing Jeremiah's
debarment (5) occurs in 33:1 and 39:15 in the sense of physical arrest
or imprisonment, but that is not the meaning here, since verse 19
shows that Jeremiah was free to escape at will. Baruch therefore was

to act as the prophet's deputy so that the people in the temple area would still hear the challenge to return and repent. The conditional nature of the prophecies should again be noted. If contrition did not follow the public reading of the scroll, the Judeans would seal their own doom.

8–10. From verse 9 it would appear that fasts were being proclaimed in times of national crisis. The ninth month was December, 604 BC, when the Babylonians overthrew Ashkelon in the plain of Philistia, an incident which probably provoked the fast. LXX shortens verse 9b. *Gemariah* was the son of Shaphan, who had been Secretary of State under Josiah (2 Kgs 22:3, 8). If this Shaphan is to be identified with the man mentioned in Jeremiah 26:24, Gemariah would then be the brother of Ahikam who treated Jeremiah kindly. The name Gemariah was fairly common in the seventh century BC, and one of the Lachish letters (Ostracon I) mentions a certain 'Gemariah ben Hissilyahu' (c. 589 BC). The *upper court* was the inner court of 1 Kings 6:36; 7:12.

11–19. A reading to the princes. Since Gemariah was attending a conclave of ruling dignitaries at the time (12), he may well have instructed his son to report on the nature and content of the reading. If Elishama the Secretary can be identified with the Elishama of Jeremiah 41:1 and 2 Kings 25:25, he was of royal descent. *Elnathan* ben Achbor was mentioned again in Jeremiah 26:22, but of the others, apart from Gemariah ben Shaphan, nothing is known. *Yehudi* ben Nethaniah ben Shelemiah ben Cushi, otherwise unknown, must have been of some importance in his day, otherwise his ancestry would not have been traced to the third generation. In bidding him be seated the rulers were evidently displaying friendship towards Baruch, who may himself have come from an upper-class family. His polite reception may indicate that Jeremiah had some following among the rulers of Judah. Their apprehensive reception of the scroll made it virtually mandatory for the king to hear about it immediately. The genuine nature of the document was attested by Baruch, who himself wrote it in ink.[35] Then the rulers became concerned for the safety of Jeremiah and Baruch, obviously profiting

---

35. For writing implements and scrolls see D. J. Wiseman, *NBD*, pp. 1343f.

from the aftermath of Uriah's utterances (26:23), as indicated by the
fact that Elnathan ben Achbor, who had extradited Uriah (26:20–23),
was present on this occasion. Jewish tradition has identified the place
of concealment with the so-called 'Grotto of Jeremiah', located outside the Damascus Gate, though with what accuracy is uncertain.

20–26. The king hears the scroll. Elishama doubtless expected
a poor reception from the high-handed Jehoiakim, who was living
in his winter residence. The Hebrew *bayit* sometimes denotes a portion of a building (cf. 1 Chr. 28:11; Ezek. 46:24). In two-storey
houses the ground floor was generally used for winter quarters, while
the upper floor, which was usually better ventilated, was more popular in the heat of summer. The burning brazier was providing heat
on a chilly winter day. LXX reads *wĕ'ēš*, 'and the fire of' (22), instead
of MT *wĕ'et*, which is the sign of the direct object and as such is not
translated. The Targum supports the MT reading, and it seems
preferable to the LXX rendering, which is a gloss. As Yehudi read the
scroll a few columns at a time, the king would cut off that section
and burn it, until the entire scroll had been used up. The *penknife* or
'scribe's knife' was used for making and repairing reed pens and for
trimming or cutting papyrus rolls. The brazen defiance of the king
and his court contrasts sharply with the reactions of Josiah when he
heard the newly-discovered law scroll read (2 Kgs 22:11). The designation *Jerahmeel the king's son* (26) may mean that he was a lineal
descendant of the king and therefore a royal prince, or else that he
was a member of the royal household (cf. Jer. 39:6; 1 Kgs 22:26;
Zeph. 1:8). The MT makes it clear that, but for divine providence,
Jeremiah and Baruch would have suffered Uriah's fate, as contrasted
with the LXX reading 'but they had hidden themselves'.

27–32. The second draft of the scroll. How soon after the
destruction of the original scroll the second edition was made is
unknown, but probably not more than a few months at the most. It
would incorporate additional material reflecting on the fate awaiting
an impious ruler. Because Jehoiakim had burned the original warning, he would be punished by being deprived of a permanent successor. His son Jehoiachin reigned for a scant three months before
being exiled himself (2 Chr. 36:9). The fulfilment of verse 30 is not
recorded in history, and 2 Kings 24:6 says nothing about the circumstances of his burial. Jehoiakim had been just as guilty as his

people in rejecting God's word, hence his fate will typify that of the nation.

37:1–21. Jeremiah's prediction and his subsequent imprisonment

Two incidents from 589–588 BC are narrated here. Perhaps in the spring of 588 BC news arrived of an approaching Egyptian relief force, and accordingly the Babylonians lifted the siege of Jerusalem for a short period to meet the new military threat. The besieged inhabitants consequently experienced a respite which many hoped would be permanent.

1–10. The siege will be resumed. The name *Zedekiah* serves to mark the transition in time from the events of the previous chapter. *Reigned as king* (RV) was a rather unusual expression for a man who was a mere Babylonian puppet, installed in 597 BC. Despite all previous warnings, king and people were still pursuing their apostate way of life. In sending to Jeremiah (cf. 21:1) Zedekiah's intention was evidently to ask him to intercede with God for Judah, so as to make permanent the temporary respite. *Jehukal* ben Shelemiah was opposed to Jeremiah, and according to 38:4 had demanded his death. *Zephaniah* ben Maaseiah had been a member of the earlier mission to Jeremiah, the latter at this point being at liberty. The pharaoh mentioned in verse 5 was Hophra (cf. 44:30), who reigned from 589 to 570 BC, and who rashly marched to support Zedekiah in his revolt against Babylon (Ezek. 17:11–21). However, he retreated before actually joining battle, leaving Jerusalem to fall to the Babylonians in 587 BC. Non-intervention by Necho II (610–595 BC) had allowed Babylon to attack Jerusalem in 597 BC, and the only consequence of Hophra's interference was a temporary lifting of the blockade, which in the end dashed the hopes of Zedekiah. Jeremiah's reply deals with the implications of self-deception, of which the coming calamity was the logical, if unfortunate, conclusion. The *wounded men* (10) had been 'thrust through' in battle by swords and daggers. The meaning is that even if the Babylonian forces were reduced to severely-wounded men lying in tents for shelter, even they would be enabled to rise up and capture Jerusalem. The rhetorical exaggeration portrays in stark fashion the fate about to overtake the capital.

11–21. The arrest of Jeremiah. While the siege was lifted the prophet tried to leave, presumably to inspect the property recently purchased from Hanamel, but his intentions were misinterpreted and he was detained on suspicion of deserting to the enemy. The *Benjamin Gate* (13) was on the north side of Jerusalem leading to Benjaminite territory. The Hananiah mentioned here is not the man of 28:10, who opposed Jeremiah. The anger of the rulers (15) shows a marked change of attitude between these men and their predecessors under Jehoiakim (26:16; 36:19), who had now been exiled in Babylonia for some time. Temporary arrangements had been made to incarcerate Jeremiah in the house of the Secretary of State. In situations of this kind cisterns were sometimes used to imprison persons arrested, and such an experience could be extremely unpleasant (38:6, 13). Accordingly Jeremiah seems to have been placed underground in solitary confinement. With the siege resumed, Zedekiah again sought Jeremiah's help. There was, however, no consolation forthcoming, only unrelieved doom because of national apostasy (cf. 32:3f.; 34:2f.). After thirty years the false prophets were appearing in their true colours (cf. 28:2f.). Begin verse 20, *Now please listen to me, my royal lord. Let me beg you with all earnestness not to send me back to the house ...* His plea was answered, and Jeremiah was moved to the palace stockade (cf. 32:2; Neh. 3:25; 12:39) from the insanitary subterranean dungeon. He now had greater liberty, and was given a ration of food daily. The *baker's street* was a name typical of the Orient, where each trade or craft was usually restricted to a particular street. As the siege drew to a close, the predicted famine became a reality.

38:1–28. The prophet is imprisoned, released and interviewed by Zedekiah

The chronology of this chapter presents difficulties because of the similarities with 37:11–21. In both accounts Jeremiah is charged with treason and imprisoned (37:15, 20; 38:6, 26). Both chapters speak of a secret interview with the king, and both end with Jeremiah being placed in the palace stockade. There are differences in the two accounts, however, including the description of the rescue in chapter 38, the actual location of Jeremiah's incarceration, and the fact that Zedekiah had sufficient authority to prevent the prophet's summary execution on a charge of treason. Perhaps this chapter is an expanded form of chapter 37, though it could refer equally well to an entirely separate incident, since Jeremiah was no stranger to the wrath of his fellows.

1–13. Jeremiah's imprisonment and release. *Shephatiah* ben Mattan was a princely ruler who is otherwise unknown. The king had already sent Jehukal (*Jukal*) ben Shelemiah (37:3) and *Pashhur* ben Malkiah (21:1) on an earlier mission to Jeremiah. If the latter had been transferred to the palace stockade at this juncture (cf. 37:21) he would have had sufficient liberty to address the people in the manner recorded here. The proclamation of 21:9 was now to be used in evidence against Jeremiah, since it appeared to the rulers as treasonable. Jeremiah's remarks were now having their effect, leading to the charge of undermining morale (4). Ironically enough, this very same charge was levelled against the *śārîm* (see note on 17:20) themselves by an anonymous patriotic official in one of the Lachish letters (Ostracon VI). While Zedekiah did not want Jeremiah proclaiming defeatist messages, he did not explicitly authorize his execution, perhaps thinking that while the prophet lived, God would defer Judah's promised punishment. In 37:15f., the *cistern* (6) was located in the house of the Secretary of State, while here it was apparently in the stockade. This may indicate two separate incarcerations. Most houses in Jerusalem had private cisterns (cf. 2 Kgs 18:31; Prov. 5:15) for storing water collected from rainfall or from a spring. They were usually pear-shaped with a small opening at the top, which could be covered over if necessary to prevent accidents or contamination of the water. By 1200 BC cisterns were lined with cement, a practice illustrated by the Qumran reservoirs. The cistern in question was apparently not in use, but nevertheless contained a residue of tacky mud in which the prophet was compelled to stand or sit. *Ebed-melek* (7) was an Ethiopian servant of king Zedekiah, who because of his nationality may actually have been a castrate. Elsewhere the term *eunuch*, omitted here by the LXX, generally designates some sort of court or palace official (cf. 29:2; Gen. 39:1, etc.). The king was evidently settling legal matters at the Benjamin Gate, making it easy for Ebed-melek to speak to him. The suggestion that food supplies were exhausted was somewhat exaggerated in the heat of the moment, since stocks lasted until just before the city fell (52:6f.). The *thirty men* of verse 10 could easily be emended to three, a more realistic number, by reading *slsh* for *slsm*, which might have been the original form. For *under the treasury* (11) MT *'el taḥat ha'ôṣār*, one could read *'el meltaḥat ha'ôṣār*, 'to the wardrobe storeroom' (cf. 2 Kgs 10:22), the latter being a more likely place for bits of old clothing.

14–23. Zedekiah consults Jeremiah again. The third entrance, unmentioned elsewhere, was perhaps the 'royal entry' (cf. 2 Kgs 16:18). If so, it would be sufficiently private for a consultation between king and prophet. The desperate Zedekiah turns to the very man whom he and his people have rejected for so long, and swears that Jeremiah will not be killed for giving frank answers to questions. The oath begins (16), 'as the Lord lives, who gave us our lives ...' God takes life just as he gives it, and hence he may be expected to take Zedekiah's life if he proves false to his oath. Being thus assured, Jeremiah sets out the frightening alternatives. The 'total' nature of ancient war should be noted again. Rebel kings who surrendered were usually mutilated and put to death, so the prospects for Zedekiah were anything but pleasant. However, he is urged to listen carefully to God's message through Jeremiah, that his life may be spared. In the utterance the prophet hears the female court-members and the royal household singing a bitter taunt-song (22) expressing the shame of their captivity and degradation by enemy military and diplomatic personnel. This would be particularly humiliating for Zedekiah, and not least because the reference to deception might have been to the members of the pro-Egyptian party at court who had given the king bad advice. *Your feet are sunk* (22): following MT, this verb, *hoṭbĕ'û*, is rendered as a passive form. It can, however, be pointed as an active causative form (*hiṭbî'û*), as with some ancient versions, so that the phrase could read, *they made your feet sink into the mud*. NEB reads, *they have let your feet sink in the mud*. In the next verse RSV *this city shall be burned with fire* (NEB *this city will be burnt down*) reads *tiśśārēp*, with LXX and Targum, for MT *tiśrôp*.

24–28. If word of the interview were to leak out, Zedekiah's position would be even more intolerable than at present, and he would be powerless to save Jeremiah's life. The excuse (26), should one be needed, was that Jeremiah was begging the king not to be returned to the dungeon where he had nearly died (37:15). This precaution was timely, since Jeremiah was subsequently (27) interrogated by several of the rulers about the interview with the king. Until Jerusalem fell, Jeremiah was kept in the stockade, where he could be under continual observation.

39:1–18. Jerusalem falls and Judah is taken captive

This chapter gives a concise account of the capture of Jerusalem, king and people, and Jeremiah's release by the Babylonians.

1–3. The fall of the city. Cf. 52:4–16; 2 Kings 25:1–12. The siege had commenced in January 588 BC, and apart from a brief respite in the summer had continued until July 587 BC, when all resistance collapsed. As Jeremiah had so forcibly pointed out, the inevitable hour could not be delayed indefinitely, and when the Egyptians decided not to go to the relief of Jerusalem, the Babylonians concentrated on breaching the walls and overthrowing the city. The weakened defenders had little choice but to capitulate. Enemy generals established a military council at the central gate of Jerusalem. MT points to some confusion in the preservation of Babylonian names, which in the circumstances is not hard to understand. Cf. verse 13, where evidently the same Nergalsharezer was mentioned twice in verse 3. The name means 'Nergal protect the king' (*Nergal-šar-uṣur*), and he is described as the Rabmag (Akkad. *rab-mūgi*), a highly-placed official whose precise duties are unknown at present. He was probably king Neriglissar (559–556 BC), who succeeded Nebuchadnezzar in Babylonia, having first killed Evil-Merodach, son of Nebuchadnezzar, in a revolt. Neriglissar's name occurs in sixth-century BC Babylonian legal texts and other inscriptions. *Samgar-nebo* may be a title rather than a personal name, with MT *samgar* being a transliteration of the Babylonian title belonging to an official of Nabu. The Rab-saris was a high-ranking dignitary who had either diplomatic or military responsibilities.

4–8. Zedekiah's capture. The king's garden was located near the Pool of Siloam (cf. Neh. 3:15), while the gate between the two walls was probably the 'fountain gate' of Nehemiah 2:14; 12:37, the two walls being those below this gate (cf. Isa. 22:11). The *Arabah* was the deep valley of Jordan north of the Dead Sea, an exit which seemingly offered the best escape route. However, Zedekiah and his followers were captured, and brought to Nebuchadnezzar in his camp at Riblah near the Hamath pass. Punishment by execution (6) was a just rather than a cruel fate, according to Near Eastern canons of warfare, for those leaders who had waged unsuccessful resistance to a siege. Blinding a person was another ancient form of punishment (cf. Judg. 16:21). The phrase, *house of the people* (8), when compared with 52:13 seems to have lost a few words in transmission. Read, *the royal palace, the Lord's temple, and the dwellings of the populace.*

9–10. The people are taken captive and Jeremiah is released. *Captain of the guard* was an archaic title (literally 'the chief butcher') which was retained long after the functions had altered (cf. Gen. 40:2). At the end of verse 9 the MT reading *the rest of the people who were left* seems to be a mistaken scribal repetition, and should be corrected from 52:15 to read, 'the residue of the skilled craftsmen'. Only peasants who seemed unlikely to cause the Babylonians much trouble were left behind (10), and to them were allotted holdings in the hill-country. The word translated *fields* in EVV (*yĕgēbîm*) is of doubtful meaning, with the Vulgate reading *gēbîm* ('cisterns'). It is uncertain if the reading should be modified in the light of 52:16 to read, 'to be vinedressers and husbandmen' (*lĕkorĕmîm ûlĕyōgĕbîm*).

11–14. Provision for Jeremiah. God's prophet was now released and treated with great deference, his arrest evidently having been based on ignorance of who he was. The superstitious Mesopotamians treated Jeremiah, as a man of God, with the same respect and deference as that accorded their own seers in Babylonia, and he was placed in the care of *Gedaliah* ben Ahikam ben Shaphan (14), later made governor over the remnants of the populace (cf. 40:5). Jeremiah and Gedaliah lived at Mizpah initially, being joined by some deserters from the forces of Judah. The latter were granted asylum there on condition that they did not revolt (40:7–12). A hostile Ammonite king plotted Gedaliah's assassination about 582 BC (2 Kgs 25:25; Jer. 41:1–3). God had honoured his promise to deliver Jeremiah (cf. 1:8), saving him when others were being destroyed. The Christian has a firm assurance of God's loving concern and care for his faithful children (cf. Matt. 10:30f.; 1 Pet. 5:7, etc.).

15–18. A message for Ebed-melek. This portion is out of strict chronological order, coming logically after 38:28, when Jeremiah had spoken privately with Zedekiah. At a critical time Ebed-melek had protested successfully to the king about the conditions of Jeremiah's imprisonment, and for this courageous act he was to be rewarded with a promise of future security. Since Jeremiah was confined in the stockade at this time, he could hardly *go* in a strictly literal sense. Ebed-melek was afraid of being punished by those who wanted revenge on a palace menial for his implied accusations of evil behaviour on their part (38:9). However, his trust in God proved to be his salvation, a situation normative also for the Christian life (cf. Acts 16:31).

40:1–16. Jeremiah remains in Judah with Gedaliah
This chapter deals with certain events in Jeremiah's life after the fall of Jerusalem. For rather obscure reasons the prophet had been rounded up with other deportees, but liberated shortly thereafter and given his choice of living in Babylonia or staying on in Judea.

1–6. Jeremiah's decision. From 39:6 it appears that Nebuchadnezzar had not actually been present in Judea when Jerusalem fell, but had been directing operations from a base camp, probably at Riblah.[36] *Ramah* (cf. 31:15), the modern Er-Ram, was about five miles north of Jerusalem, and had been selected as a general staging area from which the deportees would leave for Babylonia. Somehow Jeremiah had been rounded up with the others, and when liberated he had been shackled, despite Nebuchadnezzar's orders for considerate treatment. This must have been a very embarrassing error, and those responsible doubtless feared divine retribution. The account complements that in 39:11f. While the statement about disaster may sound curious in the mouth of a pagan Mesopotamian soldier, the Chaldeans were apparently aware to some extent of the metaphysical causes for Judah's collapse. Jeremiah's reputation as a prophet had evidently preceded him, judging from the admonition in 39:12. LXX has a shorter form of verse 3. The commander of the guard undertook to care for Jeremiah should he accept the offer to go to Babylonia. To be recognized as the patron and benefactor of such a powerful prophet would add to the status of the commander in his home city. When others were being taken unwillingly into captivity, Jeremiah was given complete freedom of choice by the enemy of Judah. The events of current history had vindicated his integrity completely, showing his opponents that he had

---

36. Cf. *CCK*, p. 26.

indeed been proclaiming the whole counsel of God. Having elected to stay in Judea, Jeremiah was given quantities of food and a present, the latter being a token of esteem from the Babylonian commander. The courteous and humane treatment from the nation's enemy contrasts markedly with what Jeremiah had received from his own countrymen. Cf. the remarks of Jesus in Matthew 13:57. It is not unknown for Christians to be treated with greater respect by the world than by the fellowship of believers. Two locations for Mizpah have been suggested; the first, Nebi Samwil, being about four and a half miles north-west of Jerusalem, and the second, Tell en-Nasbeh, situated on a hilltop about eight miles north of the capital. The latter site was occupied from the Early Bronze Age to the Maccabean period.

7–12. Gedaliah as governor. The units still at large may have been fighting a guerilla action against the Chaldeans. The economically deprived classes in Judah (cf. 39:10) would present few difficulties to the Babylonians when left in sole possession of the land. Gedaliah's responsibility was to help this remnant settle down, work the land and pay tribute to Babylon from the harvests. Halting guerilla activity was the first step towards political and economic stability. *Ishmael* (8) was a man of royal blood responsible for Gedaliah's murder soon after Jerusalem fell in 587 BC, and therefore just a few months from the time of this encounter. Variations occur between some names in this verse and their counterparts in 2 Kings 25:23, being reflected in LXX and some Hebrew MSS. LXX has *Johanan* ben Kareah, whereas MT includes an extra individual, *Jonathan*. *Ephai* is the marginal reading of MT, where the consonantal text reads *Ophai*. For *Jezaniah*, 2 Kings 25:23 and some Hebrew MSS read *Jaazaniah*.

Gedaliah's first act was to pacify the guerilla commanders and gain their confidence in his capacity as the new governor of Judea. In 2 Kings 25:24 the commanders were urged not to fear the Babylonian officials, a reading followed by MT of verse 9. The occupied towns (10) were apparently the ruins of cities overthrown preparatory to the last attack against Jerusalem. The Jews in Moab and elsewhere were refugees who had fled when the Babylonians occupied the land. So confident were they in Gedaliah's abilities that they returned to farm the desolated land.

13–16. A plot is hatched. Gedaliah's sincerity was unquestionable, as was his avowed intention to bring stability and prosperity back to the land. The Ammonite king *Baalis* (14), otherwise unknown, may have had plans for occupying the territory, hence his desire to see Gedaliah removed from office. Since Ishmael, the would-be executioner, was of the royal house of David, he may have been slighted in being passed over for the responsible office of governor. When informed, Gedaliah was evidently unable to accept the fact that others were less sincere than himself in his desire for national stability. His tragedy lay in his inability to make a critical assessment of situations and people alike. His degree of commitment to the welfare of his charges precluded the requisite amount of emotional detachment from his task. This mistake, repeated before and since, cost him his life. Contrast the attitude of Christ in John 2:24f.

41:1–18. The execution of the plot and its sequel

This chapter continues the narrative of the preceding one, and indicates how the remnant was first abducted, then rescued by Johanan.

1–3. The assassination of Gedaliah. The tragedy of this event was marked in later Judaism by a fast in the seventh month, i.e. October (cf. Zech. 7:5; 8:19). However, the actual year in which Gedaliah was killed is not stated. A harvest had just been gathered in (40:12), but whether this was in 587 BC or not is unknown. Perhaps at least one year had intervened between the fall of Jerusalem and Gedaliah's murder, if only to allow refugees to return and cultivate the land. In verse 1 MT seems somewhat confused. After *of the royal family* the Hebrew reads, 'and the chief officers of the king', presumably meaning *one of the chief officers of the king* (RSV). This phrase is absent from the corresponding section in 2 Kings 25:25 and also from LXX. The assassin Ishmael violated all the laws of oriental hospitality in murdering his host in a shocking act of perfidy. Such a reprehensible crime could only have been committed by a man utterly blinded by jealousy and by indifference to possible Chaldean reprisals.

4–9. Further atrocities. *Shechem*, *Shiloh* and *Samaria* were all towns which had flourished in the northern kingdom and had been depopulated by Assyria (2 Kgs 17:6). These pilgrims may have been descendants of Judeans who had moved north after Samaria fell in 722 BC. Shechem is identified with Tell Balata on the east end of the valley between Mount Ebal and Mount Gerizim. Shiloh is the

modern Silun, about nine miles north of Bethel (Beitin). The pilgrims had shaved off their beards, evidently in mourning for the
recently-destroyed temple, and their offerings were probably
intended for a ceremony in the area of the sacrificial altar. Self-
inflicted cuts in the skin also betokened mourning, although forbidden under the Law (Lev. 19:28; 21:5; Deut. 14:1. Cf. the injunction
in Jer. 16:6). The LXX renders verse 6 as though the pilgrims were
weeping as they went up to ruined Jerusalem. While this may well
have been the case, the MT reading is correct in pointing out the
treacherous character of Ishmael. A few pilgrims saved themselves
by revealing the existence and location of a valuable cache of food
supplies. Dry wells or cisterns were frequently used as underground
silos for storing grain. Although AV, verse 9, had *because of Gedaliah*
(*bĕyad gĕdalyāhû*), MT hardly seems appropriate to the context. Read,
with LXX and RSV, *a large cistern* (*bôr gādôl hû'*). Three centuries earlier
Mizpah had been fortified by Asa of Judah (911/10–870/69 BC)
against Baasha of Israel (909/8–886/5 BC. Cf. L Kgs 15:22; 2 Chr.
16:6). There is no record of Asa's cistern being constructed, and it
remains to be identified archaeologically.

   10–18. The remnant abducted and released. Other captives
included the princesses of the royal household who had been placed
in Gedaliah's custody by Nebuzaradan. Jeremiah and possibly Baruch
may have been among those removed from Mizpah, since the
prophet was among those encamped near Bethlehem following the
rescue (42:2–6). Ishmael's flight indicates that he now feared reprisals.
Johanan was as prompt in pursuing Ishmael as he had been in warning Gedaliah of his murderous intentions. The *great pool* of Gibeon
(12) is probably a reference to the large, rock-hewn cistern found at
el-Jib (cf. 2 Sam. 2:13), dating from the early Iron Age. This pit had
been excavated thirty-five feet down into the rock, with steps leading down into a tunnel a further forty feet to a water chamber. In the
seventh century BC wine-making was carried on in the area of the
pit, and sealed jars were stored in cool cellars cut out of the rock.[37]
The suggestion that Geba should be read here and in verse 16 for
Gibeon is of doubtful value. Although Geba (modern Jeba), which

---

37. Cf. J. B. Pritchard, *BA*, XIX, 1956, No. 4, pp. 66ff.

was about three miles distant from Gibeah, was also fortified by Asa and regarded as the northern limit of Judah, no trace has been found of any structure corresponding to a great pool. The reading *soldiers* (16), which appears to conflict with verse 3, is probably a gloss on the Hebrew *gĕbārîm* (men), apparently mistaken for *gibbôrîm* (warriors), whose consonants are very similar. The *habitation of Chimham* (17) was apparently part of a grant of land by David to Chimham in appreciation of the services rendered by Barzillai the Gileadite (cf. 2 Sam. 19:37f.). Refuge in Egypt seemed preferable to a return to Mizpah and possible Babylonian reprisals for Gedaliah's murder.

42:1–22. Jeremiah is consulted about the flight to Egypt

The plight of the refugees compels them to approach Jeremiah for advice about migrating, and after a brief interval the prophet gives them a message of assurance and consolation.

1–6. The consultation. *Jezaniah* ben Hoshaiah was not the man mentioned in 40:8, but seems identical with Azariah ben Hoshaiah (43:2). LXX reads *Azariah* here and in 43:2, but has a different patronymic. This man may well have been known by more than one name. The survivors had still not learned the lesson of implicit trust in God for all areas of life (cf. Phil. 4:19). Self-interest has predominated once again, and now their concern is merely to know if God will approve of their plan to migrate to Egypt. Thus they are not seeking spiritual guidance in the usual sense of that term (cf. 41:17). While promising obedience, they apparently felt that God would readily honour their plans, and thus their obedience would involve little effort or sacrifice. The degree of submission required of the Christian was exemplified by Christ (cf. Luke 22:42; Phil. 2:8, etc.). Jeremiah must have been very perturbed by the request, for he was being asked to stand in the ancient tradition of a seer or diviner and to convey a message from God to the enquirers. From his reply Jeremiah evidently senses divine disapproval of the plan to migrate.

7–12. Ten days later the reply was given. God would prosper them if only they would stay (10), reading *'im yāšôb*, with LXX and Syriac for MT *'im šôb*, which seems to have been copied incorrectly. God's punishment is remedial, not wilful, vindictive or capricious, and arises from the same responsible concern which a father shows towards his son's misdemeanours (cf. Heb. 12:5f.). By remaining the people have nothing to fear in the way of reprisal, since God will forestall further punitive action. *He will permit you to remain* (12): if MT *wĕhēšîb* is read, the sense is 'that he may make to return', which could be interpreted as referring to the entire exiled nation. Since, however, these words are spoken as God's message to a small, select group, it seems better to modify the vowels of MT and read *wĕhôšîb*, 'and he will allow to remain'. The Vulgate and some other versions reflect a reading of this kind, but preserve it in the first rather than the third person.

13–22. A warning about going to Egypt. Jeremiah outlines what would happen if divine leading was ignored. While his listeners imagined that safety would come with distance, he pointed out that Egypt was no more immune to attack than Jerusalem had been. Two consequences of disobedience will be famine and the sword, so lately at work in the desolated capital, and these will prove that the group has still not learned the need for implicit obedience. In warning them Jeremiah invokes on the group some of the strongest denunciatory categories familiar to Ancient Near Eastern peoples. He exposes the duplicity of their pretended consultation for guidance when their minds had been made up all along. They have shown themselves no better than their disobedient forbears, and thus equally deserving of the same kind of punishment. Far too many Christians also expect God to honour plans which are none of his making.

43:1–13. *The move to Egypt*

Although divine guidance was at variance with their plans, the small group of survivors decided to take refuge in Egypt.

1–7. The flight. Despite the vindication of Jeremiah's personal integrity by the events of recent days, they accuse him of lying because he told them things which they did not want to hear. By projecting their own emotional insecurities on Baruch, the dissidents imply that he has manipulated Jeremiah's feelings so as to present an adverse message from God. Jeremiah can see how hopeless the situation is, and does not bother replying to this accusation (cf. the attitude of Christ in Matt. 26:60–63). As noted in 40:11, many Judeans had managed to leave the homeland for neighbouring countries just before Jerusalem fell, including, apparently, princesses of the royal court (cf. 41:10). It is probable that the group compelled Jeremiah and Baruch to accompany then to Egypt. *Tahpanhes* was a frontier city in the east Delta region. LXX forms of the name (Taphnas, Taphnais) identify Tahpanhes with the Pelusian Daphani, mentioned by Herodotus. It is located at the modern Tell Defneh, about 27 miles south-west of Port Said.

8–13. The conquest of Egypt predicated. Verse 9 has been preserved with certain variations in most versions, and some MT terms are of uncertain meaning. *Meleṭ* is supposed to describe 'mortar', and *malbēn* a 'brick terrace' or 'mastaba'. RSV renders *in the mortar in the pavement*, while other translations have *in the mortar under the pavement*, but these are conjectural. Flinders Petrie, who excavated Tahpanhes in the nineteenth century, cleared a paved area in front of the entrance to the royal dwelling, identifying it with the 'platform' mentioned in this verse.[38] The Elephantine papyri also speak of the 'king's house' in this important frontier city. Just how Jeremiah was to accomplish his task is not stated, but it was evidently to be in the nature of an acted parable. As the divine servant Nebuchadnezzar will build on the occupational foundation laid by Jeremiah, and spread his canopy over the land. The Hebrew *šaprîrô* occurs nowhere else in the Bible, and is thus of uncertain meaning, with 'pavilion' or 'carpet' being suggested. The meaning of the parable, however, is clear. Though the Judean refugees have buried themselves in populous Egypt, they will be discovered and feel, as their compatriots had done, the weight of Babylonian might. A fragmentary inscription records that Nebuchadnezzar actually invaded Egypt in 568/7 BC, when Amasis (570–526 BC) was pharaoh. The attack was more of a punitive expedition than a wholesale reduction of the land. Amasis appeared to heed the warning, for thereafter he was careful to remain on good terms with Babylon.[39] EVV render the Hebrew verb *'āṭāh* (12) in a variety of ways, including *fold up*, *array* and *clean*. While unusual, the simile of the shepherd points to some such use as 'picking off', as for example pieces of grass, insects, and the like. The conqueror will pick his prey clean, and this seems to be the best

---

38. W. M. F. Petrie, *Tanis II* (1888), pp. 47ff.

39. Cf. *CCK*, pp. 20ff.

sense of the term. *Heliopolis* (13), read by RSV following LXX, is the *Bethshemesh* of MT and NEB. The term means literally 'house (temple) of the sun', designating an Egyptian city most probably to be identified with Heliopolis, near Memphis.

44:1–30. A prophecy of judgment containing the last recorded utterance of Jeremiah

Having arrived in Egypt, the prophet quickly denounces the refugees' indulgence in pagan religious practices. Their substitution of Egyptian for Canaanite paganism showed that they had failed completely to grasp the significance of the catastrophe which had overtaken Jerusalem.

1–6. A recapitulation of recent events. Some of the Jewish colonies in Egypt antedated considerably the fall of Judah. *Migdol* is a Canaanite term meaning 'tower' or 'fortress', and in Egyptian is a loan-word designating a fortification, or else the proper name of a city such as the *Ma-ag-da-li* mentioned in the Tell el-Amarna tablets. For Tahpanhes, see on 43:7. *Noph*, a variant form of Moph, the Hebrew name for Memphis, was the chief city of Lower Egypt (northern Egypt). *Pathros* was the general designation of Upper or southern Egypt, known in Assyrian inscriptions as *Pa-tu-ri-si*. In Jeremiah Pathros is specifically identified with Upper Egypt (cf. 44:15), as distinct from the cities and land of Lower Egypt (cf. 44:1). Jeremiah is incredulous that anyone could fail to observe the consequences of rebellion against God, and in this chapter he proclaims the same vigorous denunciation of sin as in earlier days to impenitent Judah. Living in a land teeming with false gods, the migrants are warned against committing the sins of their ancestors.

7–14. Denunciation and judgment. The ultimate punishment of apostasy will be the obliteration of all survivors among the remnant, an extremely serious matter, since individual survival after death was bound up with the continued existence of progeny. For *their wives* (9) MT has the singular, *his wives*, while LXX reads *your princes*. LXX preserved the succession 'fathers ... kings ... princes', as in verses 17 and verse 21, but it does not seem necessary to alter MT here. The wives were being castigated for enticing their husbands into idolatry, a tradition which originated in Israelite life in the Solomonic period. Despite all warnings, the remnant was determined to follow its own inclinations (10), thereby making the same mistakes as earlier generations. This attitude, however, will be met by a God who is equally intent on executing his own will. Apart from a very few fugitives (cf. verses 14 and 28), none of those planning to flee to Egypt will survive. The prearranged plan is now stripped of the last vestige of pretence. The threat of punishment (13) alludes to the punitive expedition of Nebuchadnezzar in 568/7 BC. Even in punishing the disobedient remnant, God will still allow a few survivors to trickle back to Judea, thereby maintaining the connection between the people and the land.

15–19. The scornful reply of the remnant. Incredibly enough, the rebellious hearers ascribe all their success to the pagan cultic forms adopted by their wives. That this was a majority opinion seems clear from the mention of the crowd of Jewish refugees from Pathros. The refusal to listen to Jeremiah shows the continued apostasy of the refugees. For *queen of heaven* see on 7:18. The rare word *mĕleket*, the *queen* of EVV, is supposedly a reference to the Assyrian deity Ishtar (Canaanite, 'Astarte'), the goddess of war and love whose numerous titles included the designation 'queen of heaven'. However, the precise object of worship is not easy to determine, since some Hebrew MSS read *m le'ket*, meaning 'creative work', 'handiwork', presumably indicating the stars and planets. LXX of 7:18 reads 'the heavenly host', while the Targum rendered it 'the star(s) of heaven'. If Ishtar is intended, the identification may be made with the Venus star, which, however, was venerated in Canaan as a male deity. The astral nature of the cult seems better preserved in Canaanite tradition in the worship of Astarte (Ashtoreth). Because Baal worship was eradicated during Josiah's reformation (2 Kgs 23:4–20), the rebellious remnant blamed all their misfortunes on this action and the instability of Judah following Josiah's death at Megiddo in 609 BC. At the beginning of verse 19 one LXX MS, followed by the Syriac, reads: 'And all the women answered and said', indicating that the women are now responding insolently to Jeremiah's words. According to ancient Jewish law (Num. 30:7–15) the validity of a vow made by a married woman rested on the consent of her husband, and if he did not approve he had the power to annul the vow. Thus the pagan worship which Jeremiah is condemning so vigorously had the full approval of the husbands in the community. The *cakes* (cf.

7:18) were presumably some sort of model intended to portray the queen of heaven.

20–30. Jeremiah's final message. The prophet's last recorded words confront the refugees with the stark spiritual realities of the situation. He reaffirms his belief that idolatry and apostasy have been Judah's undoing, and will be the nemesis of the remnant in Egypt also. While the term *people of the land* may occasionally refer to the landed classes, it frequently alludes to the general populace, as here. Jeremiah ends as he began by stating that, because God enjoys specific rights under the covenant relationship, there comes a point where he has to insist on them if his own spiritual integrity is not to be compromised. Despite centuries of divine forbearance, retribution ultimately came because pagan sacrificial rites had been offered (cf. 44:3) instead of the legitimate prescriptions of temple worship. Disaster would not have occurred had Israel obeyed the covenantal stipulations, here described as *law*, *statutes* and *testimonies*. The first of these terms was reserved exclusively for divinely-revealed material through human intermediaries; the second, coming from a root meaning 'to engrave', referred to permanent rules of conduct prescribed by lawful authority and recorded for the guidance of individuals or society, while the third, derived from a root meaning 'to attest', 'to affirm', 'to admonish', was uniformly used to refer to the testimony of God. Jeremiah brings the confrontation to a climax by challenging the populace to continue indulging in pagan rites and see whether or not God will punish them. Their doom will be heralded by the overthrow of the pharaoh Hophra (30), the fourth king of the Twenty-Sixth Dynasty, whose career (589–570 BC) was marked by interference in Palestinian affairs. He had gone to the help of beleaguered Jerusalem (37:5), but withdrew in the face of Babylonian pressure in 588 BC, after which Jerusalem fell. After his Libyan campaign of 569 BC a young relative, Ahmose, was proclaimed pharaoh in a revolt. Hophra tried to defeat Ahmose in a battle in 566 BC, but was slain, as Jeremiah had prophesied. Whether the latter lived to see this or not is unknown.

8. A message to Baruch (45:1–5)

This brief chapter recapitulates an event occurring in the fourth year of Jehoiakim (605/4 BC). Chronologically this passage is out of order, and should follow 36:8. Baruch is reproved for being depressed about his future, and is given a promise of personal survival to sustain his hopes. The *words* written by Baruch ben Neriah (cf. 36:4) formed the contents of the scroll described in 36:2–4. Verse 3 is the only place where Baruch reveals anything about his own reactions to the current situation in Judah. His distress has arisen from realizing the implications, personal and national alike, of the utterances which he has been recording. Jeremiah has to remind Baruch of God's own sorrow at destroying that which he had laboured so hard to preserve. Yet such a calamity was inevitable because of the wilful disobedience and apostasy of those chosen to exemplify a much higher calling. So appalling will be the tragedy that Baruch will count himself fortunate to have emerged alive (cf. 21:9; 38:2; 39:18). The Christian should have as his sole objective that holiness of life which will witness to the new birth in Christ and sanctification of the Spirit, regardless of environmental considerations. As with the ancient Israelites, he is commanded to trust God alone to keep him and meet his needs (cf. Matt. 10:25–30; Phil. 4:9; Heb. 12:14, etc.).

B. ORACLES AGAINST FOREIGN NATIONS
(46:1 – 51:64)

The conviction that God exercised supreme control over individuals and nations alike is characteristic of the Hebrew prophetic spirit. At all periods of their activities the prophets felt that they were participating in events which would have more than purely local or national significance. A lively interest in the behaviour of foreign peoples was one consequence of this attitude, and at times it expressed itself in the condemnation of neighbouring nations. In this section of his writings Jeremiah stands in the tradition of other Hebrew prophets who proclaimed divine judgment upon pagan peoples (cf. Isa. 13 – 23; Ezek. 25 – 32; Amos 1:3 – 2:3). LXX diverges from the order of the MT by inserting this section in the middle of chapter 25.

1. Against Egypt (46:1–28)

1–2. Jeremiah commences with Egypt because Palestine had long been a sphere of Egyptian political influence. Furthermore, the

Hebrews had never forgotten their oppression there in the Mosaic period. Pharaoh Necho had killed Josiah at Megiddo in 609 BC when he attempted to stop an Egyptian relief force from going to help the Assyrians in beleaguered Harran. *Carchemish* was one of the most decisive battles in Egyptian history. The city had been occupied by the Egyptians in 605 BC, but in that year Nebuchadnezzar stormed it and routed the occupants, sending them scurrying home. The Babylonian Chronicle stated that Nebuchadnezzar marched against Egypt again in 601 BC, with both sides suffering heavy losses. While this situation might have tempted Jehoiakim to revolt against Babylon (2 Kgs 24:1), the Egyptians could actually have been of no help.

3–6. Verses 3–4 depict Egyptian officers giving commands to their chariots and infantry units as they prepare for battle. The small shield (*māgēn*) was generally circular in shape, while the large one (*ṣinnâ*) was either oval or rectangular, being designed to protect the entire body. *Helmets* were most probably made of leather, and seem only to have been worn by the soldiers during battle.[1] The attackers are already confident of victory. Begin verse 5, *What do I see? Their courage falters. They are retreating* (NEB *what sight is this? They are broken and routed*). With true prophetic insight Jeremiah envisages the dramatic collapse of the much-touted Egyptian military power, and captures the spectacle in vigorous phraseology reflected in the NEB rendering. Their apparently high morale crumbles as soon as they encounter Babylonian troops and are cut off either at the site of the battle or at the natural barrier of the Euphrates, making flight impossible.

7–12. The *rivers* (7) allude to the Nile and its irrigation canals, hence the plural form. The onrushing Egyptians seem like the Nile when it is inundating the surrounding countryside (cf. Isa. 8:7f.). *He said* (8) is presumably a reference to pharaoh as the commander of Egypt's forces, whose exploits had been in eclipse since the days of Shishak (c. 945–924 BC). Under Psammetichus I (c. 664–610 BC) the armed forces were reorganized around a core of Greek mercenaries, strong fleets were based on the Mediterranean and Red Seas,

---

1. See *NBD*, pp. 82f.

and maritime trade generally was greatly enhanced. Verse 9 contains a series of orders similar to those in verse 3.² *Cush* (Ethiopia) and *Put* (Libya? Or Somalia?) supplied mercenary troops for Egypt. The Ludim were apparently Africans also (cf. Gen. 10:13), perhaps living in Libya. The description of their skill in archery contains an apparently unnecessary repetition, 'handle' (MT *tôpĕśĕ*), copied from the previous line. *Gilead* (cf. Jer. 8:22) was the proverbial home of balm. Egyptian medical skills were in developed form from the end of the third millennium BC, and the autographs of the great medical papyri can be assigned approximately to this period. The reference to *many medicines* (11) is a sarcastic comment on Egypt's inability to heal the wounds of defeat, her final humiliation being that others have now heard this news.

13–17. After the Egyptian defeat at Carchemish, Babylon would act as the divine servant in punishing the vanquished nation, the expedition actually being launched against Egypt in 568/7 BC (see on 43:11). For *Migdol* and *Tahpanhes* see on 44:1. In verse 15 RV reads *Why are thy strong ones swept away?* MT *nišḥap* ('swept away') has sometimes been divided and taken as *nās ḥap*, following LXX being translated, 'Why did Haf retreat?' (RSV *Why has Apis fled?*), the reference being to the Egyptian bull-deity Apis (Haf). In Ancient Near Eastern thought the conquest of a nation entailed the defeat of its gods. The thought of Apis-worship is carried on by the question, 'Why did not your choice bull stand firm?' Here MT *'abbîreyka*, a possible Semitic plural of majesty, applies concepts of courage, distinction and nobility to an animal, and while characteristic of Near Eastern thought seems better when applied to pharaoh as head of state. The phrases would then read, 'Why has your powerful one been beaten? Did he not stand his ground?' MT presents transmission problems in verses 16–17. For AV *He made many to fall* (16) read, with LXX, *your multitude stumbled and fell*. In verse 17 MT has *qārĕʾû šām* (*they cried there*), but LXX understood the same consonants differently, reading the imperative verbal form *qirĕʾû* and the noun as *šēm*, for the translation, 'Call pharaoh by the (nick)name … For this latter NEB has *King*

---

2. On the chariot see Y. Yadin, *The Art of Warfare in Biblical Lands* (1963) I, pp. 4f., 37ff., 86ff.

Bombast, while RSV reads *Noisy one*. However, 'Loudmouth' seems to reflect the scorn of MT better, since it depicts the pharaoh as a braggart who has missed his opportunity.

18–19. Both *Tabor* and *Carmel* were conspicuous in relation to the neighbouring terrain. Nebuchadnezzar towers in an analogous fashion over other monarchs, and even pharaoh must yield to his power and majesty. Thus the Egyptians will have to pack up the necessities required for the long journey into exile (cf. Ezek. 12:3).

20–24. The likening of the Babylonian punitive attack to that of a gadfly was apposite. MT reads *bā', bā'* ('it has come, it has come'), but on the basis of LXX, Peshitta and other MSS it seems preferable to read *bā' bāh*, 'it has come upon her', with RSV and NEB. The mercenaries mentioned were Ionians and Carians whom Psammetichus had hired, and had been retained by his successors. The reference to Egypt *gliding away* like a snake (22) is a sarcastic comment on the humbling of one of the most vaunted national deities, and one which was so prominent in the royal insignia.

25–26. Amun was the chief deity of Thebes (No), the capital of Upper Egypt. The phrase, *and Pharaoh, and Egypt and her gods and her kings* is omitted by LXX. God is punishing rather than destroying Egypt, so that later on she will be repopulated.

27–28. This section is almost identical with 30:10f., which recaptures Isaiah's thought concerning restoration in the language of Jeremiah. Exile will discipline a wayward and wanton nation, guiding it back to the spiritual obligations of the covenant.

2. Against Philistia (47:1–7)

This poetic utterance describes the destruction of Philistine cities by a foe from the north. The chronological note *before pharaoh attacked Gaza* is obscure, and is omitted by LXX. The attack may have occurred when Necho was marching to Harran in 609 BC. The image is that of a flood which will engulf the Philistine plain. Cf. 46:8, where the Egyptian armies are similarly depicted. Here the reference is to the Babylonians. So great will be the panic that fathers will abandon children to their fate. The obscure clause *to cut off from Tyre and Sidon* (4) seems to mean that any available Phoenician help would be prevented from reaching Philistia. *Caphtor* is the Old Testament designation of Crete, the land from which the Philistines came originally (cf. Amos 9:7).³ *Baldness* (5) was either a symbol of mourning (cf. Jer. 16:6; 41:5) or a description of the complete razing of Gaza. The site of Ashkelon, about ten miles north of Gaza, had been occupied from Neolithic times. In the Amarna Age it was ruled by an Egyptian king (cf. Deut. 2:23), and was mentioned in the Execration Texts.⁴ In the Assyrian Annals it was known as *As-qa-en-na*, and became a vassal city of Tiglathpileser III in 734 BC. It was sacked for resisting Nebuchadnezzar in December 604 BC, and its people were deported to Babylonia. In verse 5 RSV, following LXX, reads *the Anakim* for MT *their valley* (Hebrew *'ănāqîm* for *'imqām*), but this is pure conjecture. As in 49:4, *'ēmeq* here is used to mean 'power' or *strength* (so NEB), as with *'mq* in Ugaritic. While Jeremiah pleads for the divinely-wielded sword to cease its ravages, he is aware that it constitutes God's judgment upon a pagan nation.

3. Against Moab (48:1–47)

The land of Moab comprised the rich elevated plateau east of the Dead Sea between the wadis Arnon and Zered. The Moabites traced their origin to Lot (Gen. 19:37), and in the Patriarchal period they were generally friendly towards the Israelites. Moabite women beguiled the Chosen People into idolatry just before the crossing of the Jordan at Jericho (Num. 25:1–3), and from that time onwards there was intermittent war between the two peoples (cf. Judg. 3:12–30; 1 Sam. 14:47) until David made them tributaries (2 Sam. 8:2, 12). In the late eighth century Assyria conquered the Moabites, but when the empire collapsed Moab regained its independence. It was again subdued by Nebuchadnezzar after 581 BC, and later came under Persian and Arab influence. In the Old Testament prophecies Moab was generally regarded as under divine judgment (cf. Isa. 15 – 16; 25:10; Jer. 9:26; 25:21; 27:3; Ezek. 25:8–11; Amos 2:1–3; Zeph. 2:8–11). Jeremiah seems to summarize what his predecessors have said, adapting the earlier material to seventh-century BC conditions, especially the citations from Isaiah 15 – 16.

----

3. See *NBD*, p. 199.
4. Cf. *ANET*, pp. 328f.

1–10. Israel's God versus Chemosh. *Nebo* is not the mountain so named, but the Moabite city of Numbers 32:3, 38, built by the Reubenites. The Moabite Stone, erected c. 840 BC, records how Nebo was captured by Mesha of Moab in his revolt against Israel (2 Kgs 3:4f.).⁵ *Kiriathaim* was also named on the Moabite Stone, and is probably the modern El Quraiyāt, some six miles north-west of Dibon in Jordan. In verse 2 the MT contains a word-play (RSV *they planned evil in Heshbon*) which cannot be reproduced in English (Hebrew *běḥešbôn ḥāšĕbû*). The particular historical occasion cannot be identified with certainty. *Madmen* is another word-play (*madmēn tiddômmî*). Its site is unknown, but may be identified with Khirbet Dimneh, two miles north-west of Rabbah. Most cities mentioned here had been assigned by Moses to the Reubenites (Num. 32:33– 38; Josh. 13:15–23). *Horonaim* was the Hauronen of the Moabite Stone, but of uncertain location. *Her little ones* (4), so MT (*ṣĕ'îrehā*). LXX modifies the text slightly to read *ṣō'ărāh, as far as Zoar*, which furnishes better sense. *The hill of Luhith* (5) was located between Zoar and Rabbath-Moab. With this verse cf. Isaiah 15:5. In verse 6, for MT 'Aroer', AV and RV read *heath*; RSV, following LXX and Aquila, has *a wild ass* (*'ārôd*), and NEB reads *sand-grouse*. In 17:6 the word *'ar'ār* occurred in a similar context and was rendered 'shrub' by RSV, following the Vulgate. The English text of the Jewish Publication Society of America has *tamarisk*, which seems preferable. The point appears to be that safety lies only in isolation. The MT of verse 7 is obscure, with the second word (*treasure*) perhaps constituting a gloss on the first. For both terms LXX has 'in your fortifications', which may have preserved the original form. Chemosh was the principal Moabite deity (Num. 21:29), and the sacrificing of children was an important part of his cult (2 Kgs 3:27). Solomon erected a high place for Chemosh in Jerusalem (1 Kgs 11:7), but it was demolished under Josiah (2 Kgs 23:13). Destruction will overtake wicked Moab, and her land will be depopulated. MT of verse 9 is obscure, and the noun *ṣîṣ* ('blossom', 'ornament') only means 'wing' in later Hebrew. LXX reads *ṣiyyûn* ('highway sign' in 31:21 and 'grave-marker' in 2 Kgs 23:17), while NEB margin suggests that *ṣîṣ* may be a Ugaritic reference

5. Cf. *ANET*, pp. 320f.

to the sowing of cities with salt (cf. Judg. 9:45). This, however, is uncertain.

11–15. The end of Moabite complacency. Partly because of location, Moab had never undergone the experience of exile, even though invaded and occupied periodically. It was thus compared with a vintage wine which had been allowed to settle on its dregs instead of being decanted from vessel to vessel. The simile is particularly apposite because of the esteem in which Moabite vineyards were held (cf. Isa. 16:8–11). However, Moabite wine will not be decanted carefully in the time of crisis, but will be emptied wantonly. LXX and Aquila read *his jars* (12) for MT *their jars*, which suits the context better. The Moabites will be disillusioned about Chemosh because in time of danger their national deity will be powerless to help them. The issue is made more pointed by reference to the fate of Israel.

16–20. Catastrophe overtakes Moab. The phraseology is reminiscent of Deuteronomy 32:35. The staff and rod symbolize authority and strength, both of which will vanish under divine judgment. The phrase *sit in thirst* (18), as in some EVV, presents difficulties. Instead of MT *ṣāmā'* ('thirst') RSV reads *ṣāmē'* (*parched ground*), as in Isaiah 44:3. Perhaps an original *ṣē'āh* ('dung') was modified by a later scribe. RSV *inhabitant of Dibon* is MT 'Daughter-Dibon'. Cf. 46:19, where the expression 'Inhabitress Daughter-Egypt' comprises a poetic personification of Egypt's population. Jeremiah frequently uses the phrase 'My Daughter-My People' to personify the inhabitants of Judah. *Dibon*, the modern Diban, was four miles north of the Arnon and thirteen miles east of the Dead Sea. The Moabite Stone was discovered here in 1868. *Aroer*, located south-west of Dibon, was the southern limit of the Amorite kingdom of Sihon, and must not be confused with the cities of that name in Numbers 32:34 and 1 Samuel 30:28. The wadi *Arnon* ran into the east side of the Dead Sea opposite En-gedi, marking the boundary between the Ammonite kingdom to the north and that of Moab to the south (Judg. 11:18f.).

21–25. This section is a prose insertion listing the chief towns of Moab. *Holon*, as yet unidentified, is not the city of Joshua 15:51; 21:15; *Jahzah* (Jahaz in Josh. 21:36) may have been a Moabite city before the time of Sihon; *Mephaath*, a Levitical city (Josh. 21:37), is perhaps the modern Jawah, about six miles south of Ammon; *Beth-diblathaim* was the Beth-diblathen of the Moabite Stone, but is of unknown location; *Beth-gamul* was probably the modern Khirbet el-Jemeil, eight miles east of Dibon; *Beth-meon* was the Baal-meon of Numbers 32:38 about five miles south-west of Medeba, and *Kerioth* was mentioned in Amos 2:2. *Bozrah* is probably the Bezer of Deuteronomy 4:43; Joshua 20:8; 21:36, not the Edomite city mentioned in Jeremiah 49:13, 22.

26–34. The proud land falls. Moab will be made drunk with terror of her divine opponent (cf. 25:15–29). The sin of pride is one of the principal reasons for Moab's downfall. Had she boasted in the righteous deeds of the Lord (cf. Pss 20:7; 34:2; Jer. 9:24) she would have prospered. The Christian must avoid all false pride (cf. Mark 7:22; Rom. 1:30; Jas 3:5, etc.), and must boast instead in God's redemptive work in Christ (1 Cor. 1:29f.; Gal. 6:14, etc.), since every human boast has been destroyed in him (1 Cor. 1:25–30). *Wallow in his vomit* (EVV) uses the Hebrew verb *sāpaq*, which, however, means to clap the hands (Num. 24:10; Lam. 2:15) and to clap the thigh (Jer. 31:19). Presumably the reference here is to a person holding his abdomen as he vomits. Once Moab had regarded Israel as a laughing-stock, but now it is Moab's turn to endure ridicule. Both Isaiah and Jeremiah may have preserved in a loose fashion a popular saying about the notorious pride of the Moabites (cf. Isa. 16:6; 25:11; Zeph. 2:8–11), which is now going to rebound on the nation. *Kir-heres* (30) was an ancient Moabite capital located sixteen miles south of the Arnon. If the original Moabite name was QRHH it would be mentioned on the Moabite Stone. Most modern writers identify it with Kerak. Verse 32 is a variant form of Isaiah 16:8f. *Jazer* was ten miles north of Heshbon, and one of the Amorite towns captured by Israel (Num. 21:32). *Sibmah* was about three miles north-west of Heshbon, and had belonged originally to Sihon. The whole area was famous for its vineyards and summer fruit, and the remains of winepresses and vineyard towers have been unearthed there. The rendering *fountain of Jazer* is preferable to *with the weeping of,* as in AV. The Ugaritic *mbk* means 'fountain' (cf. Job 28:11) and is a wordplay on the verb *bkh* ('weep'). AV *sea of Jazer* follows MT, which repeats *yām* ('sea') erroneously from the previous line, and should be omitted, with LXX and Isaiah 16:8. Verse 33 is a variant of Isaiah 16:10.

The implication is that the shout will not be the glad cry of the vintagers, but the noise of warriors bent on destruction (cf. 25:30; 51:14). In verse 34, the MT reading 'because of the cry of Heshbon, they utter their voice as far as Elealeh' seems to have been followed by LXX. Isaiah 15:4 reads *Heshbon and Elealeh cry out*, and this has been followed by RSV and NEB. However, it should not be assumed that the text of Isaiah is automatically superior to its counterparts in Jeremiah. *Elealeh* was about two miles north of *Heshbon*; *Jahaz* was further south-west, while *Zoar* and *Horonaim* were in southern Moab. RV, RSV and NEB, following LXX, treat AV *heifer of three years old* as a proper name, *Eglath Shelishiyah*. *Nimrim* was probably the wadi en-Numeirah, ten miles from the southern tip of the Dead Sea.

35–39. A lament for Moab. For *him who offers sacrifice* (35) LXX reads 'going up on the high place' (*'ōleh 'al bāmāh*), but this seems inferior to MT (cf. Isa. 16:12). God is the cause of Moab's mourning, for he has brought to an end the hateful veneration of Chemosh. For the mourning signs of verse 37 see on 16:6. The simile of an unwanted pot was applied in 22:28 to Jehoiachin. Now it is Moab that will be shattered and discarded.

40–47. God's judgment on Moab. LXX omits from verse 40 the words *Behold … Moab*, as well as the latter half of verse 31. The *eagle*, ready to swoop on its prey, was an apt figure of Nebuchadnezzar (cf. Deut. 28:49; Jer. 49:22). Moab's predicted extinction began with a heavy Nabatean settlement in the first century BC, and culminated under the Arabs in the Byzantine period. Numbers 21:28f. and 24:17 provide the basis for the remarks in verses 45–46, which are omitted by LXX. Balaam's oracle against Moab is about to be enacted. The MT *mibbên* ('from between') is apparently a transcriptional error for *mibbêt* (*from the house*), as in RSV. Assyrian texts used the expression 'House of Omri' (*Bit-Humri*) as a technical synonym for Samaria, and here the word 'house' carries exactly the same sense. Despite predictions of slaughter and destruction, the prophet can contemplate a future occasion when God will again be gracious to Moab. Similar prophecies of disaster for Israel and Judah are also accompanied by promises of restoration. The MT phrase *latter days* might well point to a messianic expectation.

4. Against Ammon (49:1–6)

Like the Moabites, the Ammonites were regarded as emerging from a background of incest (Gen. 19:38), but despite this the Israelites were commanded to treat them kindly (Deut. 2:19). In the Settlement period the Ammonites had the Moabites as their southern neighbours, along with the Reubenites, while the tribe of Gad was located to the north-west. In verse 1 MT has *malkām* (*their king*), but the consonants should be vocalized *Milcom*, as in 1 Kings 11:5. Milcom was the national Ammonite deity, otherwise known as Molech (LXX Moloch). In this oracle the Ammonites, described in terms of their god, are censured for their greed in robbing the Gadites of certain territorial holdings, an incident which apparently occurred when the tribe of Gad and other Transjordanian peoples were made captive by Tiglathpileser III (2 Kgs 15:29). The Ammonites assumed that the owners would never reoccupy it, ignoring the issue raised in verse 1 that descendants of the captives would return one day and claim the land. *Rabbath-Ammon* was the capital city, located on the Jabbok fourteen miles north-east of Heshbon. It is now Amman, the capital of the Hashemite kingdom of Jordan. The site claims the longest continual occupational history of any in the entire Ancient Near East. The reference to the destruction of *Ai* (3) is puzzling, since no Ammonite town is known by that name. Ai as a Hebrew proper name always has the article (*hā'ay*, 'the heap', 'the ruin'), and since MT does not have an article here it would suggest something other than the name of a city. Since *Heshbon* was to become a desolate mound (Hebrew *tel*), the idea of 'ruin' would be appropriate here. The vocalization could thus be changed to '*î* ('ruin'), and read, 'Wail, Heshbon, for it is laid waste in ruins'. Another curious allusion in this verse is to the *hedges* (AV, RSV) or *fences* (RV). The Hebrew *baggĕderôt*, omitted by the LXX, introduces a pastoral idiom, and is probably an incorrect transcription of *bigĕdûdôt* (*with gashes*), as in NEB. This involves a slight modification of the MT consonants, and suits the context better. MT and most EVV speak of 'boasting of valleys' in verse 4, which is a curious rendering. If '*ēmeq* is treated here according to the suggestion for 47:5, the verse could then be rendered: 'Why do you boast about your power, your diminishing power?' The Ammonites were guilty of a rather crude materialism which could only harvest corruption (cf. Gal. 6:8). Christ specifically condemned the accumulation of material things for their own sake (Matt. 6:19f.). When divine retribution strikes Ammon, everyone will flee hurriedly, with no thought for others, least of all the stragglers. But even this judgment will not be complete, for God will bring Ammon back again from captivity. Historically the Tobiad family persisted until the second century BC, as shown by archaeological findings in Egypt and Transjordan. In the first century BC Judas Maccabaeus fought against the Ammonites (1 Macc. 5:6).

5. Against Edom (49:7–22)

Edom was the Transjordanian territory occupied by Esau's descendants, and formerly known as the land of Seir (Gen. 32:3; Num. 24:18). It extended from the wadi Zered to the Gulf of Aqabah for about 100 miles, and included the wilderness of Edom. Though not uniformly fertile it had good areas of cultivation (Num. 20:17, Num. 19). The King's Highway (Num. 20:14–18, passed along the eastern plateau of Edom. Edomite kings who succeeded the tribal chieftains of the patriarchal period (Gen. 36:15–19, 40–43) were hostile to Israel (Num. 20:14–21; Judg. 11:17f.), but despite this the Hebrews were forbidden to abuse them (Deut. 23:7f.). This prophecy, like that concerning Moab, comprises poetic stanzas interspersed with prose utterances. It recapitulates the general sentiments of the pre-exilic prophets, especially the denunciations of Obadiah. The theme is that no mercy will be shown this traditional foe of Israel, because divine judgment will be final and complete.

7–13. *Teman*, the grandson of Esau (Gen. 36:11), gave his name to the tribe living in northern Edom and also to the territory which they inhabited. Teman was also used as a synonym for the entire land (Hab. 3:3), whose inhabitants were renowned in antiquity for their wisdom. The Dedanites, an important commercial people living in north-west Arabia (cf. Jer. 25:23), will be well advised to find some inaccessible place of refuge so as to escape divine judgment. Verses 9 to 10a are parallel to Obadiah 5–6. Verse 9 can be interpreted interrogatively throughout, or can be rendered, *If vintagers came to you, they would leave no gleanings behind; if thieves came by night, they would loot to their heart's content.* God will make Edom completely desolate, flushing its peoples out of hiding-places which others might have overlooked. At the end of verse 10, MT, which introduces a brief quotation from Edom's neighbours, seems poorly preserved. For the Hebrew *we'ênennû* (*and he is not*) one LXX MS and the Symmachus version read *we'ên 'ômer* ('nobody says'), which the sense seems to require. The concept of the *cup* (12) of divine anger (cf. 25:28f.) applies specifically to Edom here, for her apostasy and idolatry demand the punishment which Israel received for the same sins. *Bozrah* was an important Edomite city (cf. 48:24).

14–16. This section parallels Obadiah 1–4. The prediction concerning the lessened stature of Edom saw its initial fulfilment in the third century BC, when Edom was overrun by Nabataeans. The Edomites who fled to Judea were later subdued by Judas Maccabaeus (1 Macc. 5:65) and incorporated into the Jewish people by John Hyrcanus. The Edomites had long enjoyed a reputation for rugged military strength, but their trust in physical prowess would fail them at the critical moment. The *rock* (16) is probably Umm el-Biyara, a site overlooking Petra, the Edomite capital.

17–22. Verse 17 resembles closely the phraseology of 19:8, recording the horrified reactions of passers-by. The kind of destruction foretold for Babylon in 50:40 is applied in verse 18 to Edom. The *jungle of the Jordan* (cf. 12:5) was the Zor, one of three physical zones of the Jordan valley, and the haunt of the Asiatic lion and other wild animals in pre-exilic days. God is likened to a ferocious beast leaving his undergrowth den to prey on sheep in nearby pastures. In the same way the enemy will scatter and annihilate the Edomites, whose howls of anguish will be heard as far as the Red Sea. The MT has *yam sûp* or 'Reed Sea' (cf. Exod. 13:18, etc.), a papyrus marsh in the swampy area between the Bitter Lakes and the Egyptian frontier post of Zilu. This area, mentioned in thirteenth-century BC Egyptian documents, was drained when the Suez Canal was constructed.

6. Against Damascus (49:23–27)

Divine judgment upon the north is now promised, with Syria's capital, Damascus, and two small Syrian states, Hamath and Arpad, being specifically mentioned. The latter two fell to the Assyrians prior to 738 BC (cf. Isa. 10:9; 36:19; 37:13), while *Damascus* was overthrown in 731 BC (2 Kgs 16:9). Hamath rebelled against Sargon II in 720 BC, but was subdued with little difficulty. 2 Kings 24:2 records that Aramean troops helped to subjugate Judah between 600 and 597 BC, but little else is known of events in seventh-century BC Syria. *Hamath*, on the Orontes about 110 miles north of Damascus, was on one of the chief trading-routes from Asia Minor to the south. *Arpad*, in northern Syria, is identified with Tell Rifa'ad, about twenty miles north-west of Aleppo. The MT of verse 23 is rather uncertain. RSV reads *kayyām dā'agû, they melt in fear, they are troubled like the sea*, though this is conjectural, as is the NEB rendering. Powerful Damascus, the once-proud capital of the Syrian régime (Isa. 7:8), is described as enfeebled, referring to its attenuation under the Assyrians when it was incorporated into the province of Hamath, thereby losing its political influence. The remark about the celebrated city (25) is put into the mouth of a citizen of Damascus. The MT negative form ('not deserted') is apparently a transcriptional error, with *lō'* ('not') probably being originally an emphatic Lamedh form (*lĕ*) rendered, 'how completely deserted the city is!' Verse 26 is repeated in 50:30, while verse 27 is cited from Amos 1:4. The name *Benhadad* was borne by several Syrian rulers (cf. 1 Kgs 15:18; 20:1; 2 Kgs 6:24; 8:7; 13:3), probably three in all though this is somewhat uncertain at present,[6] even by reference to the damaged Benhadad stele found in 1940 at a north Syrian site and now in Aleppo.

7. Against Kedar and Hazor (49:28–33)

This brief oracle is directed at certain nomadic tribes located in the Syrian desert east of Palestine. They, too, will be punished, and are warned to flee from the worst effects of calamity. *Kedar* (cf. 2:10) designated a nomadic Arab tribe living in the Syro-Arabian desert, but used also to denote Bedouin generally. They bred sheep (Isa. 60:7), traded with Phoenicia (Ezek. 27:21) and were skilled archers (Isa. 21:16f.). The tribe was mentioned with the Arabs in certain Assyrian inscriptions. *Hazor* was not the celebrated city of northern Palestine, but an area occupied by semi-nomadic Arabs.

---

6. Cf. *HIOT*, pp. 187f.

The designation could also refer to the small villages (*ḥăṣērîm*) where some Arab tribes had settled (cf. Isa. 42:11.) The *kingdoms* (*mamlĕkôt*) of some EVV is better rendered 'village chiefs' (NEB *royal princes* is too exalted a designation for the circumstances). The advance against Kedar was that of Nebuchadnezzar in 599 BC, as recorded in the Babylonian Chronicle. The Eastern People had lived in the desert from an early period (cf. Gen. 29:1; Judg. 6:3; Job 1:3). In verse 29 Jeremiah uses a favourite phrase (cf. 6:35; 20:3f., 10) to describe the panic resulting from the unexpected enemy attack. Carefree living was frowned upon in Old Testament times, since even the most heavily fortified location could be overthrown. The life of the Christian, who has been bought with a price (1 Cor. 6:20; 7:23), must be spent in the service of God and man, not in selfish indulgence. Verse 33 was fulfilled when Nebuchadnezzar finally subjugated the tribes and devastated their dwellings.

8. Against Elam (49:34–39)

This prophecy is dated in 597 BC, the accession year of Zedekiah (cf. 46:1; 47:1 for the formula). *Elam* lay east of Babylonia in the plain of Khuzistan, and was an extremely ancient centre of civilization. It had fought with various Assyrian rulers, and was ultimately conquered by Ashurbanipal about 640 BC. After he died it regained its independence, and in 540 BC its forces helped to overthrow the Babylonian empire. The oracle refers to some event in Elamite history about which there is little information at the present.

Not even the vaunted Elamite archers will be able to resist God's power (cf. Isa. 22:6; Jer. 25:25; Ezek. 32:24), and they will be dispersed among other nations because they had provoked divine anger. The *throne* to be set up is that of a righteous God sitting in judgment upon the people. Despite this calamity, Jeremiah's prophetic universalism can entertain the restoration of Elam, perhaps in the messianic age. See on 48:47. Elamites were in Jerusalem when the Spirit was given to the primitive Christian church (Acts 2:1ff.).

9. Against Babylon (50:1 – 51:64)

The two chapters in this section deal with the downfall of Babylon.

Even more than Egypt, this land was thought to be the scourge of the Hebrews, and though it would serve as the rod of divine anger for punishing Judah, its own condemnation was at hand. Most of this material would antedate 539 BC, since the Persians are unmentioned as a world power, and the similarities between these oracles and Isaiah 13 – 14 might even indicate 580 BC as the approximate time of compilation.

50:1–20. The fall of Babylon heralded

The Chaldeans were descended from a semi-nomadic tribe which had settled near Ur in the third millennium BC. From the tenth century BC their land was known as *Kaldu* in cuneiform inscriptions, and in the following century some Chaldean chiefs were vassals of Adadnirari III (805–782 BC). They became famous when Nabopolassar, a native Chaldean, came to the Babylonian throne in 626 BC and laid the foundations for the brilliant New Empire period of Babylonian history (612–539 BC).

1–3. In a passionate outburst Jeremiah speaks of retribution overtaking Babylon, putting her protective deities to shame. *Bēl* ('lord') was the title of the storm-god Enlil, and when *Marduk* became head of the Babylonian pantheon in the second millennium BC he received the designation of Bēl also. The Babylonian Creation Epic was probably composed in honour of Marduk, 'king of the gods'. At the end of verse 2 the word *her idols* (MT *gillûleyhā*) seems to have referred originally to dung pellets, and is applied disparagingly to pagan idols in Leviticus 26:30; Deuteronomy 29:17; 1 Kings 15:12; 21:26, etc. Ezekiel uses the term no fewer than 38 times in as many chapters. For the Hebrews *the north* (3) was the location from which anything sinister originated, and hence it was used colloquially rather than as a specific geographical location on many occasions.

4–7. Exiled Israel is now moved to penitence at the calamity which has overtaken her erstwhile captor. She now exhibits that spiritual attitude which will ensure her return to the homeland. In this expectation she faces Zion (cf. Dan. 6:10), promising eternal fidelity to the Lord's covenant (cf. Jer. 32:40). Again the *shepherds* (priests and prophets) are blamed for Israel's transgressions. If, however, covenant loyalty is renewed, the nation will be restored quickly. Though Israel's enemies had disclaimed any wrongdoing, all those who have *devoured* Israel are to be accounted guilty (cf. 2:3).

8–10. Just as the male goats try to leave the enclosure first, so Judah ought to be at the forefront of captive peoples leaving Babylonia for home. The group of powerful nations (as enumerated in 51:27f.) will include the *skilled warrior* (pointing MT *maśkîl*, as with the marginal variant) who returns successfully from battle knowing that his arrows have found their mark.

11–16. In verse 11, RSV *as a heifer at grass* reads *kĕ'eglê deše'*, with LXX, for MT *kĕ'eglāh dāšāh* ('like a calf threshing'), which does not suit the imagery of a frisky animal very well. Powerful Babylon will be reduced to minor status in the Near East when God punishes her, and once more the passer-by will gasp in astonishment (cf. 18:16; 19:8, used of Judah and Jerusalem; 49:17, used of Edom). Once she has been battered into submission, the captive foreign elements will be freed (16).

17–20. The mention of Assyria alludes to the exile of the northern kingdom by Sargon II in 722 BC. When Babylon has succumbed, as Assyria did, the remnant will be pardoned by a merciful God and will return to Palestine to begin life afresh (cf. 31:33). Verse 20 begins with the usual messianic formula, indicating that this vision of pardon and blessing belongs to the days of the Messiah.

50:21–32. Judgment upon Babylon

21–27. *Merathaim* and *Pekod* (literally, 'Double Rebellion' and 'Visitation') are sarcastic wordplays on specific Babylonian localities. The former is the *Mat Marratim* district of southern Babylonia, while the latter is the name for *Puqudu*, an eastern Babylonian people (cf. Ezek. 23:23). When divine retribution comes, all will be put under the ban (cf. Josh. 8:26, etc.). In verse 21, MT *after them* (MT *'aḥārêhem*), which is omitted by LXX, can be revocalized with only one consonantal change to *'aḥărîtām* ('the last of them'), this being a preferred reading. Babylon the hammer, which at its peak had shattered others, is now to be broken. The city ultimately fell in October 539 BC to Cyrus, who is said to have diverted the river Euphrates so that his troops could enter the strongly-defended city. Whereas the Cyrus Cylinder credited the easy victory to the guidance of Marduk, Jeremiah attributed Babylon's fall to the activities of Israel's God, who used the Medes and Persians to accomplish his punitive purposes (cf. Isa. 13:5). The *bulls* of verse 27 are the youthful Babylonian warriors (cf. Ps. 22:12; Isa. 34:7; Jer. 48:15).

28–32. Here Jeremiah sees the returning exiles jubilant over divine retribution. Babylon is depicted as the personification of insolence (cf. 21:13f.), and as such suffers all the consequences of the sin of pride. Verse 30 is repeated verbatim from 49:26, where the fate of Damascus was described.

50:33–46. Further condemnation of Babylon

33–40. Though the Babylonians will not release their captives voluntarily, those who conquer Babylon will do so. Jeremiah uses the concept of a near kinsman (MT *gô'ēl, redeemer, advocate*), whose duty it is to avenge a murder and serve as protector (Lev. 25:25; Num. 35:21), to depict the nature and functions of the God of Israel. When retribution comes, this world's wisdom, as enshrined in the divinatory priests, will become folly with God (cf. 1 Cor. 3:19). These deceivers, along with foreign mercenary troops, will be destroyed (37). In verse 38, the word *drought* (MT *ḥōreb*) has the same consonants as the word 'sword' (*ḥrb*). The latter seems preferable, since the enemy sword will cause the irrigation canals, on which Babylonian prosperity depended, to dry up through neglect. Verses 39–40 reflect Isaiah 13:19–22, while verse 40 repeats Jeremiah 49:18.

41–46. The warning about a northern nation addressed to Judah in 6:22–24 is now directed at Babylon, with appropriate changes. See on 50:3. The *many kings* are the allies of Persia (cf. 51:27f.) who are just as terrifying as the Assyrians were. Small wonder, then, that the Babylonian king is petrified with fear. Verses 44 to 46 repeat substantially the prediction against Edom in 49:19–21, but apply it to Babylon. Little Edom's cries would resound no further than the *Yam Sûp*, but Babylon's anguished howls would be heard throughout the Near East. Hearing them, people would recognize the Lord's handiwork.

51:1–19. Winds of change in Babylon

1–5. In verse 1, RSV *inhabitants of Chaldea* is literally 'the heart of those who rise up against me', but is generally interpreted as a cypher for *kśdym* or Chaldea (cf. 25:26). MT is difficult in verse 3, with the consonants *ydrk* being read consecutively at the beginning and left unvocalized the second time by the Massoretic scribes. As it stands MT could be rendered, *Against him who bends, let the bowman bend his bow, and against him who dons his armour.* RSV omits the repeated 'let bend', and in both occurrences of the MT form *'el* ('unto', 'against') it reads the prohibition *'al* ('not'). But since the sense requires the archers to attack Babylon, the text could well read, *Let the archer draw his bow, rise up against her in full armour.*[7] Babylon is to be put under the ban, as many other great Near Eastern cities had been. Israel, however, has still not lost her Protector, and thus will not be exterminated completely.

6–10. Verse 6 is addressed to the people of Judah (cf. 50:8) who are urged to seek self-preservation. The cup of wine (7) frequently symbolizes disaster (cf. Isa. 51:17, 22; Jer. 13:12f.; 49:12, etc.). The potion was such as to make those who drank it behave like madmen. Israel's wounds could be healed by balm from Gilead, but Babylon's fate would be absolute. By punishing Babylon God has justified the remnant, so that they can emerge from captivity to new life in the homeland.

11–14. The RSV of verse 11, *take up the shields* (NEB *fill the quivers*), is an attempt to render an obscure MT phrase. The term *šĕlāṭîm*, variously rendered 'shields', 'suits of armour' or 'quivers', is of uncertain meaning, but may perhaps be related to the Akkadian *šaltu*, 'shield' (cf. 2 Kgs 11:10). While *many waters* (13) refers primarily to the Euphrates, it also alludes sarcastically to the great subterranean ocean, a theme prominent in ancient Babylonian mythology. The Babylonians had lived by these erroneous beliefs for many centuries, and they would now die by them.

15–19. These verses follow the wording of 10:12–16 very closely, except for omitting 'Israel' in verse 19. The quotation shows the impotence of the Babylonian gods in an emergency, and the consequent certainty of divine judgment upon Babylon. In verse 16 MT has been poorly transmitted, as in 10:13, and some words seem to have been omitted. A thoroughgoing condemnation of pagan idols was a prominent feature of pre-exilic prophecy, and was reiterated in the New Testament (cf. 1 Cor. 5:10; 6:9; 8:4; 10:7, etc.). God's people must be dedicated exclusively to his service.

---

7. Cf. J. Bright, *Jeremiah* (1965), p. 346n.

51:20–26. An agent of judgment is to be judged

The allusion in verse 20 is to Babylon's past role as the 'hammer of the entire earth' (50:23). A similar figure occurs in Isaiah 10:5, in reference to Assyria. Babylon's irrevocable destruction will be God's recompense for past iniquity (cf. Deut. 32:35; Rom. 12:19). The phrase *destroying mountains* (RSV, NEB) of verse 25 is obscure, and perhaps was used originally of marauding mountaineers who made sorties in strength upon Babylon from the Zagros ranges, or upon Palestine from the craggy heights of Edom or Moab. However, the allusion may describe towering Babylon in her prime.

51:27–33. The nations ally against Babylon

Other peoples are now to be used by God to punish wicked Babylon. *Ararat* was ancient Urartu, located north-west of Lake Van in Armenia, and prominent in Assyrian inscriptions. *Minni*, the Mannai of Assyrian texts, was also near Lake Van, while *Ashkenaz*, the cuneiform *Aš-ku-za*, was an ally of the Mannai in their seventh-century BC revolt against Assyria. The reference to *bristling locusts* (27) is apparently to a highly destructive stage of locust life during which the wings are encased on the back in rough horny covers. The much vaunted courier systems of the Babylonians (31) now announce ruin in breathless haste. The marshes (32) were apparently burned to prevent refugees from hiding there and thus escaping destruction. Babylon's enemies will reap the harvest of devastation, while she herself will be destroyed in the process (cf. Isa. 17:5; Joel 4:13).

51:34–40. Judah's complaint against Babylon

In verse 34, the marginal readings of MT, which have first personal singular forms, should be followed. Nebuchadnezzar had devoured Jerusalem with the greedy gulp of a *monster* (NEB *dragon*), and for this excess his land would be punished. The idiom of recompense (35) is that of Genesis 16:5. The mythological wellsprings of life (cf. verse 13) will be dried up, thus demonstrating God's superiority over all opposition. The same power is able to save the sinner through the cross, and support him thereafter for ever. Begin verse 39, *As their appetites sharpen …* For MT *ya'ălôzû* (*that they may rejoice*), read, with LXX and some other versions, *yĕ'ulāppû* ('that they may swoon'), which suits the sense better.

51:41–58. God brings destruction upon Babylon.

Sheshak (41) is a cypher for Babylon (cf. 25:26). The celebrated city (cf. Isa. 13:19) has finally succumbed to a horde of enemy troops who have poured in like a flood. The land and its patron deity are identified (44), so that the defeat of one involves the destruction of the other, a concept well known to Ancient Near Eastern peoples. Political intrigue and internal dissension characterized imperial Babylon for some years before its fall. Throughout this period God's people were instructed to remain calm (cf. Matt. 24:6; Mark 13:7; Luke 21:9), in the conviction that God was the mighty judge of all the earth. His creation, called upon to witness other powerful divine acts (cf. Isa. 44:23), will rejoice over Babylon's fall. Verse 49 can be rendered variously. By adding the preposition *lĕ* ('for') to 'the slain of Israel' (on the pattern of 'for Babylon' in the next line), the verse begins, *Even Babylon must fall for Israel's slain, just as the whole earth's slain have fallen for Babylon.* If MT is elliptical, the text could be rendered, *As Babylon has caused the slain of Israel to fall, so at Babylon the whole earth's slain shall fall,* as adopted by RV. The RV margin construes 'the slain of Israel' as a vocative, and translates, 'Both Babylon is to fall, O ye slain of Israel, and at Babylon shall fall the slain of all the land.' The towering ziggurats (cf. NEB *their high towers*) and palaces of Babylon are neither inaccessible nor impregnable, and soon will collapse in ruins (cf. Isa. 14:13–15; Jer. 49:16). In verse 58 the singular *wall* should be read, with the LXX and several versions, so that *broad* agrees with it rather than with *Babylon*, as against NEB. Under Nebuchadnezzar, Babylon was surrounded with a double wall of defensive fortifications which, according to Herodotus (1:178ff.), enclosed an area of 200 square miles. The latter part of the verse is reminiscent of Habakkuk 2:13, and may have preserved a popular saying.

51:59–64. The charge of Jeremiah to Seraiah

This commission can be dated in 594/3 BC, according to verse 59. The MT implies that Zedekiah was compelled to visit Babylon, apparently to pledge his loyalty to Nebuchadnezzar. *Seraiah* ben Neriah ben Mahseiah would thus be the brother of Baruch (cf. 32:12). He was the officer in charge of bivouac arrangements (RSV, NEB *quartermaster*) when the party stopped to camp. He was instructed to take the oracle predicting the destruction of Babylon and read it aloud to the exiles once he arrived there. This done (63), the sinking of the oracle in the Euphrates symbolized that Babylon, like the scroll, would never rise again. Massoretic scribes apparently copied the word rendered *and they shall be weary* (AV, RV) from the end of verse 58 when verses 59 to 64 were inserted. It can be omitted, with LXX, RSV and NEB. The chapter ends with a compiler's notation which was probably intended to separate the foregoing material from chapter 52, which follows closely the contents of 2 Kings 24:18 – 25:30 with minor variations.

C. HISTORICAL APPENDIX (52:1–34)

This section deals with the last days of Jerusalem and was probably excerpted from a larger historical work used also by the compiler of 2 Kings 9, and of which Jeremiah was not the author. The material was perhaps placed here to show how Jeremiah's prophecies had been fulfilled. Some differences of content exist when compared with chapter 39, including a description of cultic equipment removed from the temple, and a surprising lack of mention of Nebuchadnezzar's instructions for the protection of Jeremiah.

1–3. *Hamutal* was the wife of Josiah and mother of Jehoahaz and Zedekiah (cf. 2 Kgs 23:31; 24:18). The MT phraseology of verse 3 is awkward, conveying the impression that divine anger was the cause of the iniquity rampant in Judah rather than being the result of it.

4–11. The siege began in early January of 588 BC, the *ninth year* being 589/8 BC. The *fourth month* of verse 6 was July 587 BC, the time being counted from the beginning of the Babylonian New Year (March/April). In verse 7 MT should follow that of 39:4 to include the flight of Zedekiah. On Riblah cf. 39:5. The imprisonment of Zedekiah was not mentioned in 2 Kings 25:7.

12–16. For the *tenth day* (12), 2 Kings 25:8 has seventh day, the difference perhaps embracing the interval between the arrival of Nebuzaradan and the beginning of the destruction. For Nebuzaradan's title see on 39:9. At the end of verse 15 AV, RV *multitude* follows MT *hā'āmôn* ('people'), which is probably a transcriptional error for *hā'āmmān* ('artisan'). This is a doubtful translation at best, since the meaning of *artisans* for *'amôn* is not fully attested, though accepted by NEB. In verse 16 the meaning of *yôgĕbîm* (RSV *plowmen*; NEB *labourers*) is also uncertain, but perhaps comes from a root denoting compulsory service, thus implying unsalaried labour.

17–23. This section contains a description of the cultic vessels carried from the temple as spoil, supplementing the parallel passage in 2 Kings 25:13–17. Some of the items are doubtful in nature. The *bronze sea* (cf. 1 Kgs 7:23–26) was a large basin ten cubits in diameter, resting upon four groups of bronze oxen oriented in terms of the compass. Many large articles were smashed to make them easier to carry off. Jerusalem had been looted once before (1 Kgs 14:25f.), and now was being pillaged again. While bronze was the commonest metal represented, there were silver and gold articles, as well as copper cups. The purpose of the *two pillars* (20) is uncertain (cf. 1 Kgs 7:15ff.), but they may have served as cressets or fire-altars. Such columns were common in first-millennium BC temples of Syrian design.[1] The reference to eighteen cubits (21) implies that the length given in 2 Chronicles 3:15 was the total for both pillars. *Pomegranates* (22) were a common form of Near Eastern decoration, being found on the High Priest's robe (Exod. 28:33). The description of the decoration of the second pillar breaks off abruptly, indicating a loss of words from the text. The MT *rûḥāh* (23) rendered *on the sides* (RV, RSV) and *exposed to view* (NEB) is probably miscopied here for *rewaḥ* ('space'. Cf. Gen. 32:16, EVV). In 1 Kings 7:20, 42, each capital had 200 pomegranates arranged in two rows.

24–27. *Seraiah* was the grandson of Hilkiah, the High Priest under Josiah, who could trace his descent from Aaron (cf. 1 Chr. 6:13–15, EVV), while *Zephaniah* was possibly the person named in 29:24–32; 37:3. The commanding officer (AV, NEB *eunuch*) was evidently a

---

1. See D. J. Wiseman, *NBD*, p. 593.

high-ranking adjutant who had mustered the populace for war. If the *people of the land* (EVV) were actually peasants, these men may have been executed representatively for the survivors.

28–30. The *seventh year* was 598/7 BC, following Babylonian reckoning. The figures given here vary from those in 2 Kings 24:14, 16. 3,023 may be the actual head count of deported adult males, while the Kings' figures may comprise the total number of deportees. The *eighteenth year* (29) would be 587/6 BC, following Babylonian reckoning. 2 Kings 25:8 preserves the Judean form of computation, as does 2 Kings 24:12 for verse 28. The *twenty-third* year was 582/1 BC.

31–34. The accession of *Evil-Merodach*, i.e. Amel-Marduk, son of Nebuchadnezzar, who reigned for only one year (561–560 BC), saw better treatment accorded to the Judean royal family. Tablets recovered from the ruined Ishtar Gate in Babylon confirm that Jehoiachin was a recipient of the king's bounty.[2] These stark historical facts come as a rather anticlimactic postscript to a period of high spiritual drama. The message of Jeremiah, so long derided by his compatriots, has been translated almost coincidentally into history. God has finally brought the promised punishment upon his apostate and idolatrous people, and the chastening discipline of exile has begun. Despite this dreadful calamity there lingers the hope that God will restore his people, bringing a faithful remnant back to repopulate the homeland.

---

2. W. F. Albright, *The Biblical Archaeologist* (1942), V, pp. 49ff.; A. Oppenheim, *ANET*, p. 308; D. W. Thomas, *Documents from Old Testament Times*, pp. 84ff.

LAMENTATIONS

INTRODUCTION

1. Title and place in canon

This small poetic work originally bore no title, but the opening
word of the MT, the characteristic lament 'Ah, how!' (*'ēkāh*), was
employed in the Hebrew Bible as a superscription. The LXX entitled
it *Threnoi* or 'Wailings', to which the Vulgate added the sub-title, 'It
comprises the Lamentations of Jeremiah the prophet'. English versions adopted the title of *Lamentations*, and following the ancient tradition of authorship designated it 'The Lamentations of Jeremiah'.
Talmudic and Rabbinic writers referred to the work simply as *qînôt*
('Lamentations'), or else as *'ēkāh*

In the Hebrew canon the book came third in the five Megilloth
or Rolls, which follow the three poetical compositions in the
Hagiographa or third division of the canon. Lamentations was read
customarily on the ninth of Ab, in mid-July, when the destruction
of the Jerusalem temple was commemorated. The LXX placed
Lamentations after the prophecy of Jeremiah and the apocryphal
book of Baruch, and this position was adopted by other versions

including the Vulgate. In the Talmud, Lamentations followed the Song of Solomon in a rearranged order of the poetical books and the Megilloth.

2. Historical background

Dirge poetry of the kind exemplified by Lamentations was by no means uncommon in Near Eastern antiquity. The Sumerians were the first to write sombre works commemorating the fall of some of their great cities to enemy invaders, one of the most celebrated being the lament over the destruction of Ur.[1] The author of Lamentations stood therefore in a long and respectable literary tradition when he bewailed the destruction of Jerusalem and the desolation of Judah in 587 BC. His poetic outpourings included a sorrowful commentary on the sufferings experienced by the Judeans both during and after the siege of Jerusalem, and also contained a representative confession of national sin. For the author this latter factor had been the real cause of Judah's downfall. There can be absolutely no question whatever as to the specific event which is being commemorated in the dirges, or the sombre nature of the calamity which they depict so forcefully.

3. Structure, authorship and date

The book comprises five poems, each of which forms the individual chapters. The first four are written as acrostics, making for a highly elaborate and sophisticated construction. The twenty-two consonants of the Hebrew alphabet are used in succession to control the length of each of the first four poems, and they also mark the commencement of the individual stanzas or strophes. However, this patternism is not applied mechanically, for although the consonants occurred in their normal alphabetical order in the first poem, the letter *pe* preceded the consonant '*ayin* in the second, third and fourth dirges to make for some slight irregularity.

The first three chapters followed a grouping-pattern involving

---

1. See S. N. Kramer, *ANET*, pp. 455ff.

three lines to a strophe, but there are two exceptions which comprise four-line stanzas (1:7; 2:19), a circumstance which may be entirely accidental. An elaboration of the simple acrostic pattern occurred in the third dirge, where each of the three verses of the stanza began with the same Hebrew consonant. The fourth poem contained only two lines in each strophe, while the fifth was not acrostic at all, but consisted of twenty-two lines and resembled certain psalms of corporate lament such as Psalms 44 and 80.

Though there is an obvious structural resemblance between them, each chapter nevertheless exhibits its own special qualities of form and content. The first poem is arranged in three-line stanzas, in which Jerusalem is depicted as mourning her destruction and crying aloud to her God for vengeance. The second elegy follows much the same pattern, except for the reversal in alphabetical order of the consonants *pe* and *'ayin*, as noted above. The thought of this poem is more developed, since the author saw that one important cause of the ruin which had overtaken the city and nation lay in the negligence of the prophets for not warning the people clearly of approaching doom. As a consequence of divine judgment, the dirge stressed that any hope for the future would have to be grounded in national contrition.

The third poem is significantly different in structure from the others, being made up of single lines grouped in threes, and commencing with the same consonant of the Hebrew alphabet. Here the personified nation is urged to turn in repentance to God and trust in divine mercy for restoration and the punishment of its enemies. The fourth chapter is very similar to the third, except that each stanza consists of two lines instead of three. After recounting the horrors of the siege and laying the blame for the depraved spirituality of the nation at the door of the priests and prophets, the poem looks towards the restoration of community life and the punishment of hereditary enemies, including the Edomites. The fifth poem, a prayer that the lamenting remnant might be delivered from its distress and restored to prosperity, contains lines equivalent to the number of consonants in the Hebrew alphabet, but is otherwise quite different in form from its precursors.

The authorship of Lamentations was ascribed to Jeremiah by the consensus of Jewish tradition (Targum at Jer. 1:1; *Baba Bathra*, 15 *a*), despite the fact that the work is anonymous. LXX and Vulgate followed this ascription of authorship, the LXX version of Lamentations being prefaced by the statement: 'And it came to pass, after Israel was led into captivity and Jerusalem laid waste, that Jeremiah sat weeping and lamented with this lamentation over Jerusalem and said ...', which the Vulgate expanded by adding the phrase, '... with a bitter spirit sighing and wailing ...' Perhaps this tradition of authorship arose from a misunderstanding of 2 Chronicles 35:25, which stated that Jeremiah composed laments over the deceased king Josiah and that these were written 'in the lamentations'.[2] Josephus (*Ant.* x.5.1) thought that the lament relating to Josiah comprised the fourth chapter of the book of Lamentations, but this seems improbable because the latter concerned a city and its people, not a defunct king. Many literary sources mentioned by the Chronicler are no longer extant, and quite possibly the 'lamentations' to which he alluded comprised some such collection of dirge material which has also perished.

Several commentators have proposed that the traditional views of authorship should be abandoned because of significant literary variations which suggest closer stylistic affinities with certain psalms, the latter part of Isaiah, and portions of Ezekiel, than with the bulk of the prophecies of Jeremiah. This argument is weakened seriously by the entirely unwarranted assumption that parts of Isaiah do not in fact belong to the eighth century BC, a position for which there is no factual evidence whatever.[3] Since Jeremiah reflects the thought of earlier writers periodically, there is no reason why the author of Lamentations should not do precisely the same, and not least if both writers happened to be identical. In favour of Jeremiah as author are the obvious similarities in style and subject-matter which both works exhibit, including such emphases as the ravaging of Virgin Daughter-Jerusalem, the appeal to the righteous Judge for vengeance, and the expectation of divine retribution being wreaked upon those nations which had rejoiced over Judah's collapse.

Whatever may be said for or against the Jeremianic authorship of

---

2. Cf. *HIOT*, p. 1069.

3. For a survey of Isaiah criticism see *HIOT*, pp. 774ff.

Lamentations, there can be no doubt that, on grounds of style and content alone, all of the poems came from the same hand, who was evidently an eye-witness of the calamity which overtook Judah. While the authorship of the work must necessarily remain unknown, it seems highly improbable that anyone other than Jeremiah would have been moved to such depths of elegiac expression by the collapse of resistance in Jerusalem and still be in a position to record his feelings in such moving verse. In the present work the anonymity of the composition will be respected, and where necessary its compiler will be referred to simply as 'the author'.

The dating of the book presents little difficulty. It furnishes adequate internal evidence as the work of a person who was an eye-witness of the disasters of 587 BC. The first four chapters may have been written shortly after the deportation of the Judeans to Babylonia, and the final dirge at a somewhat later period, though there is no certainty on this matter. There seems to be no convincing reason for placing the extant composition later than 550 BC, whether or not portions of it were written at rather different times.[4]

4. The patterns of Hebrew poetry

Many pre-exilic and post-exilic prophetic oracles are actually poetic in form, and this has been recognized adequately in the format of such modern renderings as the RSV and NEB. Since Lamentations consists entirely of poetry, it would seem desirable to comment briefly on the nature of Old Testament poetry.

From an early period the Hebrews were renowned throughout the Near East as singers and musicians. The largest collection of Hebrew poetry is, of course, the Psalter, although poetic sections are scattered liberally throughout the Old Testament. One of the most striking features of such poetry is that of parallelism, this being particularly evident in the psalms. In its simplest form this structure is expressed by a restatement in the second line of a couplet or distich of the thought which has already been expressed in the first. The basic unit of composition is thus the line, and this generally

---

4. Cf. A. S. Herbert, *Peake's Commentary on the Bible* (1962 ed.), p. 563.

comprises one half of the parallelism. It is of importance because it formulates a complete thought, and thus possesses grammatical and syntactical coherence and unity. Unfortunately there is no uniform nomenclature for describing the units of parallelism, so that the terms 'stich', 'stichos', 'hemistich' and 'colon' are all used variously to express the concept of 'line'.

Given this basic unit, however, the Hebrews demonstrated how adept they were at devising sophisticated variations of parallelism, with the result that the relationship between the first and second lines of the couplet could be one of synonymous, synthetic, antithetic, introverted, climactic or emblematic parallelism.[5] Where the unit involved three lines (tristich), all three components were integral to the parallelism. Metre, as commonly understood in occidental compositions, does not occur in ancient Hebrew poetry. Thus there is nothing corresponding to the foot as a unit of metrical measure, whether in terms of accentuation or vowel-quantity.

Hebrew poetry, however, exhibits a strong accentual quality of its own, with the stresses or ictus which are placed on the varying words being used to determine the rhythm of the passage concerned. Each major word in a verse can carry one stress, whereas minor words may either be unstressed or else linked with others by a hyphen to receive one stress for the unit thus formed.[6]

The groupings resulting from this procedure tend to exhibit quite regular rhythmic patterns, though they are never of a purely mechanical order. All that is now known of Ancient Near Eastern poetry suggests that there was a degree of accentual freedom available to Semitic composers which was unknown to the Greeks and Romans. It cannot be urged too strongly, therefore, that analogies from Classical poetry can be misleading, since in Hebrew the number of unstressed syllables which can occur between stresses is variable. Hebrew poetry is concerned primarily with intellectual rather than phonic or rhythmic considerations, and has as its predominant aim

---

5. See *HIOT*, pp. 966f.

6. For a survey of the problems presented by Hebrew poetry see R. C. Culley in J. W. Wevers and D. B. Redford (eds.), *Essays on the Ancient Semitic World* (1970), pp. 12ff.

the balancing of one thought against another by using syllabic accentual values which most probably never corresponded to strictly measurable units.

Apart from rhyme, which does not occur in Hebrew poetry, the Old Testament authors made abundant use of all other literary devices found in poetic writings, including assonance, various figures of speech, and alliteration. Some poems were organized in terms of acrostic configurations, the most familiar example being provided by Psalm 119. Lamentations, as noted above, also follows the acrostic pattern with some variation.

5. The theology of Lamentations

Like all truly inspired poetry, the imagery of the Hebrew lays hold on eternal values and brings them in all their splendour to the notice of mankind. The book of Lamentations is no exception to this, despite the rather obvious fact that its harmonies are written consistently in a minor key. Divine sovereignty, justice, morality, judgment, and the hope of blessing in the distant future, are themes which emerge in solemn grandeur from the cadences of Lamentations. The composition is in many respects *sui generis*, and it is perhaps this general divergence from all other Old Testament books which has prompted the view that Lamentations has little if any theological content. However, if the book of Job describes calamity and its outcome in the area of personal life, Lamentations can be said to deal with the problem of suffering at the national level, treating as it does of the supreme crisis which saw the end of community life as previously experienced in Judah.

This latter theme is paramount in all the poems, even though each chapter can be regarded as a complete and self-contained composition. There appear to be times when the author finds it virtually impossible to believe that the promised catastrophe has at last occurred. Yet the ruined city bears mute testimony to this tragic event, and hence it falls to the author to determine as satisfactorily as he can the real meaning which underlies this dramatic reversal of the fortunes of earlier days.

In the light of Jeremiah's teachings, the reasons for the collapse of Judah are not hard to find. The author knows full well that the people of Judah had long been apostate, and that, even more seri-ously, they had consistently ignored the hard lessons taught by the captivity of the northern kingdom for a similar repudiation of covenantal obligations. Now that a like fate had overtaken Judah, everyone was suddenly acutely aware of the serious penalties which a righteous and holy God attached to sin.

In a real sense the poems present a vindication of divine right-eousness in the light of the covenant relationship, and like the book of Job they show that God, not man, is the central figure in the drama of history. As the poems of Lamentations unfold, they make it clear that the real tragedy inherent in the destruction of Judah lies in the fact that it could almost certainly have been avoided. The actual causes of the calamity were the people themselves, who were determined at all costs to pursue the allurements of a false and debased paganism in preference to the high moral and ethical ideals inherent in the Sinai covenant.

The irony of it all lay in the fact that over the generations they had been warned time and again by various servants of God that con-tinued indulgence in this immoral way of life would result in dras-tic punishment, warnings which, in the event, went unheeded. Whereas the book of Job is a theodicy which attempts to explain and justify the ways of God with men, Lamentations consists of a sad commentary on the outworking of the prophetic conviction that those who sow the wind will reap the whirlwind. The ashes of a dev-astated Jerusalem thus testify at once to the demonstration and the vindication of divine righteousness (1:18).

The recognition of national sin as the real cause of destruction brought with it a pressing consciousness of guilt (1:8; 2:14; 3:40, etc.), and this in turn impels the author to make full confession of sin on behalf of the apostate people and their leaders as the first step towards claiming divine forgiveness and restoration. Even though it had been long prophesied, the severity of the blow which finally fell on Judah seems to have taken the author somewhat by surprise, and in the second poem he remonstrates with God and reproves him for such drastic action. At the same time, however, he recognizes that divine justice is a complement to divine righteousness, and laments over the grave folly of a covenanted people being so wilful and indif-ferent as to have lived for so long in evident unawareness of that fact.

As with Jeremiah, the author sees a ray of hope permeating even the darkest cloud. Although Judah has been desolated, her plight is not absolutely beyond any expectation of restoration and renewal. Nevertheless, the nature and content of the poems are such that it is difficult to state this explicitly, though the author can always cling to the assurance that God always keeps his covenantal undertakings (Lam. 3:19–39). In such an internally-consistent and reliable deity it is possible to place one's trust, and in complete resignation to his sovereign will to pray that he may yet again look favourably upon his apostate people and restore them to a measure of their former greatness. Like the author of Job, the writer of Lamentations recognizes that a positive reaction to an experience of suffering is a necessary prerequisite to spiritual maturity. This awareness furnishes the basis for his expectation that, in the goodness of God, the experience of tribulation will be followed by a time of restoration and blessing (Lam. 3:25–30) for a truly penitent people. Such a prospect was a firm part of the covenantal relationship (cf. Deut. 30:1ff.), for God will not reject his covenant people completely, as Paul pointed out (Rom. 11:1ff.).

The reader should be cautioned against any attempt to discover logical doctrinal coherence or a development in theological insight between one poem and the next. While the separate poems manifest a degree of external structural control, the flow of the thought is not by any means as rigorously directed, and in fact is apt to move rather haphazardly as befits the spontaneous outpourings of a grief-stricken spirit. Yet the theological sentiments adumbrated in the poems are timeless in nature, and if the book was not actually used in some manner by the exiles in Babylonia as a means of commemorating the fall of Jerusalem (cf. Jer. 41:4f.; Zech. 7:3), there is little doubt that it would form much the most suitable means of conveying a sense of national contrition and a reliance on the future mercies of God.

6. The Hebrew text and the Septuagint

It is most probably because of the nature of the poems that the Hebrew text has been preserved extremely well, and as a result it exhibits very few corruptions. There are occasional obscurities, however, and these will be noted in the commentary section. The LXX translators seem to have employed a Hebrew text closely resembling, if not actually identical with, the one familiar to the Massoretes. There are some variations in the LXX, however, and these may have arisen from the Greek text itself suffering damage during transmissional processes.

ANALYSIS

1. FIRST DIRGE (1:1–22)

    a. Jerusalem destroyed (1:1–7)
    b. Destruction follows sin (1:8–11)
    c. A plea for mercy (1:12–22)

2. SECOND DIRGE (2:1–22)

    a. God's hostility towards his people (2:1–9)
    b. Sufferings consequent upon famine (2:10–13)
    c. True and false prophets (2:14–17)
    d. A tearful prayer to God (2:18–22)

3. THIRD DIRGE (3:1–66)

    a. The lament of the afflicted (3:1–21)
    b. Divine mercies recalled (3:22–39)
    c. A call for spiritual renewal (3:40–42)

COMMENTARY

1. FIRST DIRGE (1:1–22)

a. Jerusalem destroyed (1:1–7)

The theme of the book is established in these opening verses which tell how mortal calamity had overtaken the southern kingdom and its capital city of Jerusalem. A brief reflective statement dealing with the causes of the destruction is followed by an earnest plea for pity. *How!* (1), the characteristic Hebrew expression of lamentation (*'êkâh*), frequently commences an elegiac composition (cf. Isa. 1:21), and is not included in the metrical structure. In normal times Jerusalem, Judah's capital, was a bustling commercial centre as well as the focal point of national cultic worship. Now she is a deserted ruin, stripped of all her former grandeur and emptied of her inhabitants. To heighten the tragedy of destruction the author uses the image of a woman bereaved of her husband and children, bitterly lamenting her vanished glories and contemplating her present sorry state in anguish and apprehension. The concept of widowhood was employed frequently to depict the depths of human loneliness and despair. While the author is the principal speaker as he describes the desolate scene, he also represents the bereft capital city as lamenting in its own right for past sin. The descriptive terms *princess* and *vassal* exemplified the level to which the once-proud city had fallen. She who in former times was ruler of such countries as Moab and Edom is now herself in captivity, ravaged and despoiled. MT of this verse can be redivided, as with AV, RV, and most modern translations, resulting in a three-line strophe which accords with the rhythm occurring in the remainder of the dirge.

While others are deriving refreshment of body and mind from their sleep, Jerusalem is wide awake (2), crying and sobbing continually with grief, harrassed by the prospect of nocturnal terrors, and deprived of all human comfort. The phrase *her lovers* was used by Jeremiah (cf. 22:20) for such nations as Egypt, the Transjordanian peoples, Tyre, and Sidon, with whom Judah had tried to ally against Babylonia. These *friends* had failed Jerusalem miserably in her hour of dire need, and some of them had actually behaved so treacherously as to contribute to her ruin by deliberately helping the Babylonians to plunder her.

All resistance collapsed when the refugees were overtaken and captured in the narrow defiles around Jerusalem. This leads to the larger figurative sense of the distress or extremity overtaking a person which the word *mēṣar* normally implies (cf. RSV *in the midst of her distress*; NEB *in her sore straits*). The routes to Jerusalem, once thronged with pilgrims going up to the temple to participate in festal rites, are now completely deserted (4). The *gates* describes the area just inside the city gates, which was generally one of the very few open spaces within the walls of most Palestinian cities. It was here that merchants gathered to sell their wares to the citizens, and here also that justice was meted out by the elders or the ruler (Deut. 21:19; Ruth 4:1, 11; 2 Sam. 18:24, etc.). The young women who survived are grieved at the loss of prospective husbands and children. For MT *nûgôt* ('be sorrowful'), most of the versions evidently read *nĕhûgôt*, from *nāhag*, 'to drive away'. Thus RSV reads *her maidens have been dragged away*. However, MT makes sense here, and there is no need to regard *nûgôt* as a contracted form of *nĕhûgôt*, as some commentators have done. For the people of the southern kingdom, who had long preferred to think of themselves as the crown and not the foot (cf. Deut. 28:44), the ascendancy of their enemies was a galling reality.

Disaster, however, was a punishment for national sin. The author forcibly exposes the real cause of the calamity which has overtaken Judah. The concept that God has punished the nation for its iniquities by bringing on it the catastrophe of the exile is developed in subsequent dirges. The reference to *princes* (6) is probably to Zedekiah and his advisers who fled from Jerusalem and were captured before they were able to make good their escape (cf. Jer. 39:4f.; 2 Kgs 25:4).

The imagery of pastureless *deer* (NEB) contrasts sharply with the situation depicted in Psalm 23, where the Lord is leading and guiding the flock. The greatest provision of all is made by Christ, the good shepherd, who laid down his life for the sheep (John 10:11ff.). The pathos and tragedy of captivity are deliberately heightened by the contrasting of past and present conditions of existence. MT *mārûd* ('wandering', 'unrest') has been thought to be a transcriptional error for a noun derived from the verb *mārar* ('to be bitter'). This sense of anguish is read here and in 3:19 by RSV. The reference to gloating is to nations such as Ammon, Moab and Edom, who were traditional enemies of the Israelites (cf. Obad. 12).

b. Destruction follows sin (1:8–11)

The theme of Jerusalem's sin, introduced in verse 5, is now examined more closely, and ultimately becomes one of the major theological emphases of the book. Continuing the image of a woman, the writer asserts that her former suitors have rejected her because she has become defiled through indulgence in sin. The *nakedness* of many EVV is a surrogate for 'ill repute'. The proud female has become a fallen woman through participating in the demoralizing rites of Baal worship. She groans and turns away because she is now shunned by her erstwhile admirers. In verse 9 MT *ṭum'āh* ('defilement') is used of the ritual as well as the moral variety. Judah had been guilty of offence on both counts. The ethic of the Sinai covenant made such a condition a very serious matter for those supposedly manifesting divine holiness. The Christian is similarly urged to avoid anything which will defile the personality (Matt. 15:18; 1 Cor. 3:17, etc.), and thereby diminish the authority and effectiveness of Christian witness. So indifferent was Jerusalem to her spiritual responsibilities that she never even considered the possibility that her repeated violations of the covenantal principles would bring destruction upon her as an inevitable consequence, and this in spite of successive prophetic warnings. Her collapse was therefore an awesome occurrence, full of portent and foreboding for any who cared to contemplate it.

Now, however, Jerusalem realizes the enormity of her crimes against God, and is depicted as breaking into the narrative sequence with her own cry of distress, as also in verse 11. Like a beautiful woman who has been ravished, Jerusalem has been dishonoured by the predatory activities of pagan conquerors who have entered the sacred precincts and carried off the spoil. Her *treasures* (MT *maḥămuddîm*), a rare word found only in the plural, means 'valuables', and occurs in this sense in verses 7 and 11. In the attack of 587 BC the Babylonians stripped the temple of all its costly ornamentation and removed the most valuable of the cultic objects to Babylon (cf. Jer. 52:17–23). For pagan peoples to enter God's holy sanctuary was much the worst fate that could overtake the national shrine, since even native Israelites who were not actually members of the priesthood were prohibited from entering the sanctuary. But now those very foreigners who had been prohibited from entering the congregation of the Israelites were polluting the sacred house in the most wanton manner. The allusion to *treasures* in verse 11 is to the inhabitants of Jerusalem selling their prized possessions in order to purchase food, reflecting conditions which obtained just before the collapse of resistance in 587 BC. Such actions were necessary if only to prolong life. The words, *Look, O Lord* comprise another interruption on the part of the city, which serves to introduce a change of speaker for the remainder of the dirge.

c. A plea for mercy (1:12–22)

Verse 12 has become a classic expression of grief as traditionally translated. There is some question as to how MT is to be construed, however. The first two words *lô' 'ălêkem* mean literally 'not to you', and if interpreted interrogatively, as in EVV, have the sense of 'does this not affect you at all?'. This then refers to the agony of Jerusalem's recent experiences and the lesson which the careful observer can learn therefrom. If interpreted as a wish, however, the verse would begin, 'May it never happen to you', which seems to be closer to the sense of the original situation than traditional renderings. The parallel to the lament of Christ over heedless Jerusalem is striking (cf. Matt. 23:37f.; Luke 13:34f.). In the first line of verse 12, better sense is obtained when the first clause ends with *fire* and when MT *wayyirdennāh* ('subdues') is read as *yôridennah* (from *yārad*, 'to descend'). The line would thus read: 'From above he hurled down fire; he made it penetrate my bones.' By employing the figure of fire, a snare and faintness, the author gives graphic expression to all the horrors of siege which have overtaken Jerusalem. The fire burns into the inner recesses of the city, the net prevents anyone from escaping, and the idea of faintness completes the picture of a demoralized community.

At the beginning of verse 14 MT is difficult, the form *nisqad* presenting certain problems. Since it occurs only here in the Old Testament, its meaning is uncertain ('bound'?). LXX and a number of manuscripts modify the consonants slightly to read a form of the verb *šāqad*, 'to be watchful', and translate, 'Watch has been kept over my transgressions', reading *'al* ('over', 'upon') for MT *'ōl* ('yoke'), which accords with the general tenor of the passage. For *nisqad* it is possible to read *hiqšāh*, from the root *qāšāh*, 'to be heavy', rendering the phrase, 'He has made heavy the yoke of my transgressions'. The simplest emendation of the text is to read *niqšāh* for the MT *nisqad*, and translate, 'Heavy is the yoke of my transgressions'. The passage implies that the iniquities of Jerusalem have been compounded, and are weighing her down like a heavy yoke on the neck of an animal. Such a crushing burden effectively prevents the city from eluding the punishment which she so richly deserves. The yoke is thus another figure which is adduced to express the range of calamities involved in the fall of Jerusalem. An *assembly* (15) would normally have a happy intent, but here it is the enemy forces which are gathered under divine summons to celebrate the liquidation of the Judean warriors. The *winepress* is a graphic way of representing the manner in which all resistance in Jerusalem has been crushed and the blood of the defenders spilled like grape juice gushing from a vat.

Because of her special position in the light of the covenantal relationship, Jerusalem, the *virgin daughter*, had considered herself inviolable (cf. 4:12). Now she knows to her cost how presumptuous she had been. The Christian must trust in Christ alone for his sufficiency (cf. 2 Cor. 12:9; Gal. 2:20, etc.), for when he thinks he stands independently he is in greatest danger of falling. Unlike the Christian, whose greatest consolation is his Saviour, the city of Jerusalem had no-one to comfort her in time of acute crisis, making her sad fate all the more poignant. Verse 17 seems to be a parenthetical insertion in which the writer takes up the lament on behalf of the stricken city, depicted as stretching out its hands in a gesture of sorrow and supplication. God is here represented as the righteous judge who has finally punished his recalcitrant people for their long-standing rebellion. Jerusalem had become contaminated through indulging in the sensuous and depraved rituals of Canaanite religion, and now the time of her prophesied punishment has come (cf. Rev. 22:10f.). The Christian is urged continually to abstain from all forms of filthiness (cf. 2 Cor. 7:1; Eph. 5:4, etc.).

In verse 18 Jerusalem again takes up the dirge and laments of sin which has brought on such dire punishment. In the remainder of this chapter there is no thought of rebellion against the will of God or any complaint about the nature of divine justice, as contrasted with the book of Job. The righteous judgment of God is accepted without question in a resigned attitude of spirit which recognizes that the gross sins of the nation and her continued rejection of covenantal responsibilities have brought upon her the predicted extinction of national life. The judgment of Judah is just because it has been administered by a righteous God (cf. Gen. 18:25). By comparison the afflictions which overtook Job were designed to serve a different purpose, since the book makes it clear that Job was not a sinner, but a man who walked uprightly in the sight of God. While all had suffered in the collapse of Jerusalem, a heavy blow had been dealt to the young men and women, the hope of future continuance for Judah, who had been forcibly uprooted and taken captive to Babylonia. At the national as much as at the personal level, the thought of extinction has always been understandably abhorrent to the Jews. The *lovers* (cf. verse 2) were allies who had failed to come to the aid of the southern kingdom when the Babylonian armies were devastating the land. Egypt in particular had thought it prudent to avoid direct confrontation with the Chaldean armies. The *priests* and *elders*, the very leaders who had disregarded the warnings of Jeremiah in favour of the soothing lies of the false prophets, had quite appropriately borne the brunt of the siege, finally dropping dead in their tracks while looking for food. The turmoil of acute emotional disturbance was described by *mēʿeh* ('bowels', 'intestines', 'belly'), which was held to be the locale of the emotions, and *lēb* ('heart'), which the Semites regarded as the seat of intelligence, will and purposiveness. After enduring the punishments of siege and destruction, Jerusalem has apparently realized that a radically new approach to life is required, since the rebellion of former days has brought upon her a curse rather than a blessing. The prodigal daughter is finally coming to her senses.

At the end of verse 20 the MT could be understood as implying that *death* in the house was the result of the sword. However, the Hebrew *māwet* can also mean 'plague', 'pestilence', as in Jeremiah 15:2; 18:21. Hence the plague has accomplished indoors what the sword has achieved in the streets. It must have been a matter of some gratification to the enemies of the Israelites (21) to know that God, who in earlier days had wrought such havoc on the foes of the Chosen People, had now recoiled in punitive wrath upon his own. The reference to the promised day at the end of verse 21 is obscure in MT. If *the day* is that of the calamity of Judah, the verb *bring* will need to be rendered in the perfect tense. If it refers to the time when the scoffing and exultant Israelite enemies will themselves experience the humiliation of punishment, the verb should be translated as a future, 'you will bring'. RSV, following the Peshitta, adopted an imperative form, while some medieval Jewish interpreters thought of it as a wish for the future, rendering it, 'Bring thou the day'. Jerusalem prays that the evil deeds of her enemies might also come before God in judgment, as the iniquity of Israel and Judah had done, being now fully aware that its punishment had resulted from antecedent sin, indulged in wilfully and continuously. The realization of a cause-effect relationship here establishes the theme of subsequent chapters. In this section also is the glimmering of that expectation for the future when the enemies of Israel will also receive the due reward for their misdeeds. This verse lays the theological foundations of the book of Lamentations with the thought that the righteousness of God, which demands punishment for sin, must also be viewed as the basis for whatever future hope the nation can expect to enjoy. For the latter to materialize there must be a 'turning' or 'conversion' and a complete submission to the revealed will of God.

The concluding verse of the chapter raises the moral issues involved in prayers for divine vengeance. In the Old Testament these pleas generally arose because Israel had already been punished for her wickedness, and desired the Judge of all the earth to requite other sinful peoples in a similar manner. This attitude rested on the sense of God's moral governance of mankind, and carried with it a degree of urgency because of the need for retribution to occur in this life if justice was to be seen to be done. The rationale seems to have been based upon the primary need for God's justice to be established, and only to a lesser extent on the desire for the rehabilitation of the sinner. The behaviour of wicked nations was in effect a denial of the divine law, and permitted them to indulge in apparently unrestricted acts of unrighteousness against other peoples. Since the Hebrews regarded crimes against mankind as being crimes committed against God, they could pray without equivocation for God to establish his righteousness and justice by punishing the wicked. In the New Testament, the executing of vengeance upon the iniquitous is strictly a divine prerogative (cf. Rom. 12:19).

2. SECOND DIRGE (2:1–22)

This lament describes in considerably greater detail the nature of the calamity which has descended upon the southern kingdom. Its vividness and vitality bear the obvious marks of an eye-witness.

a. God's hostility towards his people (2:1–9)

Divine wrath is poised over the kingdom of Judah like a thunder-cloud, ready to be unleashed in all its awesome power. To change the figure somewhat, this outpouring will result in the complete eclipse of Daughter-Zion. This latter expression occurs fairly frequently in Isaiah and Jeremiah (cf. Isa. 1:8; 4:4; 52:2; 62:11; Jer. 4:31; 6:2, 23, etc.), and is prominent in Lamentations. The nation had imagined that it occupied a privileged position because it stood in covenant rela-tionship with God, and was seemingly unaware that such a status involved important obligations in the moral and spiritual realm. Now her degradation was as sudden as it was complete, and reduced her in an embarrassing fashion to a level even below that of other peoples. Not merely has the glorious capital of the nation been levelled to the ground, but the hallowed sanctuary in particular, long considered inviolable, has been defiled by the conqueror. The sacred shrine (cf. Ps. 132:7) has fallen foul of destruction in order to illustrate the measure of divine anger with the Chosen People. RSV *habitations* refers to the places where shepherds lived with their flocks, and so would imply the open village areas of Judea. These undefended settlements are then contrasted with the fortified towns of the next phrase. What in God's purpose had been destined as a kingdom of priests and a holy nation (Exod. 19:6) had profaned itself by gross indulgence in idolatry and immorality. Now God had achieved the final humiliation of Judah by rescinding her privileged status and reducing her to a position somewhat below that of the other nations which she had striven so desperately to imitate. In New Testament times, Capernaum was promised a share in the fate of Chorazin and Bethsaida (Matt. 11:21ff.) because she, too, had resisted the challenge of God's redemptive works.

In verse 3, MT *qeren* (*horn*) depicts a favourite Old Testament symbol of power or strength. The implication is that even the most heavily fortified strongholds will be unable to stem the engulfing tide of divine fury as it sweeps down upon the southern kingdom. God has no longer interposed his power as a barrier between his people and their enemies. In consequence the devouring fire prophesied by Amos (2:4f.) has burned down the habitations of Jacob. In an anthropomorphic passage (4) the author represents God as the strong enemy of his people, who has become antagonized by their prolonged indulgence in sin and idolatry. The same power which in times past had so often achieved wonders on behalf of the covenant nation has now been brought against it in judgment. The imagery of a tent reflects a marauding conqueror who plunders whatever attracts his attention. However, in the despoiled nation there is very little of significant worth. Fire was employed by Christ as a symbol of punishment in Matthew 18:8; 25:41; 13:42, etc.

Because of the continued apostasy of his covenant people, God has become disaffected and has brought upon them their just deserts. RSV *mourning and lamentation* (5) is an inadequate attempt to represent in English the alliteration and poignancy of two synonymous Hebrew words, *ta'ăniyyāh* ('sorrow', 'grief'), and *'ănniyyāh* ('lamentation', 'mourning'). God's *booth* (AV, RV, NEB *tabernacle*), though of flimsy construction, was meant to be holy, and to typify his presence among his people. But now, because of national wickedness, the holy structure is demolished as though it were merely a worthless garden shed. Therefore the celebrations prescribed by the Law can no longer be observed because cultic rituals have been terminated abruptly. The mediations of the altar, where the faithful had claimed and found reconciliation with God throughout the ages, are now a thing of the past. More significant, however, is the implication that no amount of outward ritualistic procedure could avert divine judgment from a people guilty of the continued rejection of covenant love.

Verse 7 describes the pillaging of Jerusalem at its most horrifying stage. Even the magnificent Solomonic temple, the pride of the nation for centuries, was not spared in the general destruction. The palace walls were those of the temple complex, as indicated by the mention of the altar and sanctuary. The temple formed part of a group of buildings, and took seven years to construct, as against thirteen for the erection of the royal palace. This discrepancy might suggest that the temple may have been intended originally to serve as a royal chapel. On the occasion being described, however, the noise (cf. 1:15) was that of the triumphant enemy forces, not the festal shouts of Hebrew worshippers.

The *wall* of verse 8 is a form of metonymy, being the container for the thing contained, i.e. the city of Jerusalem. The planned destruction was a striking testimony to the sovereign activity of Judah's Creator. Just as a builder measured levels carefully in process of construction, so God had been equally precise in the work of demolition to ensure that one stone did not stand upon another. This fate was to overtake Jerusalem once again in the early Christian period (cf. Matt. 24:2; Mark 13:2; Luke 19:44; 21:6). All the defences of the city had been obliterated by demolition, as though the earth had swallowed them up. In Deuteronomy 5:14; 12:15; 14:27f., *ša'ar* ('gate') was used for the city or town itself.

Jerusalem's fall was a signal vindication of the righteous nature of Judah's God. His complete disavowal of sin, long a matter for urgent warnings by a succession of prophets, had now been implemented in realistic terms which all could see and understand. Once the priests and civil administrators had been exiled, there was no-one left to instruct the few remaining Judeans in the traditions of the Mosaic law (cf. Ezek. 7:26; Amos 8:11f.). The priests normally assumed the responsibility for making decisions relating to the religious aspects of the Torah, while the court officials and the king administered the civil law. For a community which professed to live by the Torah to be deprived of its normative basis of existence was as demoralizing spiritually as it was disabling socially. Because the people had lost their spiritual vision they had perished (cf. Prov. 29:18). The Christian must always keep his eyes fixed on Christ, the author and finisher of our faith (Heb. 12:2).

Not all prophets in the time of Jeremiah, whether cultic officiants or not, were necessarily false, as the case of Uriah (Urijah) indicates (Jer. 26:20–24). Even those persons whom Jeremiah denounced were at least recognized for the position which they claimed in society, and were castigated not so much for professing to be prophets as for being false ones. The fact of the exile had at last made the will of God clear to all, and had silenced those who had been holding out false hopes of peace and prosperity. Similarly, those who may have supported Jeremiah in his denunciations had no further utterances for the present.

b. Sufferings consequent upon famine (2:10–13)

In a patriarchal culture the *elders* were probably heads of families, though in Numbers 11:25 seventy such men were appointed to share with Moses the jurisdiction over the people (cf. Exod. 24:1). In the Settlement period each city had its own elders who exercised control over local affairs (cf. Deut. 19:12; 21:2; Judg. 8:14, etc.). The national body known as the 'elders of Israel' exerted considerable influence both before and after the exile. They were the ones who petitioned for the appointment of a king (1 Sam. 8:4), and their position claimed the recognition of various rulers of Israel and Judah including Solomon (1 Kgs 8:1–3), Ahab (1 Kgs 20:7), Jehu (2 Kgs 10:1), Hezekiah (2 Kgs 19:2), and Josiah (2 Kgs 23:1). Now that the land had been desolated, the elders had no civil duties to perform, and were reduced to grief-stricken impotence by the calamity of the exile. Placing *dust* on the head was a characteristic sign of mourning (cf. Job 2:12; Ezek. 27:30). *Sackcloth* was worn as a token of mourning for the dead (Gen. 37:34; 2 Sam. 3:31, etc.), to signify penitence for sins (1 Kgs 21:27; Jon. 3:5, etc.), or to betoken lamentation for personal or national calamity (Esth. 4:1; Job 16:15). It was usually made from goats' hair, and was black in colour.

The AV reference in verse 11 to *bowels* and *liver* (NEB *bowels, bile*) is to acute emotional disturbance (cf. 1:20). In particular the liver (MT *kābed*, 'heavy'), which is actually the weightiest organ of the human body, was held in antiquity to be one of the locales of psychic life, being associated with profound emotional reactions, generally of a depressive nature. AV and RSV render liver here by *heart*, with similar affective functions in view. The sadness described has been occasioned by reminiscence about the terrible fate which overtook young children during the siege of Jerusalem, a theme which recurs in verses 19–21 and in 4:4, 10. The harrowing scenes described here are obvious marks of an eye-witness, who seems to have been so utterly appalled and revolted by them as to be incapable of eradicating them from his memory. As the children gasped out their last pathetic breaths they were pleading for food, MT *corn and wine* designating normal sustenance (cf. Deut. 11:14). Even while they were crawling among the rubble, searching for scraps of food, they collapsed in their tracks and died. In their extremity the children sought the kind of security which they had known as infants, and in this helpless posture they expired from hunger. This pathetic and tragic scene stands in stark contrast to the ideal of happy, carefree children playing in the streets of Jerusalem, a situation which is promised when the nation is restored (Zech. 8:5).

Because the conditions affecting the fall of Jerusalem are unique in the light of the covenantal relationship, it is impossible for the author to offer her any consolation (13) by comparing her present agonies with those of others. Divine retribution has burst in on Zion in the same manner as the sea forces its way through a gap in the protective wall. One of the tragic aspects of much human suffering is that the innocent are frequently involved with the guilty in the consequences of sin, Jesus Christ being the supreme exemplar (cf. 1 Pet. 2:22ff.). By isolating the fall of Jerusalem from the historical chain of cause and effect, it might be possible to regard God's actions in decimating the population as unjust, unethical or unloving. But when the sequence is viewed as a whole, the destruction of the nation is seen as the fulfilment of the many promises of punishment for wilful and open sin against God. Thus the deeds which provoked divine retribution were prohibited acts in the first place. Although it is theoretically possible to regard nursing infants and young children as innocent, they were nevertheless a formal and recognized part of an iniquitous, apostate nation. Like all children, their destiny was deeply involved with that of their parents, who showed little if any signs of rearing their offspring in the ethical and spiritual traditions of the covenant. The parents were responsible for their children's doom in another sense also. Ancient Near Eastern rules of war permitted the inhabitants of a city which surrendered to escape the sword. By obstinate resistance to the Babylonians, as previously to God, they sealed the fate of the community. The corporate nature of the Sinai covenant carried with it corporate responsibility, but the seventh-century BC Judeans seemed strangely indifferent to this important fact. Thus, while some community members might be relatively innocent, the group of which they were an integral part was unquestionably guilty, and as such fell under divine judgment. The callous indifference of the wanton, selfish parents to the destiny of their offspring shows the depths of depravity to which the Judeans had sunk. Instead of bringing their children up in the fear and nurture of the Lord, they had sold them in emotional and spiritual bondage to Baal. Christian parents have an important responsibility in the matter of instilling Christian spiritual values in their children, while the latter in turn must be obedient and considerate (cf. Eph. 6:1; Col. 3:20; 1 Tim. 5:4).

c. True and false prophets (2:14–17)

The author takes up the censure of the contemporary *prophets*, a theme which had formed such an important element of Jeremiah's message. Here also the prophets are made to bear a large share of the responsibility for the fate which has come upon the nation. Instead of confronting the people with the implications of the covenantal relationship, the prophets had proclaimed a completely false message of peace and future prosperity (cf. Jer. 2:5; 10:15; 14:13; 16:19, etc.). As a result they were encouraging the inhabitants of Judah to indulge in immoral Baal worship at the expense of ignoring righteousness and the ethical ideals of the Sinai covenant, despite the severe warnings of Amos, Hosea and others. Because the prophets had failed to expose and castigate national sin, they were held responsible in large measure for the irreversible trend towards destruction and exile. To describe the utterances of the false prophets as misleading oracles was the most devastating form of criticism possible. Their intrinsic worthlessness had already been demonstrated in practical terms by the sheer progress of events. Now, to add insult to injury, the malicious glee which the enemies of Jerusalem experienced (15) was expressed by a variety of contemptuous gestures (cf. Jer. 19:8; 25:9, etc.). David's capital had been the proud boast of its inhabitants for centuries (cf. Ps. 50:2), but now their praises had been made to recoil on them in the form of taunts. The long-smouldering resentment of Judah's enemies could now be given full expression over her helpless, prostrate form.

The normal order of the Hebrew consonants *'ayin* and *pe* in the acrostic structure of the poem is reversed in verse 16, as in the two subsequent dirges, for unknown reasons. The theology of the pre-exilic prophets makes it clear that there is nothing capricious about the nature or actions of God (17). Jeremiah's oracles in particular stress divine forbearance and reveal the conditional nature of prophecy, one implication of which is that man himself plays a large part in the outworking of God's purposes for weal or woe. The reference to what God has decreed is to the threats of punishment for disobedience of the divine will as revealed in the Pentateuch (cf. Lev. 26:1–45; Deut. 28:15–68). Since the spirituality of the covenant relationship had been rejected so consistently, there could be no possible doubt as to the fate which would engulf the nation. The military might of enemy kingdoms, acting as divine agents, would accomplish this purpose.

d. A tearful prayer to God (2:18–22)

The theme changes abruptly in verse 18, a feature occurring elsewhere in this book. The author calls on the distraught city to make supplication to her God. MT of verse 18 begins, *Their heart cried* (RSV *Cry aloud*; NEB *Cry with a full heart*), this being a collective reference to the populace, and continues, *O wall of the daughter of Zion* (so AV,

NEB; RSV reads, *O daughter of Zion*). Here MT construes 'wall' in apposition to 'Lord'. For the concept of God as a protective wall cf. Zechariah 2:5. Jerusalem is now weeping in abject sorrow because she has neglected to 'let judgment roll down as waters, and righteousness as a mighty stream' (Amos 5:24, RV). She is instructed to continue her weeping (RSV *your eyes no respite*). MT has 'do not let the pupil of your eye cease', the 'pupil' (AV, RV *apple*) being a surrogate for the whole eye. It described a part or the whole of its functions, and regarded it as an organ of extreme sensitivity. At times of great emotional stress, weeping can be a profoundly therapeutic activity, and those who would internalize emotional turbulence by deliberately refraining from tears are inviting even more serious emotional, and possibly physical, repercussions. Cf. Christ at the grave of Lazarus (John 11:35), his tears shed over Jerusalem (Luke 19:41), and Paul's advice in Romans 12:15.

The *watch* (19) was a unit of time into which the twelve hours of the night were divided equally. The division was a threefold one of four hours each (cf. Judg. 7:19), hence the reference here would be to the uttering of a lament at specific intervals during the night. The purpose of this, apparently, was to break up the sleep of the surviving remnant and remind them that their sorrows were actually a punishment for earlier sin. The interruption of sleep has been employed in more recent times as a powerful psychological weapon in the eliciting of confessions for ideological and other misdemeanours, real or imaginary, and seldom fails in its exercise.

The poetic eloquence of this sad, tragic book has resulted in some particularly expressive descriptions, of which the phrase *pour out your heart like water*, relating to sincere prayer, is especially eloquent. In another brief glimpse of utter tragedy, the terrible scene of children dying from hunger reappears. The sight of these pathetic mortals, collapsing and expiring in the ruins of Jerusalem with nobody to help them, had obviously left a lasting impression on the author's mind, as indeed it would have done upon anyone of such artistic sensitivity. The dying children seem to have crawled from their homes towards the main city streets in a desperate, though vain, search for food. A personified Zion turns away in shock from this horrible scene with a desperate plea to God (20), reminding him that the persons afflicted are his chosen ones. The author is quite correct in urging his fellow-countrymen to give full expression to their turbulent emotions, which under the circumstances would be comparatively easy for them. As a result of this outpouring of grief they would go far towards achieving psychological catharsis. Such godly sorrow, if it worked towards repentance, would ultimately secure their deliverance (cf. 2 Cor. 7:10). These concluding verses contain no reproach or recrimination, but constitute an acknowledgment of the fact that the tragic events attending the fall of Jerusalem resulted from a prolonged violation of the covenant relationship. But because Zion can still consider herself to be within the scope of divine mercy even in punishment, the author feels, albeit dimly, that there is some prospect of national restoration in the distant future. The extremes to which the capital had been reduced seem implied by the reference to cannibalism, one of the most reprehensible crimes which can be committed against the human person. The Hebrews only seem to have entertained it as a last desperate resort when all other supplies had been used up (cf. 2 Kgs 6:26–29). Priest and prophet, who with such callous frequency had debased the high spiritual traditions associated with the Lord's house, had now met their end at the scene of their crimes. No cultic object, ceremonial procedure or ritual association can ever be considered superior to the Deity whose spirituality alone furnishes its validity. God desires the service of the human heart in the highest ethical and spiritual form possible, and therefore his perennial insistence is upon true motivation of spirit rather than the mechanical pursuit of ritual procedures in a cultic setting. The priests of God, like the Lord himself, must be clothed with righteousness (cf. 1 Sam. 15:22; Amos 5:21, etc.), of which the act of consecration and the robes of office are only the outward and visible signs. The believer in Christ participates in a royal priesthood in which holiness is also a prime qualification.

As noted above, the slaughter of the young men and women (21) was particularly serious because it precluded the appearing of another generation. Despite the widespread nature of the destruction, the author recognizes that the Chaldeans are nothing more than agents of the destruction, who operate under divine approbation to punish the recalcitrant Israelites. Zion has now learned the bitter lesson that the sowing of the wind inevitably reaps the whirlwind, and that this cause-effect nexus is based strictly upon the immutability and consistency of the divine nature. Hence the lack of reproach or sense of injustice on the part of the author is entirely appropriate here. His likening of Judah's besieging enemies to birds of prey hovering over their victim is particularly striking (cf. Matt. 24:28; Luke 17:37). MT *mô'ēd* (cf. 1:15) means 'an appointed time', 'a meeting', 'an appointed place', and is used of sacred seasons and calendar feasts as well as those participating in them at given locations. So in Isaiah 33:20 Zion was described as 'the city of our appointed feasts', and the term *mô'ēd* was applied to the temple in Psalm 74:4; Jeremiah seems to have used the phrase 'terror on every side' (cf. Jer. 6:25; 20:3) to emphasize the horrors of encirclement and extinction at enemy hands. Considering herself as the mother of her inhabitants, Jerusalem uses the imagery which a mother would employ in alluding to her offspring (22). The high esteem in which children, particularly males, were held made their untimely destruction all the more tragic.

3. THIRD DIRGE (3:1–66)

This lament takes the form of an acrostic in triplets, each alphabetic consonant supplying the first letter of each sentence in the strophe and constituting a highly elaborate arrangement. The sequence of the thought does not follow this pattern, however, but traverses the various groupings in a fashion encountered previously. In many respects this elegy crystallizes the basic themes of Lamentations, and as a foreshadowing of the passion of Jesus Christ has definite affinities with Isaiah 53 and Psalm 22.

a. The lament of the afflicted (3:1–21)

The sufferings of the people of Judah are described as though one man had experienced them. It is possible to interpret this chapter as a record of the feelings of Jeremiah himself, or as a personification in an otherwise unknown individual of the nation's tragic sufferings. In the mention of God's angry *rod* the author reflects the thought of Isaiah 10:5 and similar allusions in the writings of the eighth-century BC prophets, which asserted to an unbelieving nation that

God both could and would use the armies of pagan peoples in order to punish the Israelites for their repeated transgressions of the law. Because of this the author is able to attribute the travails which have been experienced to the direct activity of God in the affairs of his people, imposed not so much in anger as in judgment. In stark contrast to the beneficent guidance of the exodus and subsequent periods, God has now turned his hand (3) against the covenant people, to their great dismay. While poetic licence is obviously indicated in the expression *my flesh and my skin* (4), this highly figurative passage nevertheless expresses quite clearly the comprehensiveness of the affliction which had come upon the nation. The tragedy was spoken of as *bitterness* (5), where MT *rôš, gall*, described a plant and its fruit of obscure identification but often associated with wormwood (cf. Deut. 29:18). It was extremely bitter to the taste, and so became used metaphorically of highly unpleasant experiences. The author's remarks about 'those long dead' seem to indicate that the survival after death which he had in mind was far from pleasant (cf. Isa. 14:9ff.), and certainly very different from the prospect extended by the crucified Christ to one of those put to death with him (Luke 23:43).

The walling-up of prisoners (7) within confined spaces so that they died very quickly was a form of torture made popular by the Assyrians. The fetters (*něḥoštî*) would have been made of bronze (Hebrew *něḥôšet*; LXX *chalkos*). The confining nature of the prison was such that even prayer could not ascend to God. Both the circumstances which led up to it, and the prison itself, were of the prisoner's own making. The reference to *hewn stones* (9) continues the oppressive figure of verse 7. Forcible confinement, distasteful at the best of times, was particularly abhorrent to nomadic peoples.

In a change of figure the author depicts God as a wild animal ready to tear in pieces whatever crosses its path. Already the nation had been dismembered by vicious enemies, who had been acting under divine authority. In yet another dramatic metaphor God is represented as a skilled huntsman shooting deadly arrows at his prey (12). These find their mark in such vulnerable organs as the kidneys (MT *kělāyôt*; AV, RV *reins*). In the sacrificial tariffs of the Pentateuch, animal kidneys were held to be one of the locations of life, this being thought true of human kidneys also. In addition, emotional attributes of joy (Prov. 23:16) and sorrow (Job 19:27; Ps. 73:21) were credited to them. In verse 14 the author's allusion to himself as a *laughing-stock* certainly reflects much that was common to the experience of Jeremiah. But whereas the individual concerned was an object of ridicule only to his fellow citizens, Jerusalem has now become the laughing-stock of the entire Ancient Near East. Verse 16 depicts a form of punishment in which foodstuffs were adulterated before being administered (cf. Exod. 32:20). A good deal of accidental ingestion of substances such as sand seems to have occurred in antiquity, as shown by many instances of worn-down teeth in Egyptian mummies. In the case of Judah, however, the teeth have become broken and ground down because God has given his people stones to eat as punishment for venerating the images of Baal. The loving Father who knows how to give good gifts to those who ask (cf. Matt. 7:11; Luke 11:13), first requires the recipients to be living in obedience to his will. In this respect the covenant people had been obviously deficient for generations. Verse 17b may also be rendered, *You have deprived me of health! I have forgotten all about happiness.* So bitter was the anguish, and so oppressive the burden of suffering, that the author could not banish it from his thoughts. Only the realization that long-overdue penitence was now clearly evident afforded any hope at all for the future.

b. Divine mercies recalled (3:22–39)

Like Job, the sentiment of the author is that 'though he slay me, yet will I trust him' (Job 13:15, AV). In a magnificent expression of faith in the unfailing mercies of God, the writer looks to the distant future with renewed hope. The Hebrew term *ḥesed*, used to describe these 'mercies', has the basic meaning of loyalty or devotion, particularly in relationship to a covenant and to God as its author. Out of the fidelity of such a bond emerges a demonstration of divine mercies, so that *ḥesed* can well be rendered in this verse by 'covenant loyalties' or 'covenant mercies'. Here the author asserts the limitless nature of divine mercies and the constant conservation of these supreme spiritual values by virtue of renewal. This affirmation crystallizes the basic concept of philosophical value-theory, which states that if values are to be maintained, they have to be augmented continually. But God is much more than supreme Value; he is Love (cf. 1 John 4:8, 16). The unchanging constancy of God furnishes a firm ground for the tentative outreachings of hope for the future. After the first clause of this verse (22) MT reads, 'We have not perished' (RV *We are not consumed*), implying that this is a result of the steadfast love of God towards his people. But for MT *tāmnû*, RSV, following the Peshitta and Targum, has read *tāmnû* with *ḥasdê YHWH* as the subject, translating the phrase, *the steadfast love of the Lord never ceases*, which conveys the sense better.

Because God is Judah's portion, any hope of restoration must be firmly grounded in him (26). Waiting upon God's will was as important for the Old Covenant (cf. Ps. 37:9; Hos. 12:6; Zeph. 3:8, etc.) as the New (cf. Rom. 8:25; Gal. 5:5, etc.). The believer has a living hope because he trusts in a living God whose promises are as sure as his judgments (cf. 2 Cor. 1:20). The reference to yoke-bearing (27) reflects the teachings of the Hebrew sages, as in Proverbs. Such burdens can best be borne in youth when a man has the requisite vigour, and when his personality needs to be disciplined more than would be the case in his more mature years. Silence as a form of resignation to God's will is found occasionally in the Psalter (Pss 39:2; 94:17). Placing the mouth in the dust was a typically oriental way of expressing or exacting complete submission. In offering his cheek to the smiter (30) the captive was conveying the idea of absolute surrender. The ruler of the nation had indeed been struck upon the cheek by the besieger, as Micah had predicted (Mic. 5:1), and now Jerusalem is submissive to the divine will in the face of her sufferings (cf. Isa. 50:6). This attitude was exemplified at the highest level by Jesus Christ just before his crucifixion (cf. Matt. 26:67; Luke 22:64; John 18:22; 19:3), where an innocent victim suffered for human sin in obedience to God's will (cf. Matt. 26:39, etc.), without any form of retaliation (1 Pet. 2:21ff.). Because divine mercy has a restorative character (Ps. 23:3), the sufferings inflicted upon the nation will pass away ultimately, since they do not represent God's final purpose for his people. The Father does not afflict his children willingly (33), and while God does chasten the Christian periodically as part of spiritual development (Heb. 12:6), it is still not sufficiently realized that the disasters which overtake people are usually related very closely to their specific way of life. While the affliction may possibly be attributable to God in the ultimate sense that he is the necessary ground of contingent existence, the incidence of calamity in individual experience is normally the end-product of a chain of causation.

In verses 34−36, the supreme justice which characterizes God's nature is illustrated by reference to human dignity and individual rights under the law. God will not condone the abusing of prisoners (cf. Ps. 69:33), and makes the releasing of captives one of the most important aspects of the work of the divine Servant (cf. Ps. 146:7; Isa. 42:7), as Christ pointed out in his first sermon in Nazareth (Luke 4:18). Precisely who the *prisoners* are which the author has in mind is uncertain, and the breadth of meaning implied by the expression would constitute an apt poetic description of mankind as a whole. Earth-bound mortals are thus promised liberation from the predicament of their crushing environment by the power of God, which frees the prisoner from bondage to sin and self. For the Christian, faith in the finished work of Christ achieves victory (cf. 1 Cor. 15:57). Since man is made in the image of God, the rights and dignity of the individual are of great importance to the Creator. By definition man possesses certain basic rights, one of which is that of equal opportunity before the law. Where a person is deprived or cheated out of his legal rights, the image of the supremely just Deity within him is defaced. The MT of verse 35 lends force to the concept of natural or inherent human rights when rendered, *to pervert the right which a man has in the very presence of the Most High*. God therefore disapproves heartily of any attempt to deprive an individual of his rights in law (36), or to condemn him unjustly.

The idea that God was the supreme arbiter of human affairs (37) was an important element in the teaching of the eighth-century BC prophets. By implication it is also a castigation of the kind of prophet who opposed Jeremiah and spread false hopes among the populace. Like Isaiah (45:7) the author of Lamentations relates the whole range of moral values (*good and evil*) to the activity of the one true God of Israel, who is the ultimate ground of existence. Since nothing can happen to an individual without God's knowledge, a man should endure misfortune patiently and without protest, trusting in the mercies of God to bring good out of evil (cf. Rom. 8:28).

This attitude should be particularly the case when an innocent person suffers unjustly (cf. 1 Pet. 2:21–25). When a transgressor is punished for his wrongdoing, he has absolutely no cause for complaint (cf. 1 Pet. 2:19f.).

c. A call for spiritual renewal (3:40–42)

A life which has never been laid open in penitence and faith before God has little permanence in eternity. Because the covenant with Israel is of an eternal nature, the nation is bidden to take spiritual stock and turn in penitence to its God. Once true repentance is in evidence, the just punishments which have been imposed can be expected to be abrogated and the nation restored to a measure of favour with God. These elements were fundamental to the message of Jeremiah, but Judah has had to endure the agony of captivity before becoming aware of their validity. The prerequisites for a rewarding spiritual relationship with God remain unchanged, however, and it is up to the people of Israel, as his vassals, to renew their long-standing neglect of the covenant responsibilities. Most EVV begin verse 41, *Let us lift up our hearts and hands*. In MT the consonants *'l* occur three times in seven words, the first being generally rendered 'with' ('our hands'), the second 'unto' ('God'), and the third being the generic term for deity, *'el*. MT may contain transmissional errors here. If the first of these is regarded as an emphatic negative form *'al*, usually associated with prohibitions, and understanding the sense of the verb 'lift up', the verse would then read, *Let us lift up our hearts, not our hands*, as in NEB. This would certainly suit the context much better than the cumbersome combination 'our heart with our hands', which is rare. The appeal for spiritual renewal is concerned with internal motivation, not the kind of external ritual performances of which there had been a surfeit in pre-exilic days (cf. Joel 2:13). The process of spiritual catharsis must begin with the awareness that the nation is still under divine judgment for its iniquity. When a full and sincere confession of sin has been made, God will then have proper grounds for pardoning his people for past sin (cf. 1 John 1:9). In this verse a beginning towards a state of forgiveness is made in the realization that the nation has been sinful and rebellious.

d. The consequences of sin (3:43–54)

In verse 43 MT uses the full second singular masculine form (*thou hast covered thyself*), the intransitive verb having a reflexive force as in RSV *thou hast wrapped thyself*. The *anger* is the righteous wrath of God which punishes the hardened sinner (cf. 2:1; Rom. 1:18). The awareness of deprivation and utter despair as expressed here typifies the conditions antecedent to all genuine spiritual conversion. There is an increasing sense of the awfulness of sin in the sight of a just and holy God; the kind of barrier which it has erected between a man and his Maker, and the absolute inability of an individual to surmount this obstacle and achieve his own salvation. This latter must be by faith, not works, both under the law (cf. Hab. 2:4) and under grace (Eph. 2:8f.). The ineffable Deity who dwells on clouds of light cannot be swayed by the pleadings and laments of sinners (44) until the sins which have caused God to withdraw and turn a deaf ear (cf. Isa. 59:2) have been truly and fully confessed and expiated. The nation's recognition of itself as *offscouring* (so most EVV) employs a descriptive term *sĕḥî*, occurring here only in the Hebrew Bible, and in the context denotes anything rejected as unfit for use. Its New Testament counterpart (1 Cor. 4:13) is equally rare, depicting the suffering of the apostles. The stark tragedy of such a humiliating situation is that it has actually happened to a nation which had boasted for so long about its God. Now this very source of national strength has recoiled in horror against the sins of the people, and in punishing them has made the Israelites an object of ridicule in the Near East. Such modern translations of verse 47 as *panic and pitfall* cannot reproduce the assonance of MT *paḥad wāpaḥat*, literally 'terror and the pit'. The latter ('fissure', 'pit') was a dreaded euphemism for utter destruction. *Devastation and destruction* is another assonant phrase, MT *haššē't wĕhaššaber*, which cannot be rendered with the sibilant force of the original. Part of the majesty and skill of Hebrew poetry lies in the ability of the particular writer to match the thought expressed with literary onomatopoeia. The verse under consideration is reminiscent of the style of Jeremiah. An increasing awareness of the seriousness of sin and its devastating consequences has given place to a sustained outpouring of grief. The noun *destruction* (48) is a cognate of a Hebrew verb meaning 'to shatter', 'to tear in pieces', 'to wreck', and thus implies the complete termination of organized life in the kingdom. Before God can begin to restore the fortunes of his people, the sincerity of their repentance must be evident (49). They must not merely weep like professional mourners hired for a funeral[1] (cf. Matt. 9:23), but must show by the consistency of their lives that the tears were indicative of profound changes in the emotional and spiritual life. The spatial dimension in verse 50 is intended to emphasize the gulf which separates God and man, and the way in which this gap can be bridged when contrition and confession lead to the forgiveness of the sinner. God is faithful and just to pardon the iniquity of the penitent wrongdoer (1 John 1:8), and will not remain aloof from those who seek him sincerely and truly. For this reason God can be expected to take notice of the nation's plight once true repentance is forthcoming. The horrors of the siege and subsequent destruction are never far from the author's thoughts, and in his mind he pictures the abject humiliation of the capital, whose fate was that of her maidens.

Verse 52 commences a section in which the author personifies the sufferings of the entire nation. He finds it difficult to understand the severity of the calamity which has devastated Judah, and which has given such malicious delight to the nation's hereditary enemies. The reference to the dungeon (53) recalls Jeremiah 38:6. *Bôr* usually means a 'pit', 'cistern' or 'well', but occasionally indicates a 'grave'. Perhaps the sense here is that the nation has to all intents and purposes been buried, and a memorial cairn has been raised above the place of interment. In a change of metaphor the nation is represented as completely engulfed by the sweeping tide of destruction (cf. Jon. 2:3ff.), and all hope for the future seems lost. Cf. Psalm 69:2 for a similar figure of acute anguish in a time of crisis.

e. Comfort and imprecation (3:55–66)

The author pictures the nation in the most remote depths of misery. Because the sinner is now penitent, his plea for mercy and forgiveness is heard. MT of 56b is rather obscure. The form

---

1. Cf. D. F. Payne, *NBD*, pp. 171f.

lĕrawḥāti is from a word *rĕwāḥāh*, meaning 'respite', 'relief', and suggests a plea that God would not abstain from relieving the sufferer
in his distress. This word is followed by *lĕšaw'ātí*, derived from
šaw'āh, 'a cry for help'. RSV conflates both readings in its rendering,
Do not close thine ear to my cry for help. The sense of the MT seems to be,
'Do not shut your ear to my plea for help, that I might obtain
relief', though this is not entirely certain. The next verse furnishes
a characteristic response of a God who answers his faithful children
while they are actually supplicating him (cf. Isa. 58:9; 65:24). Having
cast himself upon divine mercy, the sinner finds that God is already
present with him as advocate (cf. 1 John 2:1) and redeemer, uttering
words of consolation and reassurance. God is the *gō'ēl*, the kinsman-
helper (58), who came to the aid of his people enslaved in sin and
ransomed them (cf. Lev. 25:25ff., 47–54; Ruth 4:1–12). Redemption
for the Christian has been purchased at the highest cost in the
blood of the cross. While the finished work of Christ has redeemed
the world, people still need to experience as individuals a personal
salvation by faith in Christ.

Despite the realization that the nation has suffered because of its
obdurate sin, there still lingers the feeling that some injustice has
been done (59). Perhaps because of their status as the Chosen
People the Jews were always sensitive to abuse and injury inflicted
from outside, whatever the source. Consequently they found it
impossible to overlook these hostile acts, with the result that the
imprecations which they hurled at their enemies, while typical of
such Near Eastern utterances, seem to possess an unexpected and
unusual degree of vindictiveness (cf. Ps. 137:9). Here the writer,
acting representatively for the nation, submits his case to the
supreme Arbiter of human affairs. Even though he is aware that the
punishment and degradation of Judah has resulted from a prolonged disavowal of the covenant obligations, he can still throw himself upon the mercy of the Judge and expect to hear a
pronouncement that is just and equitable. Most EVV speak of the
vengeance of Israel's enemies (60), but 'vindictiveness' suits the
context better. Such acts were a normal constituent of total warfare
in the Ancient Near East. Mocking or taunt-songs were also frequently used to express derision or contempt for an enemy. For
examples of taunt-songs or fragments in the Old Testament see

Numbers 21:27–30; Isaiah 47:1–15; Habakkuk 2:6–19. Here the author is praying for the punishment of those who have been the agents of divine anger upon Israel, not so much because of the destruction which they have wrought, but because of the malicious delight which they took in executing their task, and in making Israel the subject of their taunt-song. A different attitude towards one's enemies is set forth in the teachings of Christ, as well as in his life. See Matthew 5:44; Luke 6:27, 35; 23:34; and in Romans 12:20 (quoting Prov. 25:21). While the assertion that God would punish those who oppressed Israel appeared alike in the Law and in prophecy (cf. Deut. 32:34ff.; Isa. 10:12ff.; Jer. 50:9ff., etc.), the decline of a sense of responsibility under the covenant had given rise to the concept that the very idea of the Chosen People experiencing anything but continuous blessing was unthinkable. Though this notion had been dispelled abruptly by the agonizing experiences of destruction and captivity, the nation still felt that she could call legitimately upon God to punish her enemies because of the special status which she had once enjoyed, and to which she was again aspiring. RSV *dullness of heart* (65) is literally 'a covering of the heart', whether relating to insensitivity of mind or stubbornness of will. Since it is the enemies of Israel who are to receive this curse, the latter seems preferable. In the mind of the author such a state would then invite divine retribution upon those who had earlier been the means of punishing Judah. The sense of particularity which depicted the Chosen People as the only significant recipients of divine blessing is in evidence here, as elsewhere in the Old Testament. The writer appears to be concerned primarily with the punishment of the nation's traditional enemies, not their spiritual rehabilitation through suffering. In verse 66, as against MT *the heavens of the Lord*, LXX reads 'underneath the heaven, Lord', and the Syriac has *under thy heavens, O Lord*, which is adopted by RSV and NEB.

4. FOURTH DIRGE (4:1–22)

a. Earlier days recalled (4:1–12)

In a mood of sad reminiscence the writer contrasts the happy conditions of former days with the sombre situation of a city and a land humiliated and shamed by enemy forces. The figures of *gold* and *sacred stones* (1) are used to depict the populace of Judah. Whereas other nations were relegated to the level of base metal, Israel considered herself to be composed of pure gold and precious stones. But due to a sad reversal in national fortunes, this lofty self-estimate has been changed suddenly. The gold has lost its lustre, and the sacred stones have been scattered indiscriminately in the streets among the dirt and rubble. The twofold figure of the pillaging of the temple and the slaughter of the desperate defenders of Jerusalem is a vivid reminder of the events narrated in 2 Kings 25:9, Jeremiah 52:12–23 and Lamentations 2:19. For those who esteemed themselves as high-quality gold, the kind of experience which reduced them to the level of base metal in the opinion of their enemies was of harrowing psychological and spiritual proportions.

The earthen pitcher (2) was a ceramic wine-jar used for storing a variety of articles, and a great many of these containers have been unearthed at sites in Palestine and elsewhere.[1] In the third verse the horrors of the siege of Jerusalem in 587 BC were recalled. During the final stages of the attack, famine conditions were rampant (Lam. 2:19), which affected the young in particular. At this juncture such children were receiving far worse treatment than that provided by nature for the offspring of *jackals*, or the fledgelings of the ostrich, the latter being traditionally regarded as cruel and indifferent to the needs of its young (cf. Job 39:13–17). Because of the shortage of food, nursing mothers were unable to satisfy the cravings of their famished infants. The pathetic scenes of young children begging in vain for food seem to have etched themselves deeply on the mind of the author, who must have witnessed the events described here and in the first two dirges.

Such was the state of reversal of national fortunes that those who had lived on delicacies and worn purple clothing as a mark of wealth (5) were struck dumb with awe, being appalled at the calamities which had descended upon their beloved city. In Ancient Eastern society the change which caused those brought up in luxurious surroundings to lie prostrate on heaps of ashes in mourning was normally that of the enslavement of a city-state. As a result, throughout Ancient Near Eastern history, the fear of an enemy attack culminating in destruction and captivity was never very far from the surface of individual consciousness, making for a real degree of emotional insecurity even when times appeared peaceful and prosperous. In the case of Judah, however, its destruction could well have been averted had its wanton inhabitants heeded the warning voices of the eighth- and seventh-century BC prophets. In the event the citizens of the desolated kingdom had no-one but themselves to blame for the calamity which had so lately devastated them. Instead of leading other nations into the way of divine truth, the recalcitrant people of Judah had been hauled into an ignominious captivity by pagan nations who were acting as God's instruments for their punishment.

---

1. Cf. A. R. Millard, *NBD*, p. 101.

Although *Sodom* (6) had been proverbial for its wickedness among the Hebrews, that sinful city had been destroyed in a comparatively brief period, and thus did not suffer prolonged agonies. For her far more serious crime of rejecting covenant mercies, Jerusalem must seemingly endure a proportionately greater chastisement. This sentiment carries with it a great deal of poetic pathos, however, and should thus be related carefully to the distraught attitude of the author. It is precarious to postulate the concept of 'degrees of sin', since all wrongdoing is abhorrent to God, however insignificant man might happen to regard certain aspects of it. There are, nevertheless, degrees of culpability, as the penal legislation of the Law made clear (cf. Amos 3:2; Matt. 5:21ff.; Luke 12:47f., etc.), but the nation had been slow to accept its responsibilities in this respect. Again, while the destruction of Jerusalem in 587 BC was carried out with appropriate thoroughness by the enemy conquerors, there is no evidence that it was perpetrated with any greater degree of competence than was normal for the period. In any event, much of the suffering and hardship associated with the reduction of Jerusalem could have been avoided by a formal surrender of the city to the enemy, a procedure which Jeremiah had recommended. Here again, however, the same wilful and obdurate spirit which had rejected divine mercies time and again brought upon itself its just deserts by insisting that Jerusalem be defended to the last.

At the close of verse 6 RSV reads, *no hand being laid on it*. The root of the verb *ḥālû* is uncertain, perhaps being derived from *ḥûl*, 'to whirl', 'to writhe', 'to tremble'. Thus a rendering such as 'no hands were trembling in it' would indicate that the inhabitants of Sodom were taken completely by surprise when they were engulfed, and therefore had no time in which to panic (cf. NEB *no-one wrung his hands*). Such a situation seems to have been the case in more recent instances of similar destruction. If the verb is from the root *ḥālāh*, 'to be ill', 'to be weak', it might imply that the Sodomites were complacent about their society and had no awareness of its impending destruction. The translation must therefore remain tentative until more is known about the root of the verb.

The dreadful conditions which obtained just before Jerusalem fell affected nobles and peasants alike. In verse 7 the plight of the latter is described in elegant literary hyperbole. It throws incidental light on the contrast between the living conditions of the two segments of the populace. AV, following MT, reads *Nazarites* for RV *nobles*, but the term seems to denote one who is conspicuous because of his rank. This distinction no longer applied to the nobility, who had become victims of famine along with the rest of the people in the beleaguered city. MT *pĕnînîm*, AV, RV *rubies*, is probably better translated *corals*. The meaning of *gizrātām* (AV, RV *their polishing*) is uncertain. The word is apparently related to the verb *gāzar*, 'to cut', suggesting the concept of bodily 'cut' or form, as in the RSV *beauty of their form*. The general idea of 'appearance' seems to be conveyed by the context. MT *sappîr* is the familiar oriental semi-precious stone lapis lazuli.

The nobility cannot be recognized on the streets because famine has reduced all the citizens of Jerusalem to a common level of physical exhaustion (8). The gauntness, malnutrition and dehydration which are described exhibit clear marks of an eye-witness. The haggard faces and parched lips would have preferred an early death by the sword to the lingering agonies of famine and pestilence to which they had sentenced themselves. So desperate were the citizens for food (cf. Deut. 28:53ff.) that erstwhile loving and provident mothers boiled and ate their own children (10) (cf. 2:20; Jer. 19:9). The stark horror of this appalling deed had become indelibly etched on the consciousness of the author, and doubtless haunted him for the remainder of his life. The outpouring of divine anger constituted the long-promised punishment for the deliberate and sustained rejection of the covenantal provisions. The resultant work of desolation in Judah had been as comprehensive as the scope of divine blessing could have been for an obedient and holy nation. The people had not come to God for life (cf. John 5:40), and therefore death had overtaken them. Their trust had not been in God their Rock, but in the imagined physical impregnability of Jerusalem. Although the hill of Zion was so difficult of access as to make a military assault upon the city an extremely difficult and costly affair, the fact that Jerusalem had been conquered twice since it was first settled by the Jebusites would have hardly led pagan kings to think that it was completely impregnable (12).

What the author seems to be describing here is the false confidence of the citizens of Jerusalem, who imagined that potential enemies considered the site as immune to reduction as they themselves did, thus making the same mistake as the Jebusites of earlier days (2 Sam. 5:6–8). Be that as it may, the very fact that the pagan adversaries of Judah were being used by God as an instrument for the punishment of his disobedient and idolatrous people meant that there was no natural obstacle significant enough to bar their advance.

b. Sin and its results (4:13–20)

In looking for the cause of the *débâcle*, the author is not merely searching for scapegoats. The experiences associated with the fall of the capital and the enslavement of the covenant people demanded more than a circumstantial explanation. The answer to the problem must be necessarily metaphysical in nature, involving the deepest motivating forces of the human spirit. The *prophets* and *priests* (13), who ought to have been proclaiming the covenant ideals in the nation, were actually the responsible agents for perpetrating much of the iniquity so characteristic of pre-exilic life. The author illustrates the depravity of the day by reference to the shedding of righteous blood (cf. Jer. 26:20–23). But now the situation has changed to the point where the wicked priests and prophets have been recognized for what they really are, and have been treated by the enraged populace in a manner appropriate to the part which they had played in encouraging the recent disaster. Their leadership has been repudiated, and they themselves are now abhorred as lepers. This latter is fitting, in one sense, since leprosy is sometimes employed in Scripture as illustrative of the ravages of sin and death. In verse 15 the false servants of God have been given the traditional treatment accorded to lepers (Lev. 13:45f.), and hurried unceremoniously out of the city. Although they attempted to settle in other places they were prevented from doing so by the local inhabitants, who no doubt held them in superstitious dread, fearing that they would bring disaster upon them also. The utterances of Jeremiah against these guilty men should be noted here (cf. Jer. 6:13; 8:10; 23:11, 14).

God has intervened directly to disperse the wicked leaders among the nations also. One of the reasons for his anger was that these impious men had actively opposed the testimony of those priests who still remained faithful to the covenant ideals. Although the people had expected material assistance in the form of a relief expedition by the Egyptians (cf. Jer. 37:7), Jeremiah had known all along that nothing would save the kingdom from destruction at Chaldean hands, and now that the captivity had taken place the people themselves realized that their hopes for outside assistance had been without foundation. The reference to their steps being dogged (18) was apparently to the stringent controls exercised by the Babylonian conquerors over those who were allowed to remain in the land under the governorship of Gedaliah. The Babylonians were determined to forestall any possible future uprisings in Judah, and after the rule of Gedaliah had provoked further dissension which culminated in his assassination, the land was again depopulated in 581 BC. If Lamentations was composed shortly after 587 BC, the author may well have sensed that the end of community life in Judah was at hand.

In the elegant literary hyperbole of verse 19 (cf. 2 Sam. 1:23), the relentless nature of the Babylonian pursuit of refugees was vividly described. To prevent any further political contacts between the remnant in the southern kingdom and the Egyptians, the Babylonians evidently set up ambushes in the desert areas south of Judah. The *anointed* one of verse 20 was king Zedekiah, who was captured in flight in the plain of Jericho, and after being brought before Nebuchadnezzar was blinded and imprisoned (Jer. 52:7–11). Zedekiah was a weak and treacherous individual who condoned the religious corruption and moral degeneracy of the time, and generally ignored the advice proffered by Jeremiah (Jer. 37:2), except on occasions of grave crisis (Jer. 21:1–7; 37:17–21; 38:14–28). For this behaviour he was severely criticized in Ezekiel 21:25 and 2 Kings 24:19. Despite his weak and perfidious nature, however, he was still the Lord's anointed one, and it is this status, rather than his actual leadership, which is being recognized here.

c. Punishment promised for Edom (4:21–22)

The command to *rejoice* (21) is a rather derisive reference to the short-lived satisfaction which the Edomites can expect to enjoy as a result of the Chaldean conquest of their hereditary enemy. The Edomites had been the bitter adversaries of Judah for centuries, and the prophets pronounced judgment upon her for maintaining this attitude of hostility (Amos 9:12; Obad. 10–16; Jer. 49:7–22; Ezek. 25:12–14; 35:15). Edom had apparently refused to join any alliance with Judah and Egypt against the Babylonians. After the fall of Jerusalem in 587 BC, Nebuchadnezzar allotted the rural areas of Judah to the Edomites as a reward for their political neutrality, and as a recognition of the active help which they had provided for Chaldean military units during the final days of the campaign (cf. Ezek. 25:12–14; Obad. 11–14). LXX omits *Uz* in this verse, as also in Jeremiah 25:20. Whether or not this territory is identical with that regarded as the homeland of Job is unknown. Since, however, Uz seems to have been consistently accessible both to Sabaean Bedouin from Arabia and Chaldean invaders from Mesopotamia (Job 1:15, 17), it would appear to have been located in the general area of Edom. The temporary ascendancy of Edom will vanish once the retribution and destruction promised by the prophets overtakes her, for whereas the Israelites will be free from future punishment, Edom still has to drink the cup of divine wrath. When this latter event finally occurred, the Israelites could interpret it as an indication of the commencement of their own restoration to divine favour.

5. FIFTH DIRGE (5:1–22)

While this dirge contains twenty-two verses, the alphabetic acrostic arrangement has not been followed, in contrast to the structure of previous laments. The chapter comprises a confession of sin and a recognition of the abiding sovereignty of God. Since it is more strictly a prayer than a lament, its spontaneous and personal character may have made it less amenable to a stylized acrostic arrangement than the preceding laments.

a. A plea for mercy (5:1–10)

The prayer commences by drawing God's attention to the misfortunes which have come upon Judah so as to form a basis for the exercise of divine compassion. The proud heritage of the Israelites (Lev. 20:24) has been desolated and occupied by foreign troops (2). After 587 BC some Edomites penetrated into southern Judah and settled south of Hebron, to be followed later by other Edomite and Arab groups. So strictly did the victorious Chaldeans control the land that even the barest necessities of life such as drinking water (4) had to be purchased by the hapless Judeans who were left behind in the countryside. Verse 5 presents certain difficulties in translation, with RSV and NEB introducing the idea of a yoke, following Symmachus (traditionally, a third-century AD Jewish convert to Ebionite teaching, who made a Greek version of the Old Testament which was included by Origen in his Hexapla and Tetrapla). MT can be rendered, *we are pursued to our very necks*, and while the meaning of this is uncertain, it may allude to the ancient practice of a victor placing his foot on the neck of a prostrate enemy to symbolize complete subjugation (cf. Josh. 10:24; Isa. 51:23, etc.). Verse 6 shows the desperate plight of the remnant under Gedaliah, which had become so critical that they would gladly ally with either Egypt or Assyria if it would ensure their survival. *Assyria* here is a surrogate for Babylonia (cf. Jer. 2:18).

The thought in verse 7 is in accord with the second commandment (Exod. 20:4f.). The continuity of the successive human generations precludes personal isolation. Consequently children reap the fruits of their parents' lives and activities (cf. Deut. 5:9f.). Jeremiah had already repudiated the common complaint that the offspring were being punished on account of the sins of their antecedents (Jer. 31:29f.), and in his espousal of personal religion he prepared the way for the revelation of the New Covenant in the blood of Christ. Judean society after 587 BC had become disrupted to the point where class distinctions were meaningless. Consequently anyone who courted the favour of the occupying Babylonians could exercise some modest degree of civil authority. A real threat to livelihood came from marauding bands (9), whether of Babylonians or Bedouin Arabs, who preyed upon unsuspecting villagers attempting to obtain a little food from nearby fields.

b. The nature of sin (5:11–18)

The author again comments upon the terrible retribution which the nation has brought upon itself. Having been betrayed by the 'slaves' who had risen to power, the princes had been further dishonoured by being suspended in mid-air with their hands bound together. Even youths and children had been coerced into doing heavy manual work because of the disrupted state of society (13). Whether or not this was part of a pattern of forced labour imposed by the conquerors is uncertain from the text. It was demeaning for young men to grind grain, this being women's work (cf. Judg. 16:21). The place where the elders and judges sat in earlier days to dispense judgment is now desolate (14). National dignity and prestige (16) have been lost because of the persistent rejection of the covenantal obligations. This image completes the concept of the degradation of Israel, and assesses the cause of her downfall with complete accuracy. The realization that sin must inevitably result in punishment has promoted the author to intercede on behalf of his people. A graphic picture of the desolation which has overtaken the once-populous Mount Zion is conveyed by the image of prowling *jackals* (18).

c. A plea for divine restoration (5:19–22)

The permanence and stability of an unchanging God furnish the author with his ground of appeal and the prospect of future hope. Even though his children have been disobedient and idolatrous, God still abides faithful (2 Tim. 2:13), and can be relied upon to pardon the penitent sinner. Verse 21 expresses the longing of the author for national renewal and reconciliation with God in the light of his conviction that he still has a sovereign purpose for his covenant people. Verse 22 can be rendered 'unless you have utterly rejected us', or alternatively by an interrogative form, 'or have you completely rejected us?' Either translation conveys the realization that the nation is still forsaken. However, in the light of former covenant mercies, the author cannot believe that God has rejected his people (cf. Rom. 11:1f.).

Several Old Testament prophecies conclude on a negative or inauspicious note (cf. Eccl. 12:14; Isa. 66:24; Mal. 4:6), as does Lamentations. Consequently in synagogue readings it became customary to conclude such compositions with a repetition of the preceding verse, so that under these circumstances verse 21 would be read again after verse 22.